Precedent

BOOK THREE: COVENANT OF TRUST SERIES

PAULA WISEMAN

MINDSTIR MEDIA

Published by Mindstir Media
PO Box 1681 | Hampton, New Hampshire 03843 | USA
1.800.767.0531 | www.mindstirmedia.com

Printed in the United States of America

ISBN-10: 0-981964-84-2
ISBN-13: 978-0-9819648-4-3

Library of Congress Control Number: 2011937117

Visit Paula Wiseman on the World Wide Web:
www.paulawiseman.com

To Kristi

Acknowledgements

Thank you

To Jon for your unwavering confidence in me and in the story. I would have quit long ago without you.

To Amanda for the endless hours of plotting, and revising. The book is better, deeper and stronger because of your help. And so am I.

To Kristi for your emotional investment from the very beginning.

To Mary for your photos, your comments and your awesome proofreading.

To Brenda for catching all of my typos and misplaced prepositions.

To my fabulous readers for their gracious support.

To J.J. for his enthusiasm for the books and his help and encouragement.

All glory to God, who gives the story, who opens doors, who accomplishes His purposes in all things.

PROLOGUE

Thursday, June 12

Edward Reynolds glanced in the window of Gateway Mission. The kid was there. His grandson. He was sure the boy was Teresa's son. He had her eyes. For the last twelve years, he had tracked Teresa's movements across the country. He finally traced her to St. Louis, only to find out he was too late.

The kid was his last chance. He would go in and drop a few hints, make a few pointed comments, and see if the boy reacted. He opened the door of the mission and slipped into one of the chairs close to the door. The kid, Jack, never looked up from his task of straightening chairs, loudly scraping them across the tile floor. A broad-shouldered, sturdily built young man, he had to take after his father's people. The Reynolds and the Hickmans were both thin and slight. Moments later, he looked up.

"Mister, I'm sorry. They packed up the food already." He adjusted his baseball cap. "I can get you a sandwich, though."

Ed cleared his throat to make sure he could speak. "Just coffee, black."

Jack moved the broom away from the counter and leaned it against the wall so he could pour the coffee. When he brought the cup over, Ed invited him to sit at the table.

"I'm Jack," he said, extending his hand. "My brother runs this place."

"I'm Ed." Teresa just had the one son. Was he mistaken about the boy? Maybe Jack had a half-brother. Teresa never married, so it couldn't be a stepbrother.

"You need a place to stay?" Jack asked.

"Nah." Ed slurped the coffee loudly. "You make good coffee, Jack."

"I learned it from my mom. She's a big coffee drinker."

He talked about her in present tense. Ed studied Jack carefully. "You from around here?"

"Pretty much. We bounced around some when I was little, but I've been in St. Louis since I was six."

"Ever been to Baltimore?"

"No. You?"

"That's where I'm from. I had a daughter. You remind me of her. Thought you might be related."

"That would be an incredible coincidence," Jack said.

Chapter 1
Fruition

"How goes it?" Jack Molinsky leaned against the doorframe of the tiny office where his brother crunched columns of numbers on an outdated adding machine.

Brad spoke without looking up. "Slow. I've got board summaries and a bunch of filings to finish up before the thirtieth. Did somebody come in?"

"Yeah," Jack said. "An old guy. He just had a cup of coffee and left."

"He didn't want anything?"

"No. Said he had a place to stay and everything." Jack twirled the broom in his hands. "It was strange. He asked me if I'd ever been to Baltimore."

Brad put his pencil down and looked up. "Your mom was from Baltimore, wasn't she?"

"Yeah. He said I reminded him of his daughter, even."

"You don't think . . . ?"

"What?"

"You don't think that was Tracy's dad, do you?"

"Here? After all these years?"

"Did he give you a name?"

"Just Ed, no last name."

"Tracy's dad was named Ed."

"He was, wasn't he?"

"He couldn't have gotten far." Brad headed for the front door.

Jack followed close behind. "He took a right when he got outside."

Once out on the street, Brad said, "Don't make eye contact with anybody unless I speak to them first. Got that?" He glanced at his watch. "I know a couple of guys who'll be transacting some business. Maybe they've seen him."

Jack stuck close to his brother, keeping his head down as instructed. Brad had become very streetwise in his years at the mission. He knew who was just down and out, and who the truly bad guys were. A couple of blocks from the mission, Jack could see a group of six or eight boys in their late teens, maybe early twenties, sporting gang colors. This was their turf. Great.

As they got closer, a black SUV with tinted windows turned onto the street and drove slowly toward the group of boys, toward Brad and Jack. "This is wrong," Brad whispered, and Jack raised his head. He watched the boys closely, but they weren't reacting. Brad's eyes darted back to the SUV, and Jack turned to see the passenger side window inching down. Even from half a block away, Jack could make out the glint of metal.

The same instant Jack's brain processed what he was seeing, the shooting began. The group of boys dove for cover behind parked cars while one or two returned fire. Paralyzed by shock and fear, Jack felt Brad's strong hands dig into his shoulders, and then he hit the sidewalk hard, feeling the burning scrape on his knee, hands, and cheek. But in that split second, Brad left himself exposed.

Jack heard a strange thud, unlike anything he'd ever heard before. He rolled over in time to see Brad splayed against the brick building, and then he crumpled awkwardly to the sidewalk.

"BRAD!"

Jack crawled to his brother and rolled him onto his back. Brad clutched Jack's shirt but didn't speak. "I think you've been shot, Brad! It's gonna be okay!" Brad lifted a trembling hand to his chest, to the spreading red stain soaking his shirt. As soon as he saw the blood, his own blood, on his hand, Brad seemed to relax.

"Brad, hang on! Hang on. I'm calling for an ambulance, right now. Just hang on." Jack fumbled with his cell phone, trying to check Brad's pulse as he dialed. Then he held the phone against his shoulder while he worked to take his shirt off. "My brother's been shot!" he yelled as soon as the operator picked up. Holding his wadded shirt against the wound in a desperate attempt to slow the bleeding, he quickly relayed all the details he could, and waited the eternal minutes for the paramedics. "Brad, they're coming. Hang in there."

Bobbi Molinsky heard the phone ring, but when she saw her husband, ashen-faced, steadying himself against the wall, her breath pressed from her lungs.

"Jack, wait," Chuck pleaded, then he looked at her. "He hung up."

"What happened? Is Jack hurt?"

He shook his head and reached for her hand. "Not Jack." In his effort to stay calm, stay in control, he sounded mechanical. "Brad. Brad's been shot. They're taking him to University Hospital."

She heard "Brad" and she heard "hospital." This was just like when his appendix ruptured when he was a sophomore in college. That's all it was. Nothing serious, right?

"Shannon!" Chuck called. "We have to go to the hospital! Brad's been shot!"

"Wait!" Bobbi grabbed his arm and pulled him around to face her. "What did you say?"

He looked into her eyes and spoke with patronizing clarity. "Brad . . . has been shot."

"What?"

"Shot. With a gun. We have to get to University Hospital."

"That's impossible." He was just there with them a few hours ago. The aroma of the roast and homemade bread from his birthday dinner still hung in the kitchen. He couldn't be . . .

"Bobbi, we need to go." He pushed her toward the front door, flipping off lights as he went. She could hear Chuck talking, but his words weren't registering with her.

"Mom?" Shannon met them in the entry hall, terror in her eyes. "What happened?"

Bobbi shook her head. "I don't know."

"But he's gonna be okay, right?"

"Of course." Of course he'd be okay. He was young and strong. And shot. That had to be a misunderstanding. Shot at, maybe. That she could believe. That had to be what happened. In the car, she reached her right hand back between the seat and the door, and Shannon immediately seized it.

Chuck drove like a maniac, but she knew better than to say anything to him. At every red light, he made another phone call. Their son Joel. Her sister, Rita. Their pastor, Glen. He kept saying, "Brad's been shot. I don't know any details." It was so bizarre, so unreal to hear her son's name and "shot" in the same sentence. People she knew didn't get shot. Shootings were for the eleven o'clock news.

Jack ran to them as soon as they bustled through the automatic doors to the emergency room. Bobbi immediately noticed his shirt was inside out. Why . . . ? He threw his arms around her neck and sobbed. "I'm sorry . . . Mom, I'm so sorry."

"Sorry? For what?" Bobbi asked gently. There was a policeman against the wall. Was he here because of Brad?

"We thought it was . . . Brad thought so, too . . ."

"Thought what?"

Jack took a deep breath. "An old man came in the mission. . . . Just . . . some of the things he said . . . we . . . We both thought he could've been my mom's dad . . ."

"Reynolds?" Chuck asked. "Edward Reynolds was in the mission? Did he threaten you?"

Jack shook his head. "No, it wasn't like that. He just asked a bunch of questions, like if I'd ever been to Baltimore."

"Your mom was from Baltimore."

"I know. That's what Brad said. So we tried to catch up with him. We weren't three blocks away before . . ." He blinked back tears. "There were these guys on a street corner. And this big, black SUV cruised in. Brad said something was wrong. He threw me down, and that's when he . . ."

Bobbi hugged him tightly and smoothed his hair, the way she did when he was a little boy. "It will be okay," she whispered.

Jack sniffled, glanced at the policeman, and took the tissue she offered him. "He's in surgery now. I haven't heard anything else."

"Where was he hit?" Chuck asked.

"Once in the chest," Jack said, "but he was conscious and everything when the paramedics took him."

"That's good, right?" Shannon asked. "Conscious is a positive thing."

Bobbi squeezed her hand. "Of course it's good, baby." Brad. Once in the chest. Your heart was in your chest. But if he was conscious, he couldn't have been shot through the heart. So, he's okay. He'd be okay.

Moments later, Rita and her husband, Gavin, arrived. Chuck got directions to the surgery waiting rooms and the six of them headed for the elevator. Chuck filled the silence with details for Rita and Gavin. How many more times did she have to hear it?

"I called Danny," Rita said. "He's gonna drive straight through so he can get here."

"I hate for him to do that," Bobbi said. "His little ones . . ."

"They were gonna get here tomorrow anyway. There was no arguing with him."

"Sounds like someone else I know."

Rita managed a smile. "He's not due in Norfolk until July first, so they should have a good visit."

"Brad's looking forward to seeing him. Joel's not on call this weekend, so it'll be like old times. Joel's . . . where is Joel, Chuck?"

"He's waiting on a delivery."

"A delivery?"

"A baby. He's doing the newborn exam. He's got a call out for another pediatrician, so I'm sure he'll get here as soon as he can."

Good. She'd feel better with Joel here. But if Danny was driving through the night . . . Was it that bad? She felt Shannon slip an arm around hers, and when the elevator doors opened, she felt the teenager's grip tighten. Bobbi took Shannon's hand and followed Chuck and Jack to the waiting room. Another policeman stood in the hallway. They were everywhere. Were they protecting Brad? Or Jack?

"You had Brad's birthday tonight?" Rita asked.

Bobbi turned her head slowly toward her sister. That was this evening, wasn't it? "Yeah, Shannon teased him about being middle-aged now."

"At thirty-five? I don't want to know what that makes me." Rita smiled and patted Shannon's arm.

"We laughed because Joel got called out, so that meant Brad had a fair shot at the pie. Then he and Chuck talked about the mission's board meeting next week . . ."

A man in scrubs walked toward them. He slowly pulled his scrub cap off and smoothed his hair. His face was drawn, his eyes weary. He had bad news. "Are you Brad's family?" he asked quietly.

Chuck extended a hand. "We're his parents." Bobbi slipped her hand into Chuck's, and she felt Shannon's hand fall away from hers.

The surgeon surveyed the room, all the anxious eyes on him. "Mr. Molinsky, Mrs. Molinsky, I'm very sorry."

A dark heaviness enveloped Bobbi. She knew the surgeon was talking, explaining to them what efforts his team had made to save Brad's life, but he sounded distant, as if she were hearing him from underwater. As her heart and mind reeled, trying to comprehend the reality that her son was dead, she caught random words—aorta, bleeding, rare. She was vaguely aware that Chuck and maybe Jack were trying to steady her, and then everything went black.

CHAPTER 2
CATALYST

Chuck shuffled down the long corridor to the waiting area and his family. What he wanted to do was collapse the way Bobbi had, but the crisis management part of his brain had taken over. It tapped some unknown storehouse and it pushed his feet forward, one step at a time.

In the waiting area, he surveyed the emotional devastation gripping his family. Shannon perched in a chair, her knees drawn tightly to her. In the opposite corner Jack held his face in his hands. Glen and Laurie Dillard were there sitting with Gavin while Rita paced. The policeman was gone.

Shannon saw him first and hopped up out of her chair. "How is she?"

"She's okay." He hugged her close, wishing he could squeeze the worry and grief away. Even as he ended the embrace, he kept an arm around her. "Everything checked out okay, heart, blood pressure, sugar. They gave her a sedative and they want to keep her overnight. I'm going to stay with her."

"I'm staying, too."

"I know you want to—"

"Dad . . . I need . . . I need her."

He couldn't argue with her. "So do I, sweetheart." He rubbed her back gently, then took her hands in his. "It would help me out if I knew you were home. Would you do that for me?"

Without raising her eyes, Shannon nodded, then pushed a tear away with her palm.

He rubbed his thumb across the back of her hand, like she was still a preschooler, then he looked to Rita and Gavin. "Would you guys take Shannon and Jack home and stay with them?"

"Of course." Rita hugged him tightly. "I am so sorry," she whispered before fresh tears began to fall.

"Dad . . . Brad's car." Jack choked on the words. "The cop brought me here, and . . . I didn't lock the mission . . ."

Before Chuck could try to sort that out, Gavin stepped up. "I'll go with you, Jack. Rita can take Shannon home, and Glen and Laurie can drop us off at the mission."

Jack hugged Chuck and whispered, "I'm sorry. Tell Mom I love her."

"Sure thing."

Glen and Laurie took their turns, giving him hugs, offering to come back and stay with him, but he put them off.

"Have you talked to Joel?" Shannon asked.

"He's not answering. He must be busy with the baby."

"Kind of ironic, huh? Those people have the joy of a new life, and we . . ."

"We'll be okay," Chuck said gently. "We made it when we lost Grandma. It's just going to take a long time to get over this." Shannon wiped her eyes and nodded. "I'll have Joel call you after I talk to him."

She sniffled and wiped her eyes again. "Tell Mom I'm okay. I don't want her to worry."

"Chuck, I'll make the rest of the calls," Rita said, draping an arm around Shannon's shoulder, squeezing her close.

"Thanks." He turned and patted Jack's shoulder. "I love you both, and I'll see you as quick as I can."

"Thanks for not telling us to get some sleep."

"If you could, that would be a good thing."

"Maybe some other day."

Chuck watched them scuff away. Now he had to tell Joel. He didn't have to be strong for Joel's sake like he did for Jack and Shannon, and that freedom made him hesitate. Then his phone buzzed.

"Dad? What's going on? How's Brad?"

Chuck tried to answer. He made the right shape with his mouth. He had enough air.

"Oh no," Joel whispered. "Dad . . . no . . ."

"They did all they could." He forced the words out. "The bullet, it hit him. . . . It ripped through his aorta."

"Through . . ."

He heard a rustle in the background. Joel wasn't the cool, detached doctor anymore. He was the tenderhearted little brother left behind one last time, and Chuck hated himself for relaying the news on the stupid telephone.

Joel blew out a deep breath. "I'm sorry. You, uh, don't need me to fall apart on you. He, uh, he didn't have a chance, then, did he?"

"He lost consciousness in the ambulance, and he'd lost so much blood . . ."

"Do you know how it happened?"

"It was a drive-by shooting. A stray bullet."

"And Jack was with him?"

"Brad threw Jack to the ground just before he was hit. Jack's not hurt, but . . ."

"Yeah, he's gotta be devastated. . . . What about . . . How are Mom and Shannon?"

"Shannon's . . . I think it would help her if you called her." Chuck eased into a nearby chair, suddenly feeling very tired, and very weak. "Your mother . . . she's spending the night here at the hospital."

"Her heart?"

"No, she blacked out. They gave her something so she could rest, and she's being monitored."

"You need me to come by?"

"No, I think I need a little time, you know?"

"Sure. I'll run by and see the kids, then we'll be over tomorrow."

"Mom and I probably won't be home before noon."

"What about the police? Do they have the guy?"

"No. Jack told them everything he saw, but I don't know how much help it was. Everything happened so fast, and he was so torn up."

"Poor kid . . . I can't imagine . . ." There was another rustle and Joel took a deep breath. "Listen, I'll, uh, let you get back to Mom, there. I love you, Dad."

"I love you, Joel, and give my love to Abby and Ryan." Chuck would never again miss an opportunity to tell his children he loved them. As he wandered toward Bobbi's hospital room, he tried to remember the last time he told Brad he loved him. Brad knew how much he loved him, didn't he?

Jack slumped into the passenger seat of Brad's car, only Brad wasn't driving it. Brad was never gonna drive this car again. He leaned his head against the window and didn't try to stop the tears silently streaming down his cheeks.

"You want to talk?" Uncle Gavin asked.

"Nothing to say."

"This wasn't your fault, Jack."

"I'm not so sure about that."

"The guy with the gun, he's the one responsible."

"Yeah, but here's the thing." He pulled himself around to face his uncle. "If Brad hadn't . . . If he . . . I would've been the one hit, only it would've been in my shoulder or something."

"You don't know that."

"Or if we'd been two seconds earlier, or two seconds later . . ." Jack wiped a tear away. "We only left the mission because of me."

His uncle eased the car to the curb, and he looked Jack in the eyes. "Regardless of why you were there, or how things developed, the only one responsible is the guy who pulled the trigger. There are enough things in life that *will* be your fault," he said with a half smile. "Don't freelance."

After a moment of uneasy silence, Uncle Gavin drove away and Jack leaned his head back against the headrest. He wasn't freelancing. He was trying to be a man and face his responsibilities, the way his dad did years ago.

"All right, if you won't believe me," his uncle the mind reader said, "there was a wise Irish philosopher who always said, 'Don't borrow trouble.'"

"Who was that?"

"Phil Shannon. He was our pastor years ago."

"Yeah, but I keep thinking about the 'what-ifs.'"

"I'm sure it's hard not to, but nothing good will come from that." He didn't say any more until he parked next to Aunt Rita's car at home. "You think you can get some sleep?"

"No." Jack doubted he'd be able to sleep for a very long time. Every time he closed his eyes, he saw Brad's face, and the calm resignation in his eyes as his life's blood drained away.

Jack dragged himself to the porch, but he froze with his hand on the doorknob.

"You okay?" Gavin asked.

"I just . . . The last time I came through this door, Brad was here. It just . . . It happened so fast. Just a few hours ago."

Gavin put a hand on his shoulder and squeezed gently. He hated that when he was a kid. "You can do it."

"I can remember the first time I walked through that door after losing my mom. It felt so weird."

"So this begins life without Brad?"

"I guess that's what it is."

Jack gripped the door handle, his palms suddenly damp. He could feel his pulse pounding in his neck. He still had a pulse. *This is stupid. Just get it over with.* He pushed the door open and immediately smelled coffee. Home.

Aunt Rita didn't hear them come in the kitchen. She cradled the cordless phone against her shoulder while she peered in the refrigerator. Surely she wasn't hungry. No, she would probably try to feed him.

"I'm gonna get the leftovers out of here," she said into the phone. "I don't want Bobbi to have to deal with them." She glanced over, and as soon as she saw him, she gave him a smile. "Kara, Dad's here with Jack. I'll talk to you tomorrow." She clicked the phone off and hugged him tightly. "You've had a terrible, terrible shock. Why don't you try to get some rest."

He shook his head. "Is Shannon in bed?"

"She's out on the deck. Do you drink coffee?"

"I'll take some, thanks." Jack got a mug from the cabinet and Rita filled it for him. As he took the first sip, he could feel Aunt Rita's and Uncle Gavin's pathetic stares. He couldn't hang around for that. "I think I'm going to go sit with Shannon for a while."

He slid the back door open and waited a moment for his eyes to adjust to the darkness. Shannon sat in one of the deck chairs, her knees drawn up close to her body. She never acknowledged him. He hoped that meant she'd drifted off to sleep. He eased down to the top step, set his coffee beside him, and leaned back against the post. The air was still and a handful of stars were out.

"Today started out so ordinary," Shannon said, startling him when she spoke.

"Yeah."

"Why didn't God protect Brad?" She dropped her knees and looked at him. "Brad was such a good person. He was in ministry. . . . Shouldn't that count for something?"

"I don't know." He couldn't answer his own questions.

"And Mom and Dad, haven't they gone through enough? I mean, there was the affair, and then you, and now this. . . . It's not fair."

"Wait a minute. Me? I'm something Mom and Dad had to suffer through?"

She nodded. "Finding out Dad had you was a tough time for them. Why doesn't God leave them alone?"

"I'm not God, I don't know. I guess we just have to trust that God knows what He's doing, and that this will all work out somehow."

"So help me, if you quote that stupid verse about everything working out for good, I will punch you in the mouth."

Jack took a long drink of coffee to hide a slight smile. If she saw him grin, she'd punch him, verse or no verse.

"I hope somebody rots in jail for this," she muttered.

"Unless one of those other guys talks, I don't know if they'll ever catch the guy that did the shooting."

"You didn't see him? Jack! You were right there!"

"I was a little busy."

She slumped back in her seat. "Great. Justice depends on a bunch of hoods. I'm sure they'll be real reliable witnesses."

"If they recovered the bullet, they can match it to the gun. They won't need witnesses." Recovered the bullet . . . from Brad's body. Jack suddenly felt nauseous.

"I don't want to talk about this anymore," Shannon said, standing. "I'm going to bed." She stopped before stepping through the sliding door. "Your shirt's inside out, you dork."

He pulled the neck of the shirt out. He sighed and pulled it over his head, then slipped it back on. That was the least of his worries when he grabbed a clean shirt at the mission.

He leaned his head back against the post and closed his eyes. He told that cop everything, every last thing . . . but he never saw the shooter. *God, if I saw him, help me remember. . . . Don't let this depend on me.*

In his wife's darkened hospital room, Chuck eased the door shut, holding the door handle, trying his best to dampen the click as it shut. He could hear Bobbi breathing with the rhythm of deep sleep, and he didn't want anything to disturb that. This might be the only decent night's sleep she got for a very long time. At her bedside, he laid his hand on hers, then kissed her gently. "I love you," he whispered. He was sure he saw her smile.

She was such a remarkably strong woman, and they had struggled through so much together. He couldn't imagine facing the loss of his son without her. He pulled his glasses from his shirt pocket so he could read the displays on her monitors, as if he knew what the numbers meant. Blood pressure he recognized, and it was good, much better than his, but he wasn't sure what her pulse and respiration should be as she slept.

He pulled a pillow from the closet and turned the wastebasket upside down, positioning it just in front of the vinyl couch. He folded the pillow in half and slipped it behind his head, using the wastebasket for a footstool. *I need to call Christine in the morning. And the assistant director at the mission, Ron, uh, Ron . . . good grief, I just talked to him last week. Moore. Ron Moore.*

Chuck tried to replay the events of the evening in his mind, but he couldn't recall the dinner they had enjoyed. The scene always changed quickly to that wrenching phone call from Jack. And then the surgeon . . .

He reached back further in his memory until he could see Brad tightly bundled in the hospital blankets, sleeping in his mother's arms. That was one of the greatest days in his life. A son. His son. Now that son was gone. That quickly. Without warning.

Chuck pulled the pillow down and sobbed into it until merciful exhaustion won out.

Friday, June 13

Before Bobbi opened her eyes, the antiseptic, chlorine, hospital smell hit her, and she remembered where she was. Oh, Brad. Her chest and stomach remained knotted with that nauseating pain. For an instant she hoped it had all been some sort of psychotic episode, detached from reality. She'd take that in a heartbeat—losing her sanity over losing her son.

If she was still at the hospital, then where was Chuck? Where were her children?

Her head throbbed when she opened her eyes slowly, making it a challenge to focus. *They must have given me enough to sedate a moose.* She started to call for Chuck, but she heard him take a deep breath. She should have known he was right there.

He was always good in a crisis, able to think and take action. Perhaps that was why they fit together so well. He was action and she was instinct. She stretched a hand out, wanting to touch him.

Laboring to turn her head, she saw him sleeping on the small sofa beside her bed. Chuck's hair seemed grayer this morning, the lines in his forehead deeper, the ones around his eyes more prominent. She'd heard stories about people subjected to extreme shocks waking up to find their hair had turned snow white. Those stories didn't seem so farfetched now.

She rolled her head back to the center of the pillow and sighed. Brad was gone. It wasn't any more real than it had been last night. He wouldn't be there this weekend when Danny was home, or for their anniversary, or for Thanksgiving or for Christmas, or for anything ever again. And for what? Nothing in downtown St. Louis was worth Brad's life. Nothing.

If she squinted, she could make out the hands of the clock. Almost seven. She needed to get home to Shannon and Jack. Last night she couldn't bear her own grief, and she left them to fend for themselves. She would never forget Shannon's desperate hand reaching for hers, or the look on Jack's face when they walked through the emergency room doors. How could she fail them this way?

After Jack's mother died, he counseled with Glen, and they discovered what an insecure little boy he was. Anytime he began to relax and feel safe in a routine, his mother uprooted him. He was so needy for attachment, for a connection to a family, when they got him. He idolized Brad. And now . . . It would take more wisdom than she had to help him recover from this.

Bobbi heard Chuck stir. "Hey," she said.

"Hey, yourself." He reached his hand out to hers. "How do you feel?"

"I haven't tried to sit up yet, and I have the mother of all headaches."

Chuck stood up slowly. "Well, I have an everything-else-but-my-head-ache, so we've got it all covered." He leaned over and kissed her. "You scared me last night."

"Did you send the kids home?"

He nodded. "Rita and Gavin were going to stay with them."

"Were they okay?"

"They both told me to tell you not to worry about them."

"It's just unreal." She stared across the room. "It's like . . . it's like smacking yourself with a hammer, you know?" She looked back at Chuck. "For those first few seconds, it doesn't hurt, because you're too stunned, but you know it's going to hurt . . . a lot . . . and soon."

Chuck nodded and said, "I wish I could shield you from that."

"I don't know if you should. If Brad wasn't such a wonderful, special young man, if I didn't love him so much . . ." Her voice trailed off, and Chuck sat on the edge of the hospital bed, taking her in his arms. She fought the tears long enough to whisper, "If I didn't love him, it wouldn't hurt so much."

As her words faded, everything melted into black sorrow. Chuck rocked her gently and cried with her.

After several minutes, she pushed away from him. "They won't let me out of here if I'm hysterical," she choked out.

Chuck handed her a box of tissues from the small cabinet that served as her nightstand. "You're not hysterical. You've never been hysterical."

She heard her door click open so she passed her tissues off to Chuck and sat up straight. A young doctor rounded the curtain, carrying her file. "Mrs. Molinsky? How are you this morning?"

"How do I have to answer that to go home?"

"That was good enough," he answered with a hint of a smile. He opened the folder and laid it on the end of the bed.

"Do you need me to leave?" Chuck asked.

"You're fine, Mr. Molinsky." He began to examine Bobbi, listening to her heart and checking her pupils. "Did you sleep?"

"Yes."

"Any hangover from the meds?"

"My head is pounding."

"You can take what you want for that when you get home. You wear glasses?"

"Occasionally."

"How long have you been married?"

"Thirty-eight years."

"Were you twelve when you got married?"

"Twenty-one, thanks. Is this a quiz?"

"Just making sure you're all the way back with us." The doctor wrote in Bobbi's folder, then closed it and tucked it under his arm. "First of all, I am so sorry about your son. I was here last night when they brought him in."

"Thank you," Bobbi said quietly. "You saw Brad?"

"I was the one who said to take him straight to surgery. That's all I did."

"Can I ask you a question? Did he . . ." She cleared her throat, trying desperately to find her voice. "Did Brad . . . Was there any chance he could . . . ?"

The doctor's eyes dropped away from hers. "You always hope for a miracle."

A miracle . . . I've used up my miracles.

Breaking the uncomfortable silence, the doctor spoke again. "Now, you can go home as soon as they process everything. If you hadn't been here when you fainted, it probably wouldn't have been such a big deal."

"I'm glad you made sure," Chuck said.

"You folks don't need two tragedies." The doctor pulled the folder out and flipped it open again. "Oh, there was one thing. Have you been sick recently?"

"No, why?"

"Your white count was a little high. Not like 'bells and whistles' high, but elevated. Emotional stress can sometimes cause that, but you may want to follow up with your regular doctor." He reached out and shook Bobbi's hand and spoke with soft sincerity. "Mrs. Molinsky, take care of yourself, especially in these next few days." He shook hands with Chuck, then left.

"I'm thankful you're okay." Chuck stepped closer and squeezed her hand.

Physically, maybe. "Did you catch his name?"

"It'll be on his bill, I'm sure."

"He was nice. Kinda reminded me of Joel."

"So you do talk about me when I'm not around." Joel Molinsky pulled the privacy curtain aside and crossed the room to her bed in three long strides.

"Honey, what are you doing here?" Bobbi said.

"I was in the neighborhood."

"No, really," Bobbi persisted.

"Dad." Joel hugged Chuck, ignoring her.

"Joel?" Bobbi said one last time.

"Really, Mom. I'm, uh, clearing my schedule." He rolled his eyes to the ceiling and took a deep breath. "Anyway, I was practically next door at Cardinal Glennon, so I went ahead and stopped in, rather than wait until you got home, so I could stop worrying."

"I thought I was the only one who worried." She reached for him, and he leaned down so she could wrap her arms around his neck.

"I love you, Mom," he whispered.

"I love you, too." Holding one of her children close was better than all the medications and all the rest in the world. Now she needed the others.

After the embrace, he looked her in the eyes. "Are you okay this morning?"

"No, but I can go as soon as all the paperwork is done."

"I talked to the kids last night," Joel said.

"How were they? What did they say?"

"Jack needs somebody to sit down with him and let him talk for about twelve hours straight, then I think he'll be fine."

"And Shannon?"

"Shannon is like her mother." He grinned, but then he grew serious. "Everything inside her is all churned up. She's angry, scared, hurt, confused and it's all very intense."

"And I was stuck here all night," Bobbi muttered.

"I don't know if you could have done anything for her, Mom. I think she's gonna have to sort this all out for herself."

CHAPTER 3
ANTIPATHY

When Shannon tried to open her eyes, they burned and scraped like someone had ground dry sand into them. She didn't know she had that many tears in her. Last night Joel just let her cry, without saying stupid things to try and make her feel better. She loved him for that.

She asked him point-blank where God was. From what the doctor said, just a fraction of an inch would have saved Brad's life. Couldn't God have given the bullet a little push, just a half inch? Joel shook his head and said he couldn't explain it. Nobody could explain it.

Still in yesterday's clothes, she pulled a sweatshirt over her head and wandered downstairs. Uncle Gavin and Aunt Rita sat in the kitchen where she'd left them last night. Rita rounded the table and hugged Shannon tightly. "Morning, baby. You feel like breakfast?"

"No. Are Mom and Dad home?"

"It won't be long. They were signing papers, and as soon as that's done, they're leaving."

"So Mom's okay?"

"She's a strong woman."

"Crazy strong. Where's Jack?"

"He went for a walk. He's desperately trying to remember what he saw last night, hoping it'll help the police. "

"For whatever good it will do," Shannon muttered, and dropped into a chair at the kitchen table. "Jack didn't see anything."

"You'd be surprised what the police can use," Gavin said. "I'd say the boys who were the actual targets would be more than willing to give their rivals over to the cops."

"You really think so?"

"God will bring this around," Gavin said with a wink and a nod. "Wait and see."

"If God had been on the job in the first place, He wouldn't have anything to bring around." She pushed away from the table and walked out of the kitchen. Uncle Gavin always said stuff like that about God. His family never had hard times of their own, just what her family went through, so it was easy to believe God was all sunshine and rainbows. Only Kara's divorce kept them from being totally plastic.

The way it looked to her, either God *couldn't* save Brad, which meant He wasn't as great as everyone said, or He *wouldn't* save Brad, which was worse. Why would anybody worship a God who just dropped you? Where was He last night when Mom needed Him, when the rest of them needed Him?

The phone rang, and she rushed to the handset in the study, hoping it was her mother. The caller ID showed Kara's number. Probably calling for Aunt Rita. Figures.

"Shannon, it's Katelyn," Rita called from the kitchen. "Do you want to talk?"

To someone who would understand? Definitely. "Got it in the study, thanks!" Shannon picked up the handset and slouched into her mother's loveseat. "Hey, Kat."

"I'm so sorry about Brad. Mom just told me."

"It's a nightmare. Mom passed out and had to spend the night in the hospital. Dad stayed with her. They still aren't home yet. Jack was there with Brad, but he didn't see anything."

"And you're stuck there with Granny."

"And Uncle Gavin." She lowered her voice, mocking her uncle. " 'God's got a plan in all this.' "

"He said that?"

"Pretty much."

"You want to go somewhere? Or we can just hang out here at my house. Mom's at work, so it's just me and Natalie and Mia. I can come and get you."

"Maybe later. I want to be here when Mom gets home."

"Yeah, just text me or gimme a buzz and I'm there. We're praying for you guys."

"Don't bother," Shannon said as she hung up the phone.

Bobbi spotted Jack as soon as Chuck turned on to Danbury Court. A young man, a kid really, with his baseball hat pulled down low and his hands deep in the pockets of his baggy shorts. He never looked up as the car eased past him.

"Let me out," Bobbi said, unbuckling her seatbelt. Jack raised his head when her car door opened. In his eyes, she could see the six-year-old Jack once again, stunned by a loss, unsure what to do next. When she reached him, he collapsed on her shoulder, but this time she didn't have any comfort for him. "I'm so sorry, sweetheart," she whispered. "I'm sorry you had to do this by yourself."

"It's okay," he said, then sniffled. "You're home now. It'll be okay."

She wished that were so.

She held tightly to Jack's arm as they walked the rest of the way up the sidewalk to the driveway, where Chuck was getting out of the car. She let go of Jack long enough for Chuck to hug him tightly.

"I'm sorry, Dad," Jack said quietly. "I've been trying to remember. . . . It was dark. . . . It all happened so fast. . . ."

"Jack, don't beat yourself up over this. Your first priority was Brad. I would have done the same thing."

Bobbi leaned on Jack as she walked up to the porch. "How long have you been gone?"

"I don't know. Since about eight, I guess. I wasn't sleeping anyway."

"Hey, we're home," Bobbi announced once they got inside the front door. Rita and Gavin came into the entry hall from the kitchen, and Shannon tromped downstairs.

Rita hugged her sister. "Are you all right, really?"

"Yes." If being robbed of your son then abandoning your other children makes you all right, then she was in tip-top shape. "Shannon." Bobbi held her arms out and Shannon fell into them. "I love you, baby," she whispered. "I'm so sorry I wasn't here for you."

"I know you wanted to be," Shannon said in a fragile, little-girl voice.

Bobbi wanted to spend the rest of the day, the rest of her life maybe, holding her children close, drawing strength from them as they tried to regain some sense of security and order.

But there were arrangements to be made. She owed that much to Brad, and she couldn't leave Chuck to handle it alone. Should she take the kids with her, perhaps? Would it help them to be involved, or was it better to shield them? In the middle of the debate, she felt a hand on her arm.

Rita said, "I've got coffee on. Let me get you a cup." She left Chuck, Gavin and Jack in the entry hall and followed Rita to the kitchen, still holding Shannon's hand. "Glen and Laurie wanted to stop by if you're up to it, and I've got a stack of phone messages."

"I owe you." Bobbi took the steaming cup of coffee from her sister and dropped into one of the kitchen chairs.

"I can stay the rest of the day and answer the phone, or I can go with you this afternoon."

"I'll let you know, thanks." Bobbi sipped the coffee, then patted the chair next to her. "Here, sit with me, baby. Did you sleep?"

Shannon pulled the chair a little closer to hers. "A little after Joel left. You?"

"I was drugged."

"Kat called me and wanted to know if I wanted to get out."

Bobbi patted Shannon's hand. "You should. There's no reason to stay around here and smother."

"What are you going to do?"

"Catch my breath, get a shower, and then . . ." Emotion was too near the surface. She took a long drink from her coffee to give herself time to regain her composure. "Then Dad and I will have to start making arrangements," she said quietly.

"Would it be disrespectful if I took off?" Shannon asked.

"Not at all."

"You don't need me?"

I need you more than the air I breathe. "Baby, if you want to go, by all means, go."

Running around with Katelyn motivated Shannon enough to shower and change clothes. When Katelyn pulled up in front of her house, she shuffled out and got in the car.

"We're going to Burger King," Katelyn announced. "And you're gonna eat something."

"I don't want anything." Shannon rested her knees against the dashboard, the way her father always told her not to. What if the airbag goes off? he said. Today, if that happened, she'd just pull her kneecaps out of her ears and go on.

"If you don't eat, they'll be on your case."

"They'll be on my case anyway."

"Why's that?"

"My brother was murdered because Jack led him on some wild goose chase trying to track down his grandfather, if the old guy even exists. It's Jack's fault. Period." She said it out loud at last, and it felt good.

"Are you serious?" Katelyn's eyes grew wide. "Mom didn't mention any of that."

Validated, Shannon dropped her knees and sat up straight. "Plus if Brad hadn't taken the time to throw Jack down, neither one of them would have been shot."

"Wait, Jack has a grandfather?"

"Maybe. Some old guy came in the mission, and Jack thought it might be his grandfather. He's the psycho that killed his wife, so even if it was him, why would Jack want anything to do with him?"

"Seriously?"

"But, of course, Jack gets a free pass because his mom died when he was little."

"This is so messed up."

"Tell me about it."

"Oh, how's your mom? Didn't she freak and have to stay in the hospital?"

"My mom *never* freaks. She's made of steel. She just fainted and they wanted to make sure it wasn't something more serious."

"Your mom's been through a lot."

"No kidding. She lost her parents, then my dad cheated on her, then she had to deal with Jack's mother, and Jack, and now Brad." Shannon shook her head. "But she just takes it. Never crumbles, never cracks. I don't know how she does it."

That evening, Bobbi sat on the loveseat in the study, alone. Going to the funeral home . . . so many stupid decisions. Did Brad really care, did anybody care, what color satin lined the casket? Then the stop at Brad's apartment drained the rest of her energy. Joel offered to take care of things with his dad to spare her, but she had to do it herself. She had to find a way to reconcile reality with denial.

Joel was like his dad, a man of action, desperate to find something to do in a crisis. When he, Abby and Ryan had arrived that afternoon, Joel had graciously taken phone calls, while Abby handled the food folks brought over and Ryan cut their grass.

She was so thankful for him. She didn't have the strength to assess what needed to be done, much less accomplish it. Every muscle, every joint ached. The sharp headache she'd wakened with never relented. Most of all, her heart hurt. The overwhelming shock was giving way to a gnawing sense of loss and injustice. Tomorrow they would have the visitation, and Sunday the funeral. After that, there would just be emptiness.

She leaned over and laid her head on the armrest of the loveseat and closed her eyes. *Dear God, how could You ask us to go through this? Is this some kind of punishment? What have I done that You would take my son from me?*

"Honey, can I sit with you?" Chuck asked. She hadn't heard him come into the study at all.

"Always." Bobbi pushed herself up to make room for him. Even from across the room she could see tears in his eyes. "You don't have to be tough anymore. It's just me."

"Thanks," he whispered, slipping in close beside her. She reached an arm around his shoulder, and with her touch, he began to cry, then sob. After several minutes, he swallowed hard and said quietly, "I've never hurt like this."

"I know."

"Shannon and Jack . . . they're looking for answers. I don't have them."

"I don't either."

Chuck reached around and took her in his arms. "I am so thankful for you. I couldn't do this without you."

Chapter 4
Impact

Saturday, June 14

Jack never took his eyes off the mirror as he worked with his necktie. "Over, around and back, then back around, and up through the top," he recited just the way Brad showed him that first Easter he spent with his family. He had his first real tie, not a clip-on, and he wanted to surprise his parents.

It was worse than learning to tie his shoes, but after a long afternoon and dozens of failures, he got it. Kind of. If he had to do this every day, he'd have to get up twenty minutes early just to tie the thing.

He adjusted the knot, then straightened his collar and his jacket. "There you go, Brad. Just like you showed me." He heaved a deep sigh and dropped on his bed. "I can't do this," he whispered.

"Jack? You ready?" His dad eased the door open.

"Does it matter?"

"Of course it matters." He stepped inside and shut the door behind him. "Is something else going on? You avoided me and everybody else yesterday and all day today."

"It just hurts." Jack barely got the words out before the tears started.

His dad sat on the bed with him and let him cry. "I know it hurts," he said gently. "We're all hurting, and it's going to hurt for a long time."

Jack twisted away and paced to the window. Being a blubbering crybaby wouldn't help anything. "I fall apart every time I hear Brad's name. How am I supposed to do this tonight?"

"Jack." The bed squeaked as his dad stood. "The folks coming to the funeral home tonight, they're grieving, too. We need to help each other through this. They're going to want to talk about what Brad meant to them, and we need to soak that in. It's a special gift to see how many lives Brad touched, and how many people love us."

Jack nodded and wiped his eyes once more. With his dad, it always came back to doing the right thing. "I guess I owe it to Brad, don't I?"

His dad patted his back. "It'll be tough, but I think it'll help you out."

"Yeah, I just don't want Mom to see me like this."

"I've got a news flash for you. Mom already knows you're like this."

Downstairs, Joel stood at the sliding glass door, staring out across his parents' backyard, wrestling with a newly realized responsibility. He was the oldest now. He was the big brother. His parents would be depending on him once they got up in years, and he had a duty to watch out for Shannon. Somehow, he also had to be there for Jack since he'd lost his hero. Joel let a deep breath go. How was he supposed to help Jack when he'd lost a hero, too?

"What are you thinking?" Abby slipped an arm around his waist and leaned against him.

Joel hugged her close and kissed her gently. "I feel kind of alone."

"You've still got Shannon and Jack."

"I know, but Brad and I grew up together. The little kids never knew Grandpa Jim, and they missed so much with Grandma. Growing up, it was me and Brad. I feel like I've lost some of my childhood, I guess. Does that make any sense?"

"Quite a bit."

"We went through Mom and Dad's separation together. Nobody else really knows what that was like." Then Joel couldn't resist a smile. "Of course, he was a jerk until he was about twenty." Abby returned the smile and gave him a gentle shove. "We were close, Abby. I confided in him, asked him for advice. . . . I'm going to miss him." Joel wiped his eyes quickly and glanced behind him. "I don't want Mom to see me."

"I don't think your mother expects you to be emotionless."

"She needs to do her own coping, and not worry about how the rest of us are doing."

Bobbi stood on the sidewalk of Bricker's Funeral Home waiting for Chuck to join her. What she wouldn't give to be one of the people in the cars driving by, scurrying to some appointment, untouched by a profound loss. Shannon and Jack stood ready to follow her inside. She straightened Jack's tie and brushed his shoulders before kissing him lightly on the cheek.

She turned to Shannon and held her for just a moment. "We will get through this, I promise," she whispered. "I'm not sure how, but we will. You're a beautiful, strong young woman. You can do this, baby."

"Thanks, Mom."

She felt Chuck's hand in the small of her back. "Are you ready?" he asked.

"No, but I never will be." He steadied her up the steps and held the door for them. Don Bricker met them with a polite smile and directed them to the viewing hall. She pulled away from Chuck without looking back. "Give me just a minute."

She closed her eyes and stepped around the corner, met by the fragrances of lilies and roses. She forced her eyes open, forced herself to look at him at the other end of that narrow room, in a place where a son should never be. Her breath caught.

With each step toward him, images blitzed through her memory. That first smile of recognition. The triumph of getting his driver's license. The prayer offered at his graduation. The Mother's Day card spelled MOMY. Tying his shoes. The football physical—"any broken bones?" the doctor asked. "Not yet," Brad said. The way he could never remember which was a pumpkin and which was a pickle—that made Halloween interesting. The heartbreak when his first real girlfriend broke things off.

He changed her life. With every "first," he redefined her. He gave her a focus, a purpose and a confidence that she never found anywhere else.

She eased her hand around his, and the unnatural coolness prompted the first tear. The left side of his mouth was slightly drawn as if in an eternal private joke. The day's stubble on his face was just as she remembered, and his hair flipped up in perfect spikes as if he'd combed it himself.

Such a fine young man. So handsome. This was so senseless. So wrong. She leaned over and caressed his cheek, then kissed him

gently, her tears spotting the shoulder of his suit. "I love you, Brad."
Then she hung her head and shuddered with great wrenching sobs.

Chuck watched Bobbi as long as he could bear, then he
crossed the room to her. Wrapping his arms around her shoulders, he
gently pulled her away from the casket and into his arms.

"This is so unfair," she whispered.

"I know it is. I hate this for you. No mother should have to go
through this." He kissed her and held her tight.

"What am I gonna say to these people tonight?" She raised her
head and wiped her eyes.

"Tell them the truth. That it hurts more than anything we've
ever experienced, and we can't really comprehend the depth of loss."

She took a deep breath and straightened up. "Just, uh, just
stick close to me tonight."

"Tonight and every night." He kissed her again and squeezed
her hand.

She glanced past him. "The kids are watching. I've got to get it
together."

"They expect you to be emotional."

"But they need me to be in control. I need to show them how
to be strong." She pushed her hair behind her ear and smoothed her
dress against her hips. "There's Rita." She squeezed his hand one
more time before walking away to meet her sister.

Chuck turned back to the casket and gently laid his hand on
top of Brad's. "That woman gets all the credit, you know." He
swallowed hard. "A middle name was all you got from me. You have

her eyes, her strength, her focus, her sense of calling. . . . It was my profound honor to be your dad."

After a long moment, he turned and was surprised to see Shannon. "I'm impressed," he said. "With Grandma, you spent the evening in that corner over there."

She dropped her eyes. "I figured it was time to grow up."

"Don't rush that." He put his arm around her. "There's plenty of time to grow up."

She waved a finger toward the casket. "You know, the other night . . . I teased Brad about being middle-aged now."

"At thirty-five?"

"Yeah, on those little check boxes when you fill out forms, it's always thirty-five to fifty-five."

"Fifty-five? Ouch. That makes me a . . . a senior citizen."

"Truth hurts, Dad." She smiled and laid her head against his shoulder. "When I was really little, like three or four, it blew my mind that some people had brothers that were kids. Brad was in college. He shaved."

"Jack's your age."

"Yeah," she mumbled. "Everybody thinks Brad's all serious all the time, but he's the only one who would play Barbies with me. And actually be Barbie."

"Brad played Barbies?"

"Yeah, I had this one brown-haired one. That was his. Her name was Carmen. He did the voice and everything."

"Pretty secure in his manhood, apparently."

"Secure in everything."

"You're a lot like him, you know?"

"Uh, no."

"Sweetheart, you're very goal-oriented, like Brad. You have that same sense of justice."

She smiled and blinked back a tear. "Thanks, Dad. That's about the best compliment you could give me right now."

"Hey, there's Katelyn." Chuck pointed toward the door where Kara Isaac and her daughters were signing the guestbook.

"So is it okay if I hang out with her tonight?"

"Of course."

"Thanks, Dad."

Chuck watched Shannon and Katelyn distance themselves from everyone else, and he thanked God Shannon had a confidante right now. He hoped Jack could find someone. Abby's son was a quiet, thoughtful kid. Maybe Ryan could be Jack's sounding board.

"I guess this is where I'm supposed to be," Bobbi said, rejoining him. "Was Shannon okay?"

"She's a strong young woman. Just like her mother."

"Her mother is a fine actress."

The crowd seemed to part for a young man in dress blues, making his way toward them.

"Danny . . . ," Bobbi said softly. "This wasn't the homecoming I wanted for you."

He hugged her gently, then shook Chuck's hand. "I'm glad I could be here."

"You're not alone, are you?"

"No, Rachel and the kids are in the foyer. Aunt Bobbi . . . When Mom told me . . . I can't imagine what this is like for you. I'm so sorry."

"Thank you. He loved you like a brother."

"Yeah, I talked to him, oh, one day last week, trying to firm up a time when we could get together. I was going to meet him down at the mission. He was doing amazing things down there. Changing lives."

"He's an amazing young man."

"I won't monopolize your time tonight. We'll talk later." Danny kissed Bobbi's cheek and shook Chuck's hand again.

"He looks more like Brad's brother than Joel," Chuck said, as Danny walked away.

"Always has. Genes are funny things sometimes." Bobbi took Chuck's hand. "Cooper DeWitt, I never would have dreamed . . ." Brad's youth minister was in his midforties now but still had a boyish smile. He hugged Chuck, then Bobbi, and Amy DeWitt followed her husband's lead.

"We were stunned when we heard about Brad," Cooper said softly.

"Thank you," Bobbi said. "He thought the world of you."

"I think you played a big role in Brad's choice of seminary over law school," Chuck said.

"I don't know about that," Cooper said. "It was a privilege to watch him mature."

As Bobbi chatted with the DeWitts, Chuck marveled at her dignity and grace. She had an unmatched elegance even in the face of such devastating grief. Small wonder her children rose to great heights. He couldn't help but fall in love with her one more time, just a little deeper.

Not long after, David Shannon, Phil and Donna's oldest son, came into the funeral home. He shook Chuck's hand and then Bobbi's. "Mom wanted to come," he said, "but Neil is failing fast, and she's afraid to leave him."

"David, I'm sorry to hear that," Bobbi said. "I didn't realize Dr. Craig was that ill."

"It's been a battle, and Mom doesn't drive anymore so I left Jan home with her."

"Give her our love, and tell her thank you for thinking of us," Bobbi said. Once David had left, Bobbi looked to Chuck and said, "Donna must be getting close to eighty by now." She shook her head. "Listening to David makes me feel old."

"You don't look it," Chuck answered with a smile.

"Looks can be deceiving," Bobbi replied.

Chuck saw John Isaac slip in, and even though his split with Kara had been amicable, he hung back, waiting for his opportunity to speak to them privately. Bobbi smiled and extended her hand to him.

He took her hand and leaned in to hug her. "I'm really sorry about Brad."

"Thank you," Bobbi said.

Chuck shook John's hand and said, "Good to see you, John. Thanks for coming."

"You know, I've always thought the world of you and Bobbi," John said, glancing past. "When Kara and I couldn't work things out, I felt like a real failure considering what you all were able to overcome."

"It takes both of you," Chuck said.

"Yeah, I don't think we had the energy to do what it was going to take to rebuild things." He glanced around the room again. "I should speak to Joel, and the rest of my family."

"John, take care," Bobbi said, reaching for his hand again. "You're still one of us."

"Thank you," John said quietly, with a gentle smile. "You're in my prayers."

John stopped and talked to Rita and Gavin briefly, then Joel, before moving on to see his girls. "I miss him," Bobbi said just loud enough for Chuck to hear her.

"I think Kara is too much like her mother," Chuck said with a wink.

"Granted, but like you said, it takes two to reconcile."

Jack spent the evening eavesdropping as partners, clients and coworkers from his dad's law firm, schoolteachers, doctors, classmates, church members and extended family all offered condolences and shared memories with his parents. He hung on every word, but each story deepened his sense of loss. Needing a break, he found a chair in the corner and slumped into it, resting his elbows on his knees, with his face in his hands.

"It's a lot to process, isn't it?"

Jack looked up slowly. Joel had pulled up a chair next to him. "Yeah," he said. He leaned back and stretched his legs out. "This wasn't part of my plan."

"I doubt it was part of anybody's plan, even the shooter."

"Yeah, but I mean, I planned on following Brad to seminary, and maybe the mission." His eyes began to brim with tears. "What do I do now?"

Joel turned to face him. "Jack, you won't hear this right now, but file it. You're Jack, not Brad. God's got something for you that only you can do. Find that."

"How?"

He grinned broadly. "The same way the rest of us figure that out. The hard way."

"Thanks," Jack said with mock aggravation.

"Looks like everybody's gone home." Joel stood and stretched.

"Finally," Jack said with a sigh.

"It'll be easier tomorrow."

"In theory." He saw Shannon look his direction, then turn her back. "Joel, I gotta check something. Thanks, man." He crossed the room and tapped his sister on the shoulder. "Shannon?"

"What?" She whipped around to face him.

"Did I do something wrong? Are you mad at me for something?"

"Jack, do you understand what happened here tonight? You're the whole reason Brad was out on that street."

"You think I don't know that?" Jack jabbed at his temple. "I haven't slept because I can't get that out of my head." Then he added quietly, "I wish it had been me instead."

"Brad gave his life to protect *you*."

"I know, I know." Jack glanced at his parents, thankful they were talking to Rita and Gavin, unaware of their conversation. Shannon must have seen him.

"Of course, it's Dad's fault you were even born," Shannon said with disgust.

"You wouldn't have been born either if Dad hadn't had the affair."

"You don't know that." Shannon leaned in close to him. "But *you* certainly wouldn't have, and if your mother hadn't been such a head case, we would have never had to take you in." Shannon walked away, leaving Jack feeling like he had been punched in the stomach. Did his mom and dad feel the same way? Did everybody else?

Did Brad regret throwing him down and out of the line of fire? He shuffled over and stood at the foot of the casket, almost afraid to look. It was Brad's idea to follow the old man, wasn't it?

"Son, are you ready to go?" His dad put a hand on his shoulder and gave it a gentle squeeze. He still hated that.

Jack sidestepped him. "Do you think Uncle Gavin would give me a ride home?"

"Why don't you want to ride with us?"

"Can we talk about it later? It's a long story."

"Did somebody say something or do something?"

"Dad, please. Not now."

Against his better judgment, Chuck gave in and sent Jack home with the Heatleys. When Bobbi questioned him about it, he gave her the same answer he'd gotten—we'll talk about it later. Shannon, alone in the backseat, never gave the slightest indication that she knew anything about it, but Chuck suspected she was the instigator. He'd seen the two of them talking moments before he approached Jack.

Later that evening, Chuck knocked on Shannon's bedroom door. "Can I talk to you for a minute?" After a long pause, she opened the door without speaking to him and climbed back on her bed. "Is something going on between you and Jack?"

"Is that what Jack said?"

"I asked you," Chuck said firmly.

Shannon fixed her eyes on him and spoke with uncharacteristic deliberation. "Jack and I had a discussion about Brad's murder."

"And?" She was holding something back.

Shannon sighed. "Okay, this was gonna come out sooner or later anyway." She twisted around and sat up on her bed, facing him. "Dad, what happened the night Brad died?"

"What are you getting at?"

"Brad and Jack were out on the street in that neighborhood because they were on some ridiculous search for Jack's grandfather. It's Jack's fault they were there. It's Jack's fault that Brad is dead."

"You're wrong, Shannon," Chuck said sharply, his voice rising. "You're upset, and you're trying to find some way to deal with it, but Brad's death was an accident."

"Of course," Shannon said, rolling her eyes. "Poor Jack could never do anything wrong. He's had such a hard life. His mother was crazy—"

"What?"

"Dad, you've always made excuses for Jack. It's like—"

"We've never expected any less of Jack than we have from you."

"Whatever," she muttered.

"Give me an example."

"I am not arguing with a lawyer. Thanks anyway." She leaned back against the headboard. "Brad was innocent. If it wasn't for somebody else, he'd still be here."

"What about the guy with the gun? How can you ignore him and just blame your brother?"

"That guy was not after Brad. Jack put Brad in that position. And he knows it was his fault! Why do you think he's avoided us for three days?"

"Grief."

"Guilt. And you let him ride home with Uncle Gavin."

"That's . . . This is ridiculous. I don't want to hear any more about this." He pointed directly at Shannon, his jaw set. "You don't mention this to your mother, and you lay off Jack."

"You're mad because you know I'm right."

"I'm not mad, and you're absolutely wrong. I'm going to overlook your disrespect because of the circumstances, but we don't need this undercurrent running through our family. I'm not going to put up with it." Shannon glared at him but said nothing. "Good night," he said at last, leaving her alone in her room.

"So what's going on?" Bobbi asked when Chuck returned to their bedroom.

"Nothing," he said, untying his tie. "Teenager stuff."

"Look me in the eyes and tell me that."

"Both kids have very strong emotions right now. It will all blow over, and I don't think you should worry about it."

"Shannon is blaming Jack for this, isn't she?"

Chuck smiled and sat on the bed beside his wife. "Do they know you can do that?"

"No, it's my secret weapon. I'm right?"

"Completely. How'd you know?"

"Shannon is cut from the same fabric as Brad, Rita, and my mother. Somebody has to be responsible. There has to be someone to blame, someone to punish. Remember how Brad was after your affair? He just wanted you to pay."

"Yeah . . . and Jack is all too ready to take that blame."

"It's a dangerous combination."

"So what do we do?"

"Reassure him. Let her vent. Keep telling her it's not Jack's fault, but she'll have to come to that realization by herself."

CHAPTER 5
EROSION

Friday, June 20

Bobbi sat out on the deck as the late afternoon sun lengthened the shadows creeping across the backyard. In a long, strange week, the four of them rarely passed each other. Chuck coped by staying busy, so he spent the week settling Brad's affairs. He closed Brad's bank account, scheduled the utilities to be shut off at the end of the month and terminated his lease. Today he was at the apartment again, sorting through Brad's personal things.

Shannon and Jack kept to themselves, making few appearances outside their respective bedrooms. Bobbi encouraged them to do something, anything, but she found it difficult to take her own advice. Her only accomplishment for the day was throwing out all the remaining food well-meaning friends and family had dropped off.

Joel stopped by daily, usually with Abby and Ryan. Rita and Gavin called or visited and the Dillards checked in a couple of times. Bobbi appreciated their concern, but the visits were so awkward for all of them. She hoped everyone would get the sympathy out of their systems soon.

"Mom?" Shannon pushed the sliding door closed and took the deck chair next to her. "It's hot out. Wouldn't you rather be inside?"

Bobbi shook her head. "I was starting to feel trapped, you know?"

"Exactly. If it's okay with you, I think I'm gonna go to Katelyn's and spend the night."

"At Kara's or John's?"

"Her dad's."

"You have plans?"

"Not really. We may catch a movie."

Good. Good girl. Getting out. She needed that. They sat in silence for a moment, watching a rabbit hop across the yard and squeeze through a hole in the fence. "Are you still mad at Jack?"

"How'd you know? Did Dad tell you?"

"I told Dad. I've been a mom for a long time. You're not going to get much past me." Bobbi smiled at her daughter, then she grew serious. "Shannon, blame is a dangerous game."

Shannon never moved her gaze from the back fence.

It was too soon. Bobbi wouldn't press her now. She turned to face Shannon and waited for her daughter to look at her. "Dad and I decided to give Brad's car to Jack."

"Of course."

"What does that mean?"

"It's what I expected."

Shannon was lying. She saw some injustice in giving Jack the car. "Did you want Brad's car? Because—"

"Mom, no. Just . . . it's okay."

"That means you can have the little Ford all to yourself."

"So can I drive it tonight?"

"I don't see why not."

"Great. I'm gonna go ahead and go."

"Dad will be home soon. Don't you want to wait for him?"

"I'll see him later."

Jack heard the gentle knock at his door but couldn't find the will to get up and open it.

"Dad's home. Why don't you come down for dinner?"

What excuse would his mother buy? Then he heard the squeak as the door opened.

"Jack?"

"I don't feel like eating." When in doubt, go with the truth.

"I don't either. Would you please, for my sake?"

The last thing he wanted to do was to make things harder on her. He pushed himself up to sit on the bed. "And I guess I'll go back to work at the store Monday. I talked to them today."

"I'm glad they were understanding."

"I would have quit if they hadn't been." He stood and dragged himself toward the door.

"Sweetheart . . ."

"I know, I shouldn't be a quitter."

"I don't think you're a quitter. You just don't realize how strong you can be. You can do this, I promise." She put a hand over his heart. "It's all in there. Get it out, and use it."

"What about you?"

"Don't worry about me," she said. "Dad wants to talk to you."

Dad wants to talk. *Well, Jack, it's been a week. It's time we discussed your responsibility for Brad's death.*

He wanted to drop back on the bed, or crawl under it maybe, but his mother was watching so he shuffled to the kitchen. His dad sat at the table and smiled at him. "Hey, Jack, sit down."

He smiled. Was that a good thing or a bad thing? Jack dropped into a chair and his mother took the one beside him, like she was on his team. Definitely a good thing.

Then his dad stood and set a cardboard box on the table. "These are Brad's books. I think you should have them."

Brad's books? Jack stood and began pulling out thick volumes. Theology . . . Greek . . . Old Testament. "These are all his seminary books." Then Jack carefully lifted Brad's black leather Bible from the box. He opened it slowly, as if he were handling an ancient text. He turned page after page, each covered with Brad's notes and marks in the margins. "This is . . . Wow, I don't know what to say. Don't you guys or Joel want this?"

"No, there was no question," his dad answered. "You should have it. I'm sure Brad would agree." His dad shifted so he could reach into the front pocket of his jeans, and he pulled out a key ring. "Here. We want you to have Brad's car."

"What if I wreck it?"

"Then we'll collect the insurance money," his dad said. "Jack, it's a thing. Take it, use it. If you don't want the car, I'll sell it, but I thought you would appreciate having it. That it would mean more to you than anybody else."

"Of course it does, Dad. It's just . . ." *I don't deserve it. Not after I . . .*

"You loved your brother, and looked up to him," his mom said, "and, if you want to honor him, then take these gifts from him and use them."

"What about Shannon?"

"Shannon wouldn't read those kinds of books if you threatened her, especially not theology," his mom said, and she smiled.

"I mean about the car. Is she okay with that?"

"I told her this afternoon. She gets the Ford outright, so she was happy."

Jack held the Bible and the keys, then he looked at his parents. "Thank you. This is . . . it means a lot to me." Then glancing at his mother, he added, "This helps."

Shannon dragged a french fry through the puddle of ketchup and stared blankly across the mall's food court. Changing her surroundings didn't change her situation or how she felt about it. Naturally, Jack got Brad's car. Not that she wanted it, but . . . And she understood how hard it had to be for him, to have witnessed the shooting, and the guilt, but . . . her grief was dismissed because his was supposedly worse.

"So which movie?" Katelyn asked.

"I don't know," Shannon muttered. She slurped the last of her drink and wadded the wrappers in a tight ball to throw them away. "None of them look very good."

"There is an alternative." Katelyn leaned across the table and grinned mischievously. "Dylan Snider's turning nineteen. He's having a party."

Shannon rolled her eyes. "Is he getting a Ferrari?"

"It might be worth finding out," Katelyn said.

"Parties aren't really my thing. Besides, I'm not dressed for it."

"Me either, but you need to get out with kids your own age and forget about everything else in your life. Even for a few hours. We wouldn't have to stay."

"You're officially invited?"

"It was more like a general invitation. On his webpage."

"You were on Dylan's webpage?"

"I confess," Katelyn said with an embarrassed smile. "I think he's gorgeous. Totally bad news, but very easy on the eyes."

"All right, we'll go, just for curiosity's sake."

From half a block away, Shannon heard the throb of the heavy bass from the stereo system. Dylan lived in an enormous two-story, the last house at the end of a cul-de-sac, sheltered from the neighbors, which tonight was more fortunate for the neighbors.

Shannon carefully negotiated her way through the cars lining both sides of the street. The last thing she wanted was to have to explain to her parents how she got a big scratch on the car, or worse, on someone else's car.

"You still want to go?" Katelyn asked.

"Yeah, I'm just looking for somewhere to park." She scanned the Sniders' yard, mentally sizing up the spaces in between the cars. "I think I can fit between the tree and the Honda." She gave the car enough gas to get up the curb, then slowly pulled in beside the compact.

"I can't open my door," Katelyn said.

"Well, scoot across." As she and Katelyn walked up to the front door, the strong smell of beer hit her. "Where are Dylan's parents?"

"Here somewhere, I'm sure," Katelyn said, straining to be heard over the music. "They'd probably rather have him home than out partying somewhere."

Shannon shook her head. "And people think I'm spoiled." Katelyn put a hand on the doorknob and started to open it, but Shannon grabbed her. "What are you doing? We can't just walk in."

"Do you honestly think anybody could hear the doorbell?" Katelyn pushed the door open and led the way inside. Shannon could feel the music vibrate in her chest as she followed Katelyn back through the house. She tried not to stare at the dozens of teenagers drinking, or brazenly pairing up in one corner or another. Shannon's jaws began to tingle the way they always did right before she threw up. This was a mistake. She knew better and her mother would kill her if she ever found out.

Finally they came through the kitchen and out the back door onto the patio. "Much better," Katelyn said, without having to shout. "Hey, food!" Katelyn dragged her to the buffet table and began piling appetizers on a plate.

Shannon pulled back. "Listen, I think we should—"

"Ladies! Thanks for coming to my party!" Dylan Snider appeared and draped an arm around each of their shoulders. He reeked of beer, and his eyes were already red from the cigarette smoke.

"Thanks . . . for inviting us," Shannon said awkwardly, stepping away from him.

"Here, you gotta try these." Dylan reached over to the buffet table and held some breaded, deep-fried thing up to her mouth.

"What are they?"

"Poppers. Jalapeño peppers stuffed with cheese and deep-fried. I love 'em."

Shannon cautiously took a bite, but before she really had time to taste anything, her mouth was on fire. "Too hot . . . I need something to drink . . ."

He handed her a cup. "Here."

Shannon gulped until the burning cooled. "Thanks, that's good punch."

"Yeah," Dylan said with a wink. "It's got a punch all right."

"It's got alcohol in it?"

He grinned. "It's a party, isn't it?"

"Katelyn, we need to go," Shannon said. "Thanks, Dylan. Happy birthday." Before Shannon could turn to leave, the music suddenly shut off and the lights came on.

Two policemen stood on the patio. One of them pointed in Shannon's direction. "Everybody in the house. Party's over."

Chuck poured the water in the coffeemaker, knowing his wife would wander into the kitchen soon, ready for her nightly cup. In the cabinet, the Sumatran blend was closest to the front. Strong stuff. He couldn't blame her. This had been a long, difficult week for all of them.

He was exhausted, but he was afraid to stop moving, afraid to go to bed before he was worn out. He didn't want his mind to wander. He didn't want to dream. Having a focus, settling Brad's affairs, helped him get through the days.

He wasn't denying his grief exactly. He just couldn't fight it right now. When the monster was more manageable, when Bobbi could help him, then he'd deal with it. Until then, he had to be strong for her.

He scooped the dark crystals into the basket and started the brewing cycle, not a moment too soon. Bobbi joined him in the kitchen, her shoulders rounded with the weight of grief. "So how did everything go?" she asked, leaning against the counter. "And thank you for starting my coffee."

"You're welcome. I got done what I could. The rest of it will have to wait until the bills start coming in."

"Going back to work Monday?"

"Unless you need me here." She didn't reply and wouldn't look at him. "Do you need me here?"

"I need Brad," she said sharply. "This is wrong. It's not fair, and it's draining the life out of all of us."

"Honey . . ." Chuck crossed the kitchen to embrace her, but she stepped away from him.

"No," Bobbi said, her voice rising in anger. "I've been strong. I've said all the right things, but I just can't do it anymore. This is my son, Chuck." Tears started to form, and she clutched at her heart. "Someone took my son's life. . . ." Chuck pulled her close. "I don't understand," she whispered.

"Honey, you don't have to be strong anymore," he said as he kissed her gently. "Not for my sake, not even for the kids' sake."

"I didn't get to say good-bye . . ." Her tears flowed freely now, and Chuck held her tightly. When the phone rang, Chuck let the machine get it.

"This message is for Mr. or Mrs. Molinsky. This is Officer Miguel Estrada, Florissant PD. Your daughter, Shannon, has been arrested. We need you to come to the police station." Chuck tried pick up the phone, but the policeman had already hung up. He replayed the message to ensure that he had heard it correctly. He had. Shannon had been arrested.

"Are you coming?" he asked his wife.

"Of course."

"I'll tell Jack."

Bobbi leaned back against the head rest as Chuck drove them to the police station. Shannon was going to a movie and then to John Isaac's to spend the night with Katelyn. What could she possibly have done . . . ? Unless she lied. But Shannon wasn't a liar. Something wasn't right.

She glanced over at Chuck and could see his jaw tightening and the flush across the back of his neck. When he jammed the car into PARK, she gripped his hand. "Before you go in there, I want you to remember one thing. No matter what happened . . . we still have her."

"Don't worry."

Easier said than done. She knew he was stuffing his grief just like the rest of them and this was exactly the kind of thing that could trigger a release, only with Chuck it would come as long dormant anger. "Promise me you won't say anything tonight."

"Bobbi—"

"I mean it, Chuck. Promise me."

"Fine. I promise."

Once inside, after explaining who they were and why they were there, Officer Estrada met them and directed them to a desk. "Mr. and Mrs. Molinsky, your daughter was at a party that got a noise complaint. When we arrived we found underage drinking and some marijuana."

Drinking. Bobbi shuddered. Her father drowned his grief over her mother's death in whiskey. Where was Katelyn? Had Shannon contrived the whole sleepover story? To drink?

"Shannon was arrested for drinking and smoking marijuana?" Chuck asked.

"She had alcohol on her breath, but she blew clean. Even so, she's underage."

"Where was she? Who was having the party?" At least Chuck had the presence of mind to ask questions.

"Dylan Snider, also underage."

"Can we take her home?"

"As soon as we finish processing everything and get a court date."

"A court date?" Bobbi asked. "Like a trial?"

"She'll have to appear, but I'd say the charges will be dropped. If you'll excuse me, I'll move things along so we can get her out here to you."

Chuck leaned back in his chair. "Do you know this kid?"

"He just graduated with Shannon. He's been a troublemaker since kindergarten."

"So how . . . ?"

"I don't know, but don't start on her tonight," Bobbi said. "Let's just get her home and deal with it in the morning."

Moments later, Officer Estrada escorted Shannon out to them. She looked away quickly when Bobbi tried to make eye contact with her. While Chuck signed the papers Officer Estrada handed him and got the court date, Bobbi maneuvered over closer to Shannon. "It's okay," she whispered. "Whatever happened, it's okay."

Shannon raised her head and started to speak, when Chuck looked at her and pointed toward the door. "Let's go."

Shannon trudged out to the car. She could hear her parents behind her, but she was afraid to turn around. Her mom said everything was okay, but her dad . . . she was dead. Maybe if she threw herself on the mercy of the court. She blew out a deep breath, stopped walking and turned around to him. "Dad, I—"

"Not now, Shannon. Let's go home."

The harsh edge made her reconsider spending the night at the jail. He would never believe that she hadn't done anything wrong, that it was just a misunderstanding.

She curled up in the back seat of the car, trying to make herself invisible. She watched her father's eyes in the rearview, but he was focused on the road ahead. She could see the tightness in his jaw, though.

That meant he'd made up his mind, and he was going to hand out a punishment without even hearing her side. Her mother said everything was okay. Did that mean she planned to step in, to be her advocate? That was her only hope of getting out of this mess.

When her dad pulled into the driveway, her mother turned around to her. "Sweetheart, I'm sure this has been an ordeal. Why don't you go ahead to bed."

"Mom, this was a big mistake. I didn't do anything wrong—"

"Shannon, you heard your mother." Her dad stood at her open car door. "I think I'd do what I was told if I were you."

"Don't you even want to hear my side?" Shannon climbed out of the backseat and stood inches from him, her eyes locked on his. Her father was a big guy, a head taller than she was with broad shoulders, but right now, she was too angry to be intimidated. "Or have you already made up your mind?"

"Don't start with this." He shook his head and stepped away. "We just had to pick you up at the police station. Whatever your side is, it doesn't change the fact that you were arrested at a party for being underage."

"I wasn't drinking!"

"Then how did it get on your breath?"

"I had one drink—"

"Which was it, Shannon? Drinking or not?"

"A sip, Dad!" She held one finger up toward his face. "I had one sip. I didn't even know that it had alcohol in it—"

"What if it had one of those date rape drugs in it? What were you thinking?"

"You're being ridiculous!"

"I'm not going to argue about this out here in the driveway. Go inside and go to bed." He slammed the car door a little too forcefully.

Shannon stormed in the house without bothering to shut the front door.

"Have you lost your mind?" Bobbi rounded the car and headed for the house without waiting for Chuck to catch up.

"She was drinking, and she was arrested. You saw the pictures of Tracy's wreck. That's where this leads."

"Will you listen to yourself? Sipping a mixed drink at a party does not lead to Tracy. That sounds like something I would say."

Chuck closed the front door and turned the deadbolt. "How can you take this in stride? She doesn't have any idea what she's playing with, and to do this to you a week after losing Brad is the height of insensitivity!"

"And I'm warning you that if you don't hear her out, you're going to do more damage than you understand!" Bobbi dropped her purse by the stairs and lowered her voice. "If she loses your approval, then nobody else matters. That's the way it is with daddies and daughters. Trust me on this one."

"What are you talking about? She's not going to lose my approval."

"But what's it look like from her side? After my mom died, all I wanted was to know that my dad loved me, and that he'd be there for me. Shannon just lost her brother. Don't abandon her."

"I'm not abandoning her. I was trying to do what you said and wait until morning to talk about it. She started it."

"Who's the grown-up here?" Bobbi shook her head. "Girls are different, Chuck. Is that how you would have talked to me?"

"You're my wife. It's a little different."

"That's not what I mean. I want to hear your heart, not your head. Lining up your facts has never worked with me, and it won't work for Shannon."

Chuck took a deep breath and let it out slowly. "So what do I need to do?"

"She needs to know that you love her, no matter what happens, no matter what she does."

CHAPTER 6
PROVOCATION

Saturday, June 21

Shannon awoke, drained and disoriented, surprised that she had slept at all. She rubbed her eyes and took a moment to regain her bearings, and as she waded back through the events of last night, and the exchanges with her father, her anger reignited.

How could he . . . ? He, of all people, should understand what it was like to be in the wrong place, to make a bad decision. Where was that grace he always talked about? "Go inside and go to bed," he said. Well, if he wanted to talk to her this morning, he could come and drag her out of her room.

When she heard the knock at the door, soft and inquiring, so obviously not her father, she convinced herself she had imagined it.

"Shannon?" It was her mother. "Katelyn's downstairs. She brought your car back."

So she had to leave her room after all. What were the chances her dad was someplace else, and she could make it downstairs and back without crossing his path? Slim to none.

"Be right there," Shannon answered. She pulled a sweatshirt on over her pajama top and opened the door just a crack. Her mom was standing there in the hallway, waiting for her.

"He's in the kitchen," her mother said with a reassuring smile. She was good.

"So can I just run downstairs and come right back?"

"I don't think so. You need to talk to him."

"I didn't do anything wrong, Mom. It was a huge misunderstanding."

"And he needs to hear that from you."

"Will you be in the kitchen?"

"If you want me to."

"He won't go off if you're there."

"He won't go off, period." Her mother patted her arm and headed down the stairs.

Yeah, right. Shannon crept down the stairs to the entry hall where Katelyn stood, shifting her weight and glancing back toward the kitchen.

"So how much trouble are you in?" Katelyn asked, just above a whisper.

"I don't know yet. I got the 'we'll talk about it in the morning' treatment."

"He's really mad," Katelyn said.

"Ya think?"

"My mom and dad had it out on the phone this morning over it. I gotta go. My dad followed me over here, and he's waiting for me. Here's your keys."

"Thanks."

"Good luck," Katelyn said as she slipped out the door.

Shannon held the keys in her hand and looked toward the kitchen, then back up the stairs. *Just get it over with.* She sighed and shuffled back to the kitchen. Her father sat at the kitchen table, newspaper in one hand, his glasses perched halfway down his nose. He sipped a cup of coffee as he read.

Her mother stood at the sink rinsing out her cup. She smiled at her. "You want a cup of coffee?" When her mother spoke, her father dropped his newspaper.

Shannon shook her head. "Here Dad," she said, sliding the car keys across the kitchen table. "I'll save you the trouble of taking them away from me."

He took off his glasses and folded his hands. "I don't want your keys. Shannon, do you know how much I love you? Do you have any idea what kind of panic I felt last night?" He spoke with a quiet intensity.

"Dad, I . . ."

"Let me finish," he said, holding up a hand. "This is not about punishing you. It's about keeping you safe. From the day you were born, all I ever wanted was to be sure that nobody ever hurt you. I know you think I went too far, that I overreacted, but I have to protect you. Now, tell me what happened."

Now she, the thoughtless, selfish child, was supposed to blubber how wrong she was, how sorry she was, and bow and thank him. She'd rather be punished than mocked and humiliated. Shannon looked at her mother then back at her father and set her jaw. "You had your chance last night."

She turned to walk out of the kitchen, but before she could get away, he scrambled around the table and took her by the arm. "You hold it right there! All I heard last night was about your side."

"And you immediately thought the worst about me!" Shannon shouted back. "Maybe I was leaving the party. Maybe it wasn't even my idea to go. Maybe there's a simple, reasonable explanation for why I had a drink." She dropped her voice and glared at him. "You know, if you don't have any more confidence and trust in me than that, then I don't care what you think." She jerked her arm loose from his grip and ran up the stairs.

"Shannon!" Chuck said sharply, as he started to follow her.

"Let her go, Chuck." Bobbi crossed the room, intercepting him just in time.

"But she's wrong about me."

"She's hurt because you didn't give her the benefit of the doubt."

"You heard the policeman. What was I supposed to think?"

"Yes, the evidence was stacked up against her. Open and shut case."

Chuck rolled his eyes and scowled at his wife. "Mocking me is not helpful."

"Did it ever cross your mind that there must be some other explanation?"

Chuck frowned. "No."

"Then she has a point."

Chuck pulled one of the kitchen chairs around and sat down, trying to sort out how he ended up the villain in all this. "So you believe her?"

"Yeah, I do. She hasn't lied to us before, and she has a good head on her shoulders. I don't think we should punish her."

"Not at all?"

"All right, Mr. Negotiator, what's the goal here?"

"We don't want her to ever do this or anything like it again."

"Exactly. You and I are not going to be beside her the rest of her life, making her decisions for her. We have to trust her and let go."

"Trust and let go?" Chuck asked, managing a smile. "That doesn't sound like a mother talking."

"I didn't say I'd done it yet," Bobbi replied, "not with any of the four . . ." She quietly corrected herself. "Not with any of them." Bobbi looked away for a moment. "Just stop trying to win, and listen to her."

He frowned and looked back toward the staircase. "I don't think she has anything to say to me right now."

"Then take Jack out somewhere, and let me try to mediate this one."

Bobbi waited a couple of hours before knocking on her daughter's bedroom door, hoping it was less obvious that she and Chuck were coordinating their efforts. "Shannon? Can I talk to you?"

"Just you?"

"Just me." Moments later Shannon opened the door, glancing down the hall. "He's not here. He took Jack and left a while ago."

Shannon dropped on her bed with dramatic flair, causing it to squeak loudly. "Mom, I promise you, I didn't do anything wrong," she said, holding back tears. "The party was Katelyn's idea. I knew I shouldn't be there. I had a hot pepper and grabbed the first drink I could get my hands on, but as soon as I realized it had alcohol in it, I was ready to go, but that's when the cops showed up. It was a horrible misunderstanding. You believe that, don't you?"

Bobbi joined her daughter on the bed, put an arm around her, and pulled her close. "Sweetheart, your dad believes that, too."

"Then why is he being such a jerk?" She sat upright, pulling away from her mother and wiping her eyes.

"Simply put, your dad is a control freak." Shannon smiled. "He just lost Brad, and he's trying to find some reassurance that things are still familiar, predictable, that they still make sense. If that means he has to impose his own order on things to get there, then he will." She patted Shannon's knee. "When the police called last night, everything spun out of his control again."

"He can't control me."

"No, but when things go nuts, he feels like he's not protecting us, sheltering us. It really shakes him up."

"He can't take this out on me, though. That's not fair."

"No, it's not. Be patient with him." She took Shannon's hand and placed her car keys in her palm.

"Patience works both ways."

Thursday, June 26

Shannon scrolled through a list of obscure science fiction titles on the store's computer, searching for a book a customer had requested. She was the last one in the house to get back to work, back to a routine . . . except her mother. After three days, things were starting to feel normal again. At least as normal as they were ever gonna be.

The security system dinged, so she reflexively checked the door. Dylan Snider walked in. He parked his sunglasses on top of his head, and she caught the glint of a diamond in his ear bigger than her mother's engagement ring. His T-shirt was at least one size too small, so it stretched across his chest. He wore the same type of long cargo shorts that Jack liked, except Dylan didn't look like such a dork in them.

I didn't know he could read. She went back to the computer, back to the search. *Maybe it's listed under fantasy instead of sci-fi.*

Within moments, Dylan appeared at the counter with a video game magazine. "I didn't know you worked here," he said.

"Two years now." She picked up his magazine and ran the bar code across the scanner. "Is this all?"

"Yeah," he said, reaching for his wallet.

"Do you have one of our members' discount cards?"

"What? No. Listen, Shannon, I'm really sorry about the party and everything. I'd like to make it up to you. Can I take you for dinner somewhere tomorrow night?"

"Serious?"

"As a heart attack," Dylan said with a smile.

Her head, her gut instinct, everything inside her screamed "say no!" but what better test of her dad's sincerity could there be? If he really trusted her, he would let the date go without much comment. If he went off, well . . . then she was right about him.

"Okay, Dylan." Shannon dropped the magazine in a bag. "I think I'd like that."

"Six?"

"Six is fine. See you tomorrow."

Friday, June 27

"I had a great time," Dylan said with as much smooth sincerity as he could muster. He eased his car to a stop in front of Shannon's house, then he twisted around to face her. "I hope this isn't the last time I get to take you out."

"I have to admit," she said, "in spite of your reputation, you're a really nice guy."

"So do nice guys get to kiss you good night?" he asked with a sly grin.

"Just a quick one." She leaned over and kissed his cheek, then hopped out of the car. "Thanks again!"

Dylan watched her walk up the driveway, then he pulled out his cell phone. "Wes, you better be saving your money. You're gonna have to pay up on this one. I'll have her in five dates, maybe three." A nice guy. He laughed and drove away.

Chuck spent a solid week encouraging and prodding, but it paid off. He convinced Bobbi to join him for an at-home movie date. He popped a bowl of popcorn and rented a couple of chick flicks the girl at the video store recommended. Two hours. That's all he was asking for. If he could take Bobbi's mind off everything for just two hours, it would be a major victory.

For a sweet hour and a half, he thought he'd pulled it off. He sat on the sofa with his arm around her, enjoying just being close to her. When she laughed gently, he felt a boost, like things were turning around, that grief was subsiding at last. Before the movie finished, he heard Shannon come in.

She shuffled in and leaned against the doorframe. "Where's Jack?" she asked.

"Upstairs," Bobbi answered, motioning for Shannon to come and sit. "Did you have fun?"

"Yeah, I did, actually." She sat on the arm of the easy chair across from the sofa.

"What'd you do?" Chuck asked, trying his best not to sound like an interrogator.

"I, uh, I had a date."

"Sweetheart, we need to meet these boys before you go out with them," Bobbi said. "You know that."

"You can meet him. That's no problem."

"Before the date, not after," Chuck said, his voice rising ever so slightly. "Who was he?"

Shannon glanced at her mother, then faced him and said without wavering, "Dylan Snider."

"The boy who had the party? What were you thinking?" He jerked the remote control off the coffee table and turned off the television. "Is this how you repay us for cutting you a break over the arrest? For believing you that you were innocent?"

"You never believed me! You only went along with it because of Mom."

"Give me your car keys." Chuck held his hand out. His voice was quiet and steady. He wasn't going to get angry and make things worse.

Shannon took the keys from her purse and dropped them in his hand. "You can't keep me here. I have a job. I'm eighteen now."

"I don't care how old you are," Chuck said. "Check the deed. This is my house, and you will live by my standards."

"So is adultery okay, then?"

"Shannon!" Bobbi stood between them. "That's enough!"

Chuck took a step back. If Bobbi intervened, things would calm down.

"Mom, I'm sorry." Then she turned to him, her eyes narrowed in bitter anger. "Just remember that whatever happens, it's your fault."

"Where is this coming from?" Chuck asked, his fists clenched in barely controlled fury. He could feel the heat on the back of his neck, the surge of adrenaline pushing his pulse. "What has gotten into you? Is it Katelyn? Is she putting you up to this?"

"Leave Katelyn out of this," Shannon seethed. "You brought this on all of us when you decided to sleep with that whore!" She pointed a finger at his chest. "You're just like King David. His baby paid, his kingdom paid, his sons and daughters paid. . . ." Bobbi reached for Shannon's arm, trying to pull her into the kitchen, but Shannon wouldn't budge. "Brad's dead. Joel and Abby can't have kids. Everyone has paid because of you, Dad."

"Shannon, you need to—" Bobbi began, but Chuck cut her off.

"No, let her say what she's got to say."

"She's said enough." Bobbi turned to Shannon. "I don't care what hurts or injustices have been inflicted on you, nothing . . . nothing justifies that kind of language and that kind of disrespect. I want you to apologize." She locked eyes with Shannon and added, "Now."

"I can't," Shannon said quietly, shaking her head. "I can't do that. I'm sorry, Mom." She turned and bolted from the room and up the stairs. Chuck snatched up the nearest thing he could get a hand on and heaved it across the room. The hardback book hit the wall with a thud, denting the drywall.

Bobbi whipped around to face him. "I thought we were past all that!" she said sharply.

He steadied himself against the wall and raised his fists to his eyes. "I'm sorry. I'm sorry, Bobbi. I lost it. I'm so sorry. Dear God, I'm sorry."

She reached out and touched his arm. "Chuck, you're shaking. What is it?"

He wiped his eyes and dropped his hands to his sides. "What if . . . what if she's right? What if this, all of this, is my fault?"

"It's not," Bobbi said quietly. "That's crazy. Shannon's upset—"

"No, she's thought about this. Reasoned it out."

"But that doesn't make it so."

Chuck frowned and looked away. People revealed their deepest convictions in times of high emotion. And why did he lash back at her with that kind of anger? Because . . . deep down . . . he suspected she was right.

" . . . and since you won't take my word for it, let's call Glen first thing in the morning," Bobbi said.

"For her or for me?" Hearing Glen confirm it was the last thing he wanted.

"All of us."

Jack's hands shook with outrage and indignation, sloshing the Coke over the rim of his glass. He should never have come down to the kitchen for a snack. He should have just waited for breakfast tomorrow. But no . . . And he heard every word. Every last hateful, spiteful word.

His mother wasn't a . . . She wasn't. She was messed up. He would admit that much, but she wasn't . . . She wasn't what Shannon called her. She just wanted somebody to love her, to tell her she was okay. That didn't make her a . . .

No. It didn't. Shannon owed him an apology. And he intended to make sure he got it.

Saturday, June 28

Before daybreak, Shannon stole downstairs and out the front door. She patted her front pocket, pleased with herself for having the foresight to get an extra set of car keys made. She eased the front door closed and checked up and down the street. No one was out, not even walkers or joggers. She quickly unlocked her car, slung her bag into the passenger seat and shut the door as quietly as she could.

She glanced back at her house, her resolve wavering just a little. She shook her head quickly as if to clear her mind. There was no other choice. She turned the key in the ignition, but nothing happened. Not even a click.

What the . . . ?

The gas gauge read three quarters of a tank. Not the battery. Alternator, maybe. Irritated, she popped the hood and got out of the car. When she raised the hood, she swore out loud. Her dad had taken the spark plug wires. "You think he could trust me any less?"

she muttered. She clicked the hood closed and took out her cell phone. "Dylan, I need some help."

An hour later, Bobbi got up after a fitful night of sleep. Chuck was asleep beside her, but she knew it had only been for the last hour or two. Before heading downstairs for her first cup of coffee, she opened Jack's bedroom door slightly, checking on him just as she had done every morning since he'd lived with them. She was relieved to hear his deep breathing. Finally, he was able to rest.

Then following her routine, she walked to the opposite end of the hall to Shannon's room. Through the night, catching each other awake, she and Chuck talked, trying to come up with an explanation for why Shannon's emotions became so intense so quickly. What could they have done differently? Where had they failed?

None of them had really processed Brad's death. Chuck suggested she take Shannon away for a weekend, someplace where they could both vent all their grief and frustration. Maybe Shannon was uneasy about starting college and leaving home now. Maybe she just needed to know she could sit out a semester, or even a whole year.

Bobbi pushed the door open just wide enough to peek in, and in the dim light she could see the bed was made, the room was completely in order, but Shannon was gone.

Bobbi flung the door open and turned on the light. An envelope with MOM written on the outside lay on the desk. Bobbi ripped the envelope open and pulled out the single sheet of notepaper. It said simply, "I love you. I'm sorry."

"No," Bobbi said. "This is not happening . . . CHUCK!"

CHAPTER 7
EXPLOITATION

Panicked and disoriented, Chuck rushed into Shannon's bedroom ready to fight somebody off or mop up blood. "Bobbi? What? What's the matter? Where's Shannon?"

"She's gone." Bobbi thrust a piece of paper at him.

He squinted to read the girlish script. "Sorry? For what? What is she talking about?"

"Mom? What's wrong?" Jack stood in the doorway, rubbing his eyes.

"Shannon's gone," she snapped. "Do you know anything about this?"

"She hasn't spoken to me in a couple of weeks," Jack answered softly.

"Get me a phone," Bobbi said sharply.

"No, Jack, check downstairs and out on the deck for her first," Chuck said. Jack nodded and left. "Don't take it out on him."

She whipped around to face him, her teeth clenched in defiant anger. "Don't tell me how . . ." Then her eyes met his and she collapsed on the bed, burying her face in her hands.

He sat beside her and held her close. "Honey, let's not jump to conclusions here. What if she just needed to get out of the house for a while?"

She pushed away from him, indignant. "At seven a.m. on Saturday? Honestly, Chuck!"

"Bobbi, you asked her to apologize last night, and she refused. She wrote you a note, and she's processing all of it by herself before she comes back to face us."

"How can you be so sure?"

"Because you're the same way. Brad was the same way. Rita's the same way. All of you react with these highly charged emotions, but then after you've some time to decompress, you work through the situation." He squeezed her hand and walked to Shannon's window. "Her car's still here. If she's not here, she's probably stomping around the park, muttering at me under her breath."

Jack reappeared, and avoiding Bobbi's eyes, he said, "She wasn't downstairs." He held the cordless phone out to Bobbi as if he expected to lose a hand. "Here's the phone."

"Thank you, sweetheart," she said gently, and he nodded. She punched in numbers then held it close. "She's not answering." She clicked the phone off and laid it beside her.

"She's not ready yet."

"When will she be ready?"

"You tell me."

"I don't know. I don't know what she's feeling, or what she's thinking."

"Then let's give her some space."

Bobbi crossed her arms across her chest and shook her head. "You have turned a hundred and eighty degrees from yesterday."

"Because yesterday I was wrong."

Just then, the phone rang and Bobbi snatched it up, then paled. "It's the police," she whispered. "I can't . . ."

Chuck took the phone from her trembling hands. "This is Chuck Molinsky."

"Yes sir, you have the law firm?"

"Benton, Davis and Molinsky, yes. Why? What happened?"

"Your building's been broken into. We need you to come and give us an idea what's missing."

He held the phone against his chest and took Bobbi's hand. "It's okay. Somebody broke into the office, that's all."

"That's all?"

"Compared to whatever ran through your mind right now, it's nothing."

"You need to get down there." She pulled her hand back and stood up, steeling herself.

"I can call Chad."

"No . . . Shannon will be home soon. You need to take care of this. I'll be fine."

"Call me when she gets home."

"I will." She kissed his cheek. "The minute she walks through the door."

Shannon stuffed the envelope full of cash deep in her purse. Withdrawing her tuition money as cash wasn't the brightest thing, she admitted, but she might need the money in the coming weeks and couldn't risk her dad shutting the account down. Monday she'd open a new account at a different bank.

"What else do you need?" Dylan asked as he pulled out of the bank's parking lot.

"Just the basics. A car, a place to stay and a job."

"Thought you had a car."

"Jack's hand-me-down? No thanks. And the bookstore will be one of the first places my dad will check, so I can't go back there."

"You don't need a place to stay." He grinned and looked over the top of his sunglasses at her.

"Dylan, I cannot stay with you. Let's grab something to eat and pick up a newspaper. I'm sure there are decent apartments around."

"What are you gonna do for a bed?"

Subtle. Real subtle. Slimeball. "Furnished apartment."

"I gotta hand it to you, Shannon. This was a bold move, kissing off your parents that way."

"Not my parents, just my dad."

"He must have said some really harsh things."

Harsh, no. Her father was a first-class hypocrite, deflecting attention away from himself by harping on her, the disrespectful wild child. He'd never acknowledge the role Jack played in dragging Brad out on that street. Oh no, poor Jack was grieving. She wasn't about to stay there.

"Look, I don't want to talk about that now," Shannon said, staring out the window of Dylan's car.

"You don't have to," Dylan said, reaching across and putting a hand on her knee. "It's all cool."

Bobbi clicked the phone off and crossed another name off her list. Shannon had been gone for six hours and no one had seen her. With Chuck still gone, she paced, gulped coffee and dialed Shannon's phone every fifteen minutes. The little reassurances she been whispering to herself all morning were losing their effectiveness.

This wasn't like Shannon. There was more than grief at work here. And she couldn't dismiss it as just anger at Chuck. Bobbi knew that feeling of trapped desperation. She knew what it was like to be drowning and smothering at the same time, but yet be incapable of reaching for a lifeline. Shannon was there, and Bobbi was only a few steps behind her.

Chuck worried about a curse. There was no curse, just a mother who couldn't function, who couldn't parent when her baby needed her. Paralyzed by her grief, she abandoned Shannon the very same way her father abandoned her.

As the minutes continued to tick by without a phone call from Bobbi, Chuck found it nearly impossible to focus on his office inventory. He brought Chad and Christine in to help him talk to the police but never mentioned what they were dealing with at home. They naturally assumed he was distraught over the break-in. Hardly. So some punks stole a half dozen computers. Insurance would replace the machines, and all the sensitive files were off-site on the server.

When Chad volunteered to stay and help the IT guys get the office back online, Chuck couldn't get to his car quickly enough. He blasted back toward home until he got to the park. Chuck rolled through it three or four times, zigging back and forth, willing Shannon to appear. When she didn't, he wheeled the car around and headed home.

What could he possibly tell Bobbi? He was certain, in the depths of his soul, that Shannon would be home by now. And he was wrong. How could he tell her everything would be okay when he no longer knew that?

You brought this on all of us. . . . Everyone has paid because of you. . . .

Chuck was all too familiar with the story of David and Bathsheba, and the judgment God levied on them after their adulterous affair—the death of their child, then violence and rebellion plagued their family.

He and Bobbi had just lost a son through violence and now Shannon was playing the part of Absalom in open defiance of him. He couldn't dismiss the connection.

You brought this on all of us. . . .

He saw Bobbi peering out the front window when he pulled into the driveway and she was on the porch before he got out of the car. The fear in her eyes spoke more than words ever could. "Call Joel," he said.

"He's on his way." She fell into his arms and clung to him. "What about your office?"

"Nothing major. Computers, the conference room TV. Insurance will cover it. The agent's already been there."

"I called . . . half her graduating class, I think. Left a message at Kara's."

"That was good thinking." He kissed her forehead and led her inside. "Rita and Gavin?"

"I hadn't yet. I guess . . . I guess I should. Did the police . . . I mean, did you think to ask them . . ."

"She's eighteen. She's not a runaway. She's not a missing person yet, and unless we suspect she's in danger—"

"What if we do?"

"Then they'll take a statement, but they're not gonna comb the city."

"So they won't do anything?"

"It's just a woman having a disagreement with her father."

She pushed away from him. "Why do we have police? Why do we even have them? Brad gets shot, Shannon disappears and—"

"Honey—"

"No, Chuck, I am at my limit. And if anything happens to Shannon . . . you'll be burying me beside Brad."

Shannon clutched the key and the paperwork for the used Civic. It was a little more than she hoped to pay, but it was a Honda. Reliability mattered now. On Monday, she'd buy her own insurance, and that would make it official.

"All set?" Dylan flipped his phone closed and slid off the hood of his car.

"Yep. Thanks for your help."

"No prob. I still feel like I owe you."

She felt her face flush when he smiled at her. Stupid involuntary reactions. "I'm gonna start checking out apartments, so I guess I'll catch you later."

He dropped his head and kicked at a rock. "I know you don't need my help, but . . . I mean, I just like hanging out with you."

"You want to follow me around looking at apartments?"

"Yeah. Is that bad?"

"Yes! It looks really bad. Like I'm looking for a place to shack up."

"I know better."

"But the landlords don't."

"Just tell them I'm your brother."

"That's even less believable."

"I'll sit in the car and wait for you."

"That's ridiculous. Why would you want to spend the afternoon sitting in your car in apartment complex parking lots?"

"You'll think it's stupid." He shuffled back toward his car, jingling his keys.

"What?" She took a couple of quick steps to catch up with him.

"I got you in really big trouble, but you don't hate me. I'm not used to somebody treating me that way. You're different . . . special, you know."

"You mean that?"

"Well, yeah."

His eyes twinkled when he smiled this time, and Shannon suddenly felt dizzy. Dylan Snider thought she was special. Dylan, the party boy who could have any girl he wanted, and he wanted to spend the day with her. A very boring day at that.

Her dad would totally blow a gasket if he knew she was with Dylan again. Imagine what he'd say if she started dating Dylan. She smiled. "So . . . are you just gonna follow me then?" she asked.

"Anywhere," he said.

He rested his elbows on his open car door, his face just inches from hers. He wanted to kiss her. Should she . . . ? Just then, her phone tweeted the arrival of a text message. "Ugh!" she muttered, digging through her purse until she found her phone. "My stupid brother." She deleted the message without reading it.

Jack sighed and snapped his phone closed. Shannon wasn't going to reply, even to an apology. Now his dad was back home, and there was no way he could watch them worry and wonder all afternoon. He had to confess.

He tromped down the steps and found them in the kitchen, his mother in her usual spot, with her usual cup of coffee, but carrying the weight of the world. His dad sat next to her holding her hand, his face drawn the way it was the day after Brad was killed. Even so, his dad looked up and smiled. "Hey, Jack. I wondered where you were."

"Mom, uh, Mom said the office got broken into," Jack said, buying some time, trying to soften his dad up.

"It was no big deal. You haven't heard from Shannon, have you?"

Jack felt the breath press from his lungs. "Why would she call me or anything?"

"Are you okay, sweetheart? You look a little pale." His mother pushed a seat out for him. "Why don't you sit."

He slumped into the chair, certain they could see his pulse throbbing in his neck. "Mom . . . Dad . . . I . . . I mean, Shannon . . . It's my fault she's not home yet."

"What?" his dad whispered. "How is it . . . ?"

"I heard what she said last night. About my mother. What she called her."

Then his adopted mother reached over and squeezed his hand. "Sweetheart, I'm sorry. I'm sorry you heard such hateful—"

"But see . . ." Jack pulled his hand back. "I wanted her to apologize—"

"And she will—"

"Mom, will you let me finish!" Jack sighed and rubbed his eyes. "I took the spark plug wires from her car. It was childish and immature, and if I hadn't done that, she would've been back by now."

"How's that?" his dad asked.

"She won't answer my texts. She's still ticked off."

"I don't understand how this is your fault, son."

"I took a bad situation and made it worse."

"Sweetheart," his mom took his hand again, "you didn't. You have to believe me. Joel will be here any minute, and Aunt Rita and Uncle Gavin are on their way over. I need you to be strong and help us." She swallowed hard and blinked back tears. "We can deal with whatever we have to when Shannon gets home."

Chuck stole upstairs while Bobbi filled Joel, Rita and Gavin in on everything that had happened with Shannon in the past couple of weeks. He gently pulled Shannon's note from its envelope, the envelope marked MOM and not MOM AND DAD.

You brought this on all of us. . . .

He dropped the note on the desk. She was sorry. For what? The argument? No. If she was sorry for that, she would have apologized. To both of them. So what was she talking about? Unless . . .

He yanked the closet door open and his heart stopped. Coat hangers. A dozen of them. She wasn't off pouting for the day, she'd left home.

Just remember that whatever happens, it's your fault.

His fault. Bobbi downstairs at her emotional limit. His fault. Jack blaming himself. His fault. All these years and his office was broken into now. Right after Brad. His wife. His children. His job. He felt a stab of pain through his chest, and he gripped Shannon's desk. His health, too?

He heard footsteps on the stairs, then in the hallway. Too heavy for Bobbi. Too quick for Jack. "Dad?" It was Joel.

Chuck doubted whether he could let go of Shannon's desk and turn around to face Joel. He felt Joel's arm supporting him almost as soon as he made a move. "I'm okay."

"Sure you are." Joel leaned against the desk. "What happened?"

There was no way he was telling Joel about the pain in his chest. It would go away. It always did. "Shannon and I had—"

"No, just now. What happened?"

"I checked Shannon's closet. She packed her clothes." He had to make Joel forget that he saw the chest pain hit. "This is more serious than just blowing off some steam."

"Mom didn't mention that."

"Mom doesn't know." He slumped into Shannon's desk chair. "She can't . . . This is more than she can handle right now. Maybe more than I can handle."

"What would make her leave home?"

He stared across the room, chewing his bottom lip. A curse. Judgment he brought on them all. That sounded crazy. He understood that, but his world had come apart in the last two weeks. Crazy had new boundaries.

"Dad, whatever you're thinking, it's not true."

"I'm not so sure, Joel."

"All right, then let me ask you this—do you love that woman downstairs?"

Love her? He'd give his life for her. He'd pay any price just to see her smile again. If he'd done this to her . . . "More than my own life."

"She needs you now more than she ever has."

"I know that, and I can't—"

"Then fake it. You get downstairs and act like everything is gonna be all right."

"Joel—"

"No excuses. Act like you're in charge."

"But I don't know what to do! She's gonna look at me and say 'what are we going to do' and I don't know what to tell her."

"You tell her not to panic. You tell her this is temporary. You tell her Shannon is safe."

"But I don't know that!"

"Yes, you do. Fear is the loudest, strongest voice you hear right now, but it's lying to you. Fear always lies, Dad."

Chuck unclenched his fists and blew out a long, slow breath. Fight or flight. He had to fight. Bobbi needed him. Shannon needed him, and Jack needed him. He took the deepest breath the tightness in his chest allowed, and he squared his shoulders. "I'll have the nervous breakdown next week. Tell Mom I'll be down in a minute."

When Bobbi saw Joel trot down the steps alone, she quit pacing the living room and caught him just before he ducked around the corner to the kitchen. "What's wrong? Where's Dad?"

"He'll be right down."

"Is he okay?"

Joel nodded. "He's in Shannon's room."

"He thinks this is his fault."

"He mentioned that."

"She told him he'd brought a curse on us. His affair was why you and Abby can't have kids, and why Brad . . ." She swallowed hard, and Joel reached for her hand. "He thinks Shannon . . . that it's part of it."

"That's ridiculous."

Words choked off, Bobbi nodded, and when Joel hugged her, she couldn't hold back any longer. Angry, frustrated, grief-stricken sobs came in waves. Joel never moved, never lied and said everything was okay. He understood it wasn't, and she wondered if it ever would be again.

"Do you know how much I love you?" she whispered. "I don't know what I would do without you and Jack."

"You don't have to worry, Mom." He leaned down and kissed her. "Uncle Gavin's here. We'll handle everything. You and Dad take care of each other."

"I'm trying, sweetheart, but . . ."

"You're doing better than you realize."

"Yes, she is."

Bobbi turned around, and Chuck stood on the bottom step, reaching his hand out to her. She took his hand and nestled against him, comforted in an odd way by the fresh scent of fabric softener.

"I was up in Shannon's room just now," he said, holding her tightly.

"Joel told me. You shouldn't torture yourself that way."

He took both her hands, staring at them for a moment before raising his eyes. "Honey, Shannon packed a suitcase."

"Packed . . . ?" She pushed around him and took the steps two at a time. She charged into Shannon's room until cold reality stopped her. Empty hangers dangled from the rod. Suddenly unsteady, she hoped she could make it to the desk chair before she vomited or passed out.

"Bobbi?" Chuck knelt beside her. He was going to say something stupid, like "don't worry" or "everything will be all right." He didn't. "I misjudged her. I had no idea how deep . . ."

"This is bad." She closed her eyes and leaned back in the chair. Gone. Shannon was gone.

"Yeah, it is."

Thank God he agreed. He wrapped his hands around hers, and she opened her eyes.

"She's not stupid, though. She had a plan. If we can figure out her plan, we can find her."

"But I've called everyone I can think of."

"Except Katelyn. We haven't heard from Katelyn."

"You're right. I left a message." She glanced at the note still lying on the desk. "If she's with Katelyn . . ."

Bobbi returned to the kitchen, her hand secure in Chuck's. When Chuck prayed just now as they huddled over Shannon's desk, God had to be listening. They would get through this. Some way. Somehow. God would intervene here in the eleventh hour and wrap this all up for her. God knew her limits, didn't He?

She walked through the doorway and immediately felt as if she had interrupted a high-level strategy session. Joel leaned over the kitchen table, poring over papers and lists with Jack and Gavin. Rita held the phone in one hand and scribbled notes with her other hand. Rita forced a smile, then looked up at the back door and waved. Kara Isaac pushed the door open, and Katelyn shuffled in behind her. But no Shannon.

"I'm sorry," Kara said, crossing the kitchen to hug Bobbi. "We've been gone all morning. I didn't know anything until Mom called. We got here as quick as we could."

"Aunt Bobbi, I promise, I promise, I didn't know anything about Shannon running away," Katelyn said, begging to be believed. "I haven't talked to her since last Saturday. I've been grounded."

Gavin looked up from his papers at Kara. "Unground her," he said, and Kara nodded. "Katelyn, you get on every online site you can to try and contact Shannon. Tell her she needs to come home."

"Yes sir," Katelyn said quietly.

"Did you take her cell phone?" Gavin asked Kara.

"Of course. You want me to give it back?"

"Yes, and her car. Katelyn, I want you out of the house. Circulate yourself. Be visible so Shannon knows she can contact you."

"Jack," Gavin said, "head down to the bookstore. Let them know the situation, but tell them not to do anything. We want Shannon to go to work just like normal."

"Okay," Jack said, and hustled out the door.

Joel motioned for Bobbi to follow him to the study. "Mom, I need you to get online with your bank, and I need you to cancel her cell phone service."

"Don't," Chuck said, following close behind them. "That's the only way we can track her."

"Can you see what calls have been made on that line?" Gavin asked. He stood in the doorway bouncing his glances between them, occasionally checking the kitchen. Bobbi knew that look. He was gathering his data, then he'd make his reasonable, rational pronouncement and give them the pathway out of this mess. She silently thanked God for Gavin, and that someone could still think clearly.

"Yes, if we can't get it online, I'll get it some other way."

Gavin then turned to Bobbi. "Did she take her class ring, jewelry, photos, anything like that?"

"Just clothes. Why?"

"Gimme a minute," Gavin said. "How much money was in her bank account?"

"She had her college money in there so we could pay her tuition in the next week or two," Bobbi said.

"Is your name on the account?"

"Yes."

"We need to get it now," Gavin said.

Joel was already on the computer, on the bank's website. "Mom, type in your password." When Bobbi did, the accounts screen appeared. Shannon's bank account showed an available balance of twenty dollars, and a pending withdrawal of the rest. "She got it this morning," Joel said.

"That was thousands of dollars," Bobbi said, and Gavin scowled. "What? You have an idea about what she's doing, don't you?"

He looked at Chuck first, then back at her. "She's the prodigal," Gavin said. "She's taken her inheritance, and she's leaving us all behind."

The prodigal? How could she have become a prodigal? She and Chuck did everything right with Shannon. They trusted her, gave her freedom, and loved her unconditionally. But that's what made a prodigal, wasn't it? Every material and emotional advantage.

She swiveled the desk chair around to face Gavin. "If you're suggesting we sit back and let her go until she's so miserable she drags herself home—"

"Not at all."

"Then what do we do?" She looked to Chuck, ready for the action plan, but he leaned against the desk, grimacing, rubbing a hand across his breastbone. "Chuck, what's wrong?"

"Nothing," he muttered.

"It's doing it again, isn't it?" Joel said, pushing back from the desk.

"Again? Doing what again?"

"He was like this up in Shannon's room." Joel took Chuck's arm and pulled him toward the love seat.

"I don't want to sit down," he said. "It'll hurt worse."

"Tell me what is going on!" Bobbi demanded.

"Honey, it's nothing. It'll go away on its own."

"What is IT? Are you having chest pains?"

"Kind of."

Bobbi felt Gavin take her arm and ease her back to the desk chair. God had to know she had a breaking point. He couldn't take Chuck, too.

"Mom, it's okay." Joel held Chuck's wrist and kept an eye on his watch. "Guys come in the ER all the time with chest pains from a whole host of things. It's not necessarily a heart attack."

"But?"

"I'm gonna take him to the ER."

"I'm going with you."

"What if Shannon calls?" Joel said.

"Then somebody can tell her where I am. You're not leaving me here."

"Joel, I don't think it's any big deal," Chuck said, standing a little straighter. "It's done this all day."

"All day! You think you should have mentioned that before now?"

"You just told your mother it was probably no big deal."

"Yeah, and you're a sixty-two-year-old guy with a sedentary lifestyle whose mother had three heart attacks. Get in the car."

"I'm not sedentary. I play golf all the time."

"I've played with you. You rent a golf cart. Go."

On the drive to Christian Hospital, Bobbi sat in the backseat, listening to Joel fire off question after question, trying to gauge whether Chuck was having a heart attack.

"I thought you were a pediatrician," Chuck muttered.

"Yep, and that's going to come in very handy." Joel pulled his hospital ID badge from his sun visor and clipped it to his shirt. "My all-access pass. Chest pain will get you fast-tracked. You shouldn't have to wait to get in." Just as Joel predicted, Chuck was taken back for an exam not long after they arrived.

Too nervous to sit, Bobbi leaned against the wall in a corner of the waiting room, watching Joel talk to nurses and anybody else in scrubs who happened to walk through the ER. When he joined her at last, she asked, "Is it a heart attack?"

"I don't think so, but we need to be sure."

"I trust you. I can relax if you say it's not a heart attack." She eased into the nearest seat. "Thank God, we got a break on something."

They sat in silence for several minutes, then Joel spoke. "This thing with Shannon will work out like everything else we've been through, Mom. Hang on to that faith."

"Faith? I'm not sure I have any left."

"You do. It's just a little overwhelmed right now."

"A little?"

"Figure of speech," Joel said with a wink. "I'm going to go check on Dad. They should know something by now." He squeezed her hand and walked down the hallway with long, confident strides. Definitely his father's son.

His father. *God, he has to be okay.* She leaned her head back against the wall, and a tear made its way from the corner of her eye. *I'm begging, Lord.* Another tear squeezed out, then another, then the floodgates opened. Alone in the waiting room with no one to be strong for, Bobbi let herself cry. For the injustice, for the uncertainty, for the disappointment of each passing hour with no word from Shannon, for the emotional exhaustion, and for the intensity of regret and failure.

Chuck sat on the exam table, fumbling to button his shirt. Muscle spasms. He knew it wasn't anything serious, and now he felt like an idiot. He'd terrified Bobbi and wasted time everybody should have been using to find Shannon.

He hoped it was the cardiologist pulling the curtain back, but it was Joel. "What's going on?"

"I'm waiting for them to let me go home."

"No heart attack?"

"No. I tried to tell you. But I get to do a stress test Tuesday, and they gave me a couple of prescriptions."

"Blood pressure?"

"A little high, but not bad."

"So it's stress."

"Most likely." Chuck sighed deeply. "I feel like a complete failure, on so many levels."

"Dad—"

"Last night, Shannon said I brought a curse on us. That's why Brad's dead, why you guys can't have children."

"You don't believe her, do you?"

"She makes a good case."

"This is not your fault. None of it."

"It's my fault Shannon left."

"No, it's Shannon's fault. She's selfish and immature, and I'd like to give her a good spanking."

"Now that sounds like a dad."

"Yeah, I've been practicing."

Chuck stood and slowly pushed his shirttails into his jeans. "But what if it *is* because of me that you and Abby . . ."

Joel held up his hand. "First of all, I don't think God operates that way. Second, God knows what He's doing. He has to be in control of all this or else He's not God."

"Yeah but . . ."

"No buts," Joel said. "Abby and I have both seen doctors. There is no earthly reason why we haven't had kids yet." Then he smiled. "No earthly reason." He pulled up a chair and sat down. "It used to give us fits. We worried and grieved over it, but then I started studying. There are plenty of children in the Bible born to parents who longed for a child and were unable to have any. Men like Samuel, and John the Baptist." Joel smiled again. "Every one of those children who were so desperately longed for grew up to do great things. Every one of them was specially used by God. He's going to do something great with our children. I know it."

Chuck smiled at Joel's boundless optimism and faith. "Your mother did a good job raising you."

"She had a little help."

"Thanks, but I know better." Brad and Joel grew up during his workaholic years, so Bobbi handled most of the parenting alone, with occasional interference from him. That's why this thing with Shannon didn't make any sense. He took his responsibility as a father so much more seriously with her and Jack. He thought they were close. He thought he knew her. "So what do we do about Shannon?"

"She'll call Mom tomorrow."

"You sound sure."

"She's a lot like Brad, and Brad would want to give you the opportunity to grovel and beg after you'd been sufficiently punished."

"Brad wasn't like that."

"He was twenty or so years ago. It was your affair. He changed profoundly after that."

Joel had a point, but was Shannon that calculating and manipulative? "She's punishing us?"

"Probably just you, but she has to reassure Mom. Mom is an innocent victim."

She's always the innocent victim. "You think Shannon's okay then?"

"She's exactly where she wants to be right now, exactly where she planned."

Relieved to be home, but no less exhausted, Bobbi left Chuck in the study with Jack and Gavin, and headed back to the kitchen, to the coffeemaker. Joel said Shannon was safe, that she would call soon. Bobbi trusted Joel, trusted him enough to send him on home. Now she just wanted a pot of coffee to sip while she waited for the phone to ring. And Rita, bless her heart, already had it brewed.

"You didn't have to stay," Bobbi said, "and you certainly didn't have to do dishes."

Rita dried her hands on the dishtowel, then reached for a mug. "Jack needed some company. We hated to leave him. How's Chuck?"

"Fine, they said it was a muscle spasm. He's got a stress test on Tuesday and they're going to put him on some medication."

"Thank God." Rita set her mug on the kitchen table and took the seat across from Bobbi. "Baby, honestly, I was more worried about you than Chuck."

"Yeah, I'm not sure how much more I can take." Bobbi took a long drink from her coffee, relishing the warmth permeating through her insides, no matter how temporary. "I've been treading water, but I'm getting exhausted."

"You haven't taken time to grieve for Brad."

"Shannon and Jack needed me. I couldn't . . ." She looked away as tears formed. "And now Shannon's . . ."

Rita reached over to hug her sister. "She'll be back."

Bobbi wiped her eyes. "Gavin says she's the prodigal."

"I don't think so," Rita said. "I think she's like a wounded animal, and she's got no idea how to deal with her heartache. She's lashed out at everybody who got close, and finally she ran."

"She should have talked to me."

"Yes, she should have." Rita let go of Bobbi and looked her in the eyes. "Now listen to yourself. You need to talk to somebody, too, whether it's me or Chuck or somebody else."

She swallowed another mouthful of coffee. "I'll be fine as soon as we get Shannon home."

"I don't think I've done this much in a single day in my entire life." Dylan dropped onto Shannon's sofa and motioned for her to join him. "I'm exhausted."

"I tried to warn you." She sat on the opposite end of the sofa from him, consciously aware of the distance. "Thanks for hanging out with me and helping me carry my TV upstairs. Saved me the delivery charge."

"Glad to do it. You're amazing."

"Not really." Shannon felt her face flush. She hated that. It made her look like a little girl who'd never had a boyfriend. Which was true, but she still hated it.

"Seriously. Think about it. Yesterday, you were a kid at home, but today, you've got a place, a car, a little money in the bank. You're a woman who's got it made."

"Hardly. When I call my folks, that's when it's really gonna hit the fan."

"Your dad?"

She nodded and slouched a little closer to Dylan. "I had to do something, though. My dad . . ."

"He hates me, doesn't he?"

"How'd you know?"

"Well, it's not rocket science. I got his princess arrested, and the big blow-up came after we went out."

"I've never done anything wrong, but that doesn't seem to count."

Dylan twisted around to face her and eased close enough to take her hand. She knew she should pull back, but his hand was warm, comforting, and truth be told she wished he'd put his arms around her and let her cry. She wanted him to tell her this wasn't the biggest mistake she'd ever made.

"Your dad's wrong." He rubbed his thumb across the back of her hand, the very same way her dad always did. "You know, since he hates me anyway . . ." He leaned forward and kissed her, his lips lingering near hers.

Her head spun, and for a moment she thought she might pass out. Embarrassed at her pathetic inexperience, she kissed him back, imitating the most passionate kisses she'd ever seen in the movies.

His smile was dreamy like he was intoxicated, the same way he smiled at his party. "Did I say you were beautiful?" he whispered, and she felt his breath on her neck, in her ear.

"I'm sure I'm not the first girl you've ever told that."

"I still mean it, and *you* are not a girl." He leaned closer still and kissed her again.

"But, I can't . . . ," she sputtered as Dylan kissed her once more.

"You can," he whispered, then slipped an arm around her. "You know you can."

CHAPTER 8
COMPUNCTION

Sunday, June 29

Shannon sat in her darkened bathroom, hugging her knees, rocking herself in a pointless attempt to stop the next round of tears. *Now* you're a woman, Dylan said. No, she wasn't. She could hear her own angry voice spitting out the word "whore" at her father. That's what she was. Not a woman. Defiant. Needy. Weak. She allowed Dylan to go too far.

Then he wouldn't stop.

She pulled herself to the toilet and vomited. She never meant for it to be this way. A precious treasure she should guard, her father said, and she let Dylan Snider snatch it away. Last night she hungered for reassurance, for validation. He made her feel wanted, capable, and for a brief instant, empowered.

That was before he pinned her arms down.

Every time she closed her eyes, she saw her father's face. "All I ever wanted was to be sure that nobody ever hurt you." Right now, she would give anything on God's green earth to crawl up beside her daddy and hear him say everything would be all right.

The muffled sound of a distant song filtered into her bathroom. That song . . . That was her ringtone! Her phone! Could it be her dad? Could it work that easily? She gathered herself up and found her phone. It wasn't her dad. It was Katelyn.

"Shannon! Thank God! Where are you?"

"I'm away."

"I knew that much," Katelyn huffed. "Listen, everybody's flipping. You gotta go home."

"I can't."

"You have to! Your dad went to the ER yesterday with chest pains!"

She gave him a heart attack. She thought all those horrible things about him, but chest pains . . . A new wave of guilt washed over her. What would happen if he knew . . . the rest of it? "Is he okay?"

"It wasn't a heart attack, but they're gonna do more tests. Tell me where you are, and I'll come and get you."

"I can't." He can't know. He can't find out.

"Of course you can."

"No, you don't understand. It has to be this way. Tell my mom I'm okay, but the less you know the better."

"Why? What'd you do?"

"I don't want to talk about it."

"Dylan?"

Everything inside Shannon ached. How could it be that obvious?

"He's there?" Katelyn asked.

"Not anymore."

"Oh no. You didn't . . ."

But she did. Her stomach twisted and she thought she'd vomit again. She hung her head, breathed deeply and squeaked out, "That's why I can't go home."

"Your parents, they'll understand. Your dad, he knows better than anybody—"

"I gotta go. Tell them I'm sorry." Shannon clicked off the phone so Katelyn couldn't call back, and made a mental note to pick up a new cell phone. She couldn't risk any more calls or deal with any messages.

Katelyn would never be able to keep it a secret, either. If she couldn't face her best friend, how could she possibly look into her father's eyes or feel her mother's soft hands on hers, and admit that she let Dylan Snider . . . do . . . that?

But when her parents found out, well, then it would make sense why she disappeared.

Chuck arrived at Preston Road Community Church early, while the Bible study classes were still meeting, so he seized the opportunity to slip into the auditorium for a few quiet moments alone. Bobbi understood he couldn't sit at home waiting for the phone to ring. He loved that about her. But he understood she wasn't leaving until she heard from Shannon.

Taking a seat in his family's usual pew, he felt a smothering burden, as real as if sandbags were strapped to his back. *Dear God, everything's a mess right now, and I don't know what to do. How can I find Shannon and get her home? I don't even know where to look, and I'm concerned Bobbi's sliding into despair. I have no idea what's going on with Jack, because I've not taken the time to sit down and talk with him. The way everything has fallen apart in the last two weeks makes me afraid for my family. Are we doing something wrong? Are You punishing us? Is this . . . is it a curse that I brought on us?*

Chuck felt someone sit down, so he raised his head. "Hey, Dad," Jack said, then looked past him back through the auditorium. "Mom made me come. Said you needed the company."

"Me? What about you?"

"I don't know." He shifted so he could cross his legs. "Things were just starting to settle down when Shannon took off." He leaned back and stared at the front of the church. "Last night I was thinking, in some ways, it reminds me of physics class. You know, when you work a physics problem—"

"No," Chuck said, "absolutely not."

Jack looked his direction. "Well, just pretend for the sake of the illustration."

Chuck could see Tracy's sideways smile in her son's. "I'll fake it the best I can."

"The first thing you do is define the problem," Jack said. "You figure out what it's really asking. Then you look at the information they give you so you can figure out what you really need and what's a red herring."

"Physics may not be as useless as I thought," Chuck said, impressed by his son's insight.

Jack shook his head. "I'm still trying to define the problem. Is it Brad, or Shannon or both, or something deeper that hasn't occurred to me yet?"

Like a curse. Chuck felt a hand on his shoulder. When he turned, he saw his pastor standing with his hand extended. "Hey, Glen," Chuck said, shaking hands.

"Any news?"

"No. You got a minute after the service?"

"Sure thing."

"I'll catch you up then."

"Is Bobbi here?"

"No," Chuck said quietly.

Glen nodded, and Chuck knew he understood. The pastor leaned across to shake Jack's hand. "How're you doing, Jack?"

"Fair."

"Hang in there. You'll never get over it, but you will get through it, I promise. Give yourself some time. It'll get easier."

Jack slumped back against the pew and watched folks file in for the morning worship service. Sure, it would get easier. Like nightmares only four nights a week? No, it was just like Shannon said—he was to blame.

He'd confessed it, begged God to take it away, and had wracked his brain to try and come up with a way to make up for it, but it was no use. God was giving him the silent treatment. Didn't that prove his responsibility for his brother's death?

The old guy who came into the mission couldn't be his grandfather, anyway. That was just nuts. His mother's dad, the ex-con, showing up here after all these years. Right. They should never have gone looking for him, especially that time of evening.

Jack glanced over at his dad, but he was paying close attention to the announcements or whatever. Maybe this afternoon he could catch his dad for a few minutes and tell him he wasn't going back to college in the fall. Then his dad, the professional negotiator, would try to talk him out of it. Let him try.

The decision made perfect sense. For starters, he didn't want to be on campus. On top of that, he was unsure what direction his life was supposed to take, so why waste time and money taking classes that might be useless?

He opened his Bible on cue like he was following the sermon, but he couldn't focus. He wished he could talk to Brad one more time. Brad knew how to coach him through anything, even dropping out of college. Who did Brad talk to when he needed advice?

He twisted in the seat and laid his Bible beside him, but his cell phone jabbed into his hip. He glanced at his dad then reached in his pocket and moved the phone over. Just touching his phone brought his other secret to the forefront of his mind.

Last night, while his parents were at the hospital, he checked the calls on Shannon's line. He knew who her accomplice was. If he could find out from Dylan where Shannon was and bring her home, that would be enough to make up for everything. After church, he'd seize this one shot to redeem himself.

As soon as the last prayer was over, Chuck left the auditorium through one of the side doors and took the long way around to Glen's office, detouring through as many empty corridors as possible. He pushed Glen's door open and took a seat. Glen startled him when he strode in a few minutes later. "That was fast," Chuck said, shaking Glen's hand.

Glen smiled. "I must've made everybody mad, so they didn't want to speak to me." He took a seat behind his desk. "So what's the latest?"

"Shannon's still not home. Joel's convinced she'll call Bobbi today."

"We'll pray that she does. How're you and Bobbi holding up?"

"Bobbi's at her limit. I don't know how she's keeping it together."

"Same way you are, I expect." Glen leaned up to the desk. "Which reminds me. I understand you were in the ER last night with chest pains and never bothered to call your pastor."

"Because it was nothing. A muscle spasm."

Glen frowned. "Well, I'll cut you some slack this time."

"I'm glad somebody is. You know, I didn't hear much of your sermon today."

"What else is new?"

Chuck smiled but then dropped his eyes. "The . . . the prodigal son was across the page."

"That was more helpful than anything I had to say. What'd you find out?"

"More questions. Is that how we're supposed to handle this? Just wait it out?" Surely not. He couldn't sit back and wait for Shannon to come home.

Glen sat in silence for several moments then folded his hands. "Chuck, can I be real honest with you?"

"Always."

"I feel categorically unqualified to tell you what to do. Laurie and I only know the grief of never having children. I can't tell you how to handle a wayward one."

"But I want you to," Chuck said. "You know God's Word, you follow His leading. I trust your counsel." He felt the weight of another door closing. "I need your advice, Glen."

"Thank you, but who am I to tell you not to turn the city upside down looking for Shannon? Maybe you should ask Gavin about this one."

"You expect me to believe you've spent your whole ministry dodging parents?"

"No, I just think you could get more credible advice."

Chuck frowned. If Glen wouldn't touch the situation with Shannon, would he tackle something as crazy-sounding as a curse?

"May as well ask the other one," Glen said. "I can tell you got something else running around in your head."

Chuck sat up straight and took a deep breath. "Shannon . . . she said all of this— Brad's death, her rebellion, even Joel and Abby's infertility—all of it was the result of some judgment against me for the affair. That it was a curse."

"What a thing to tell a grieving father."

When Glen dropped his eyes and took a deep breath, Chuck braced himself for the yes.

"The answer is yes and no," Glen said at last.

"Great." Chuck slumped back in the seat.

"Now, hold on. Before you take all this guilt on yourself, hear me out. It's an oversimplification to say action A causes result A to the exclusion of all others. Bad things happen as a result of a combination of things."

"But one of those things is judgment."

"Not always judgment on us. It could be someone close to us, and we're caught by the fallout. Sometimes we're completely innocent and just a victim. It's impossible to say for sure."

"You're not helping."

"I know. It's a gift." He leaned back in his chair. "Thing is, on the surface, Shannon's got a point. You committed a grave sin with lasting, far-reaching consequences."

As if Chuck needed reminding.

"But to say your action is responsible for her willful rebellion . . ." He shook his head, leaving the sentence unfinished. "Plus, it's presumptuous to declare how God has chosen to deal with His children. You ever feel like Job?"

"Yesterday, yes."

"Job's a perfect case. He never understood why all those tragedies happened in his life. Everything his friends said was theologically sound, but none of it was applicable. In the end, his conclusion was, 'God is God, and I'll shut up now.'"

"So is that a hint?" Chuck asked. "Do I need to go?"

Glen smiled and shook his head. "Remind me to pray more for Bobbi. She has to deal with you all the time." Then he leaned forward and snapped his fingers. "You ever see one of those mosaic pictures made out of a whole bunch of little pictures?"

"Yeah, so?"

"Each of us lives out our lives in one of those little pictures. God sees the whole mosaic, and He ordains how each of those little pictures fits together. You and I, because we can't see the big picture, we struggle to understand what it all means. When we run up against things like why weren't Laurie and I given a chance to be parents, or why God called Brad home, there's just no discernable answer."

"Or why does Bobbi has to go through so much?"

"Perfect example. None of it makes sense, and we'll never get a satisfactory reason for the 'why.'"

"But what about sin? How does that affect the picture? God doesn't ordain sin."

"I'd say it affects the little picture quite a bit, but God brings it around in the little picture so that it still fits in its place in the mosaic."

"Shannon and I are different pictures?"

Glen nodded. "Yeah, I think everybody gets his own picture."

"But if our sins affect innocent people, your analogy fails. How can the pictures affect each other, and remain discreet at the same time?"

Glen rolled his eyes. "You know, I'm making this analogy up as I go. It's not perfect."

"Even so."

"Lemme think a minute." He stared past Chuck for a moment, then nodded slowly. "What if the mosaic deals less with the actual events, but more with our responses to them?"

"Keep going."

"When you sin, you choose how you respond to that. You can repent. You can deny it. Whatever. Our little picture reflects our responses to the whole gamut of situations God allows us to experience. Our sins, the sins against us, random events that don't fit anywhere, they all shape us. God keeps throwing events at us, allowing things in our lives—including the fallout from the sins of other people—to get us where He wants us."

"What if we fail? He allowed Tracy to cross my path and I failed."

"Bound and determined to blame yourself, aren't you? You think when you were with Tracy that God was surprised? That you caught Him off-guard?"

"No, but—"

"Either God can work around us and through us in spite of everything, or I need to turn in my preacher Bible."

Chuck closed his eyes for a moment and tapped the armrest, absorbing everything Glen said. Everything he'd done to change, to make up for his sin, it was part of a process. His picture wasn't done yet. So he still had hope. "I knew you'd know the answer," Chuck said at last.

"Hallelujah." Glen smiled and pushed his chair back from the desk. "I don't know if it's *the* answer, but it'll get you out of here so I can go eat lunch."

"Seriously, you make a lot of sense, Glen. It gives me a lot to think about and pray about."

"That's where you'll get the real answer."

Jack parked Brad's car beside the schoolyard at Stoneburner Elementary. A half dozen guys, three without shirts, were playing a pick-up basketball game. He quickly spotted Dylan Snider, wearing mirrored sunglasses with his T-shirt tucked in the back of his shorts. Jack blew out a deep breath and wiped his palms on his jeans. His one chance.

He got out of the car, leaned against the fender and waited. He wanted to talk to Dylan without the audience, figuring that would increase his chances of getting a straight answer, plus one-to-one odds were way better than six-to-one.

Moments later, Dylan bounced the ball behind him and shuffled toward Jack. "What do you want, Josh?"

"It's Jack." He crossed his arms across his chest, doing his best impression of the cops who questioned him about Brad. Jack was taller and heavier than Dylan, and he hoped that mattered. "When was the last time you talked to Shannon?"

"Not since we went out Friday night."

Now Jack understood why Dylan needed the sunglasses. It made it easier to lie. "Shannon disappeared sometime between Friday night and Saturday morning. We're trying to do all we can to find her before we bring in the police." Jack was bluffing, not lying. There was a difference.

"Sorry, can't help you." Dylan turned to walk away.

"I thought you might be concerned. Girl out there somewhere, all alone."

"Oh, she's not a girl anymore," Dylan said. "Not after last night."

"What's that supposed to mean?"

Dylan took a step toward Jack, laid a hand on his shoulder and sneered. "Someday when you're a man, you'll understand."

Jack brushed the hand off and jabbed Dylan in the chest with his index finger. "So help me, if you touched her . . ."

Absorbed by his outrage, Jack never saw the windup. Dylan landed a quick punch in Jack's stomach, and a second one on the left side of his mouth.

Jack doubled over and gasped for his next breath as salty blood seeped in between his lips. Dylan hissed, "There's no 'if' about it. Go home, Jack. Get over it."

CHAPTER 9
UNFULFILLED

Bobbi swung her feet down from the love seat and slid to the opposite end. Except for quick trips to the bathroom or the kitchen to refill her coffee cup, she'd spent the last twelve hours clutching the phone and whispering desperate prayers for it to ring. So far the prayers hadn't been answered.

Yesterday was a long, hard day for Shannon, too. She was still a teenager. She still slept until noon from time to time. It wasn't time to panic yet. Maybe Shannon was afraid Chuck would answer. Or Jack. Maybe she was waiting until Monday to call, until her dad and brother weren't home.

Unless she was hurt.

Or worse.

No, it couldn't be worse. God wouldn't ask that of her. He knew she could handle anything else but that. God would be merciful. He was just that way. She hoped. She sipped her coffee, then closed her eyes and held the phone to her cheek. "Please, dear God. Just a phone call. A phone call will get me through today."

But the phone never rang. She set her coffee on the end table behind her, then slouched a little lower in the seat. At some point, she dozed off until she felt a touch on her arm.

"How are you doing?" Chuck asked quietly as he sat down beside her. At least he had the good sense not to mention the phone call that hadn't come.

"When I start to feel things again, I'll let you know." She reached for her coffee cup and took a sip, and grimaced. Room temperature coffee, ugh. "How was church?"

"I talked to Glen for a little while." He reached for her, but she didn't move. She didn't want comfort. "He said we should ask Gavin what to do about Shannon."

"If Gavin knew, he would've already told us." Bobbi left the loveseat, paced to the window and stared down the empty street. "We're stuck, aren't we? Until she decides to come home, there's nothing we can do."

"I don't know that we've exhausted everything yet."

"What if she doesn't show up for work Monday? Then is she a missing person?"

"Maybe, I don't know."

She whipped around to face him. "For crying out loud, Chuck! You're a lawyer. Don't you know what the law says?" It came out angrier and more frustrated than he deserved.

"I don't do criminal law. I'd have to look it up."

He responded gently, with more grace than she showed him. "I'm sorry. I didn't . . ." She closed her eyes and took a deep breath. "Where's Jack?"

"He said he had something to do before he came home." Chuck glanced at his watch. "He ought to be here just any time."

"You probably should take him to get some lunch. I don't have anything ready, and I doubt there's anything to cook."

"Will you go?"

He'd lost his mind. There was no way, not as long as Shannon . . . "No, thank you."

"Will you eat if I bring you something back?"

She couldn't. "I'm not—"

Then the phone rang. She charged to the loveseat and snatched up the phone. Chuck took her hand as she clicked it on. "Hello?"

"Aunt Bobbi, I talked to Shannon just now." It was Katelyn.

Crushing disappointment pressed tears from her eyes, and she slowly shook her head so Chuck knew. Focus. Katelyn talked to Shannon. She had information. She wanted to help. That was more than anyone else had right now.

"Where is she? Is she all right?"

"She's okay. I mean, she's not injured or anything. But she wouldn't tell me where she was. I said I'd go get her—"

"What else did she say?"

"Not much, and she won't pick up now. She said to tell you she was sorry, but she couldn't come home."

"Why not?"

"She wouldn't say. Just that it had to be this way."

"Did you tell her about her dad?"

"Yes! I told her she needed to come home, and Uncle Chuck had chest pains and everything, but it was no use. And I've called back every five minutes."

"Sweetie, listen to me, when you talk to her again . . ." When. Not if. When. "When you talk to her, I will do anything to get her home. You make whatever promises you have to."

"But Aunt Bobbi—"

"No limits, Katelyn. Whatever it takes. And can you conference me on the next call?"

"Sure."

"You have my cell?"

"Yes, but there's something you need to know. Things . . . things have changed since she left."

"What things?"

"She's not mad at Uncle Chuck anymore. She's ashamed to come home—"

"It doesn't matter. Tell her, Katelyn, I don't care what it is. It doesn't matter."

"But she—"

"It. Does. Not. Matter. I will go anywhere. I will do anything. I need her home."

"Yes, ma'am. I'll keep trying to get her."

Bobbi nodded and clicked off the phone. "Katelyn talked to her." She felt Chuck's arm around her and she let him guide her down to the loveseat. "She says she can't come home. She's ashamed."

"You said exactly what she needs to hear." He gave her a little squeeze.

"If she's listening." She tried to smile as she patted his knee. "She's a lot like her daddy. No matter how many times we tell him something's not his fault, he still blames himself."

She heard the front door open and Jack's footsteps on the stairs. "There's Jack."

"Speaking of blaming himself," Chuck said. "It would help him out if you went to eat with us."

Help Jack. Cling to what she had left. That was her only option right now. "Someplace not too busy," Bobbi said.

Chuck kissed her cheek. "I'll go get Jack."

By the time Chuck made it upstairs, Jack had holed up in his bedroom. He knocked lightly on the door. "Hey, Jack, let's take Mom out to eat." No response. He leaned close and listened at the door. The only sounds were the air conditioner and a faint rustling. No, not rustling. Jack was crying.

Chuck opened the door just wide enough to step through. Jack sat on the edge of the bed, his head hung almost low enough to touch his knees. "What happened? What's wrong?"

Jack shook his head and moaned. "I blew it, Dad. I blew it again."

"What are you talking about? Blew what?" Chuck sat on the bed beside his son.

"I know who helped Shannon leave." Jack wiped his eyes and glanced up, then quickly looked away. "I got the cell phone records. It was Dylan Snider."

The name stabbed through Chuck's heart. Because he overreacted, he drove Shannon straight to the one person he didn't want her near.

"I thought if I could talk to him and find out where she was . . . I could get her home, and that would make up for everything."

"Make up for what?"

Jack's eyes darted to the floor several times as his jaw clenched and relaxed. Finally, he said, "For Brad."

"Son, I don't know how much more plainly I can tell you. Brad's death was not your fault. You handled it the absolute best way you could have. Nobody blames you."

"Shannon does."

"Shannon is wrong."

"It doesn't matter." He stood and leaned over his desk. "Dylan wouldn't tell me anything. He said he hadn't talked to her since

Friday night." He gripped the corners of the desk. "I could already see the look on Mom's face when Shannon came home."

"She'll come home."

"I wanted to make it happen."

When Chuck stood, he noticed Jack's swollen lip. "What'd you do to yourself?"

"Walked into a door," Jack muttered and looked away.

"Turn around here. Did that kid hit you?"

Jack huffed and faced him. "He made a smart remark about Shannon, then I got mad."

"You hit him?"

"I never had a chance."

"Are you listening to yourself?"

"What?"

Chuck smiled broadly at his son. "You're willing to get punched in the mouth standing up for your sister after the way she's treated you lately. You're amazing, Jack."

"It's no big deal."

"It's a very big deal," Chuck said. "It's exactly the kind of thing Christ would do."

"Really?"

"Yeah, and it's what Brad would've done."

"Brad . . . he would've, wouldn't he?"

"Yeah." Chuck winked at his son. "Come on. Mom's waiting."

"I'll be right there," Jack said. "I gotta clean this up so Mom won't notice."

"Good luck, but I wouldn't get my hopes up. Not much gets past her."

After a long, awkward lunch watching Bobbi and Jack pick at their food, Chuck needed a moment to regroup, to absorb what Jack had told him about Dylan Snider, and to come up with a plan.

Certain that the heat and humidity would discourage anyone from following, he slipped out to the deck. He leaned on the railing and stared out across the backyard.

God, where do I even begin . . .

He heard the door slide open, and Bobbi joined him. "Thanks for going to lunch," he said.

"I could tell it really helped Jack," she smirked. "So what's he keeping from me?"

She stepped up beside him and leaned her elbows on the rail, her forearm brushing against his. Even that touch energized him in a way she'd never understand. She loved him. She trusted him. She believed in him.

"Jack found out who helped Shannon leave. It was the Snider boy."

"As if I didn't have enough to worry about."

Chuck took her hand in his. "Let me tell you about your son, though. He went to talk to this kid to find out where Shannon was. He wanted to bring her home all on his own. The boy made a smart remark about Shannon. Jack defended her, and the boy punched him."

"Why didn't you guys tell me this earlier?"

She pushed away from the rail, but Chuck tightened his grip on her hand. "The last thing he needs right now is his mother hovering over him. He didn't want you to know at all."

"Why not?"

"Because he failed. He failed himself and he failed you."

"Me? How did he fail me?"

"He wanted to fix things for you, and he wasn't able to."

"Fix things for me? Am I that pathetic?"

"Honestly?"

She slumped back against the rail. "I don't know how to do this, Chuck. I don't know how to handle losing my children."

"You haven't lost Shannon."

"She's not here. She doesn't want to be here. In some ways, that's worse."

Chuck interlaced his fingers with hers. "It's not you. I'm the one she's mad at."

Bobbi drew up the corner of her mouth, trying to smile. She raised their hands, turning her rings toward him. "We're a package deal, remember?"

"Thank God." He kissed the back of her hand and risked adding to her burdens. "Glen and I discussed whether or not this was my fault, you know, like Shannon said."

Bobbi shook her head. "Chuck . . ."

He squeezed her hand gently. "I'm working on it."

"Glen said it wasn't, right?"

"Yeah, he was a lot of help, but I can't let this paralyze me like it did yesterday. I can't sit by while things fall completely apart. I'm going to go talk to the Snider kid in the morning. Maybe he'll open up to me because I'm old."

"Oh dear God, please . . ."

She was silent for several moments, praying Chuck suspected, then she took her free hand and wiped her eyes.

"Now, here's a perfect example of why I'm losing it. You tell me this, and I start to have some hope, and then in the back of my mind, I hear, 'What about Jack?' What will it do to him if you succeed where he failed? He's so fragile right now."

"He's still the hero. He tracked her to the Snider boy." He leaned in closer. "And you're not losing it. You want the best for everybody. It means you're a good mother."

"And you're a good father. There. I'll believe you when you believe me."

Monday, June 30

Chuck started Bobbi's coffee and quickly dialed Christine Gardner at home. She answered before the second ring.

"Mr. Molinsky, what's wrong?"

She was good. After working together for twenty years, Christine knew him almost as well as Bobbi did. "I'm not going to be in today or tomorrow."

"Of course. Mr. Mitchell and I can handle things with the insurance people."

"I have no doubts, but something else came up. . . . If anyone asks, I was in the ER with chest pains Saturday night, and I'm doing a stress test in the morning."

"Mr. Molinsky!"

"It's no big deal. They said it was a muscle spasm."

"Thank God. You should have called me—"

"Before the lecture starts, listen to me. For you and Chad only, Shannon left home early Saturday morning. She left a note for her mother, and we don't know where she is, or who she's with."

"I knew it. I knew something else was going on. I just couldn't believe you were that upset over some computers being stolen." Then she gasped. "And Mrs. Molinsky, bless her heart, so soon after your son."

"Yeah, I don't know how much more Bobbi can handle. Jack found out who helped Shannon leave, and I'm on my way to talk to him now."

"We'll be praying you find her. Don't give us another thought, though. We can cover everything."

"I know," Chuck said. "You should give yourself a raise."

"As soon as you approve the new budget."

"Leave it on my desk, on top of everything."

Chuck clutched the notepaper with the scribbled address for Dylan Snider's house against the steering wheel. Stay calm and matter-of-fact. Never let the kid know how desperately he needed his help. Bobbi begged him to bring Joel. He was rational and reasonable, she said. Chuck couldn't argue with that, but he had to do this by himself. Besides, if he did lose it, he didn't want anyone here to see it.

Before he double-checked the paper, he knew it had to be the big house at the end of the cul-de-sac. It all made sense. The spoiled brat who'd never heard the word no painted a glorious picture for Shannon. *Your parents are the problem. Ditch the parents, and everything will work out.* And she was vulnerable enough to soak it all in.

He wheeled his car around before he parked, in case he needed to make a quick exit. Before he got out, he took a deep breath and whispered a prayer for a level head, for a restrained temper, and most of all, for help bringing Shannon home today. Bobbi and Jack were praying. He knew Christine would be, too. God had to hear one of them.

He left the car unlocked and walked the long sidewalk up to the porch. The air conditioner hummed, but no other sounds came from the house. Surely, somebody was awake. Somebody in there had to have a job to be able to afford the house.

Chuck rang the doorbell and a full fifteen minutes later, a bleary-eyed man in his early forties opened the door. He raised his hand as a shade from the morning sunshine. "This better be important."

Buddy, you don't know . . .

"My name is Chuck Molinsky. My daughter is missing, and I know your son has talked with her in the last few days. I want to talk to him."

"I don't even know if he's home."

"Where else would he be?"

"How should I know? I don't keep up with him." He leaned out the door slightly. "His car's here. Hang on." The man disappeared inside the house. Another fifteen minutes later, Dylan stepped out onto the porch, dressed in a wrinkled T-shirt and shorts. Chuck guessed he'd slept in them.

"Dylan, I'm Shannon's father. She's disappeared, and I know you've talked to her recently."

"Did Jack send you over here?"

"Jack?" Chuck played dumb, letting Dylan believe he'd gotten away with punching Jack. "I'm here about Shannon. Where is she?"

"Like you care." Dylan smirked and crossed his arms across his chest, flexing his biceps.

Chuck wasn't impressed. *Don't let him bait you.* He fixed his eyes on Dylan's and never moved.

"Well, I don't know where she is."

"You were with her Saturday."

"You can't prove that."

"Don't press me, boy." Chuck felt a flash of heat move from his neck across his face.

"What? You want to yell at her some more? Is that it?" Dylan leaned back against the door, dropping his hands to his hips. "She doesn't want anything to do with you."

"So you put her up to leaving home?"

"She called me because she knew I would help her. Because I didn't judge her. Unlike you."

"You didn't help her."

"I helped her become a woman."

The part of Chuck's brain that comprehended that statement refused to let the information out. "What?"

Dylan looked Chuck in the eyes, his mouth curling into a malicious grin. "I said, Shannon's a woman now." Chuck felt the punk's breath as he leaned in closer. "And you know what else? She liked it. She begged me—"

In a flash, Chuck had Dylan by the shirt and slammed him up against the house face first, pinning Dylan's arm behind him. "You shut your filthy mouth." Dylan squirmed, trying to work himself free, but Chuck wrenched his arm even tighter. "You've never dealt with a father who cares about his children. You don't know who you're messing with."

"Don't threaten me, old man. I'm not afraid of you."

"It's not me you have to worry about." Chuck shoved Dylan away and walked off the porch.

"Who are you talking about?" Dylan asked, but Chuck ignored him. "Crazy old man," he muttered, adjusting his shirt.

Chuck sprayed gravel as he tore out of the neighborhood. "God, forgive me, I wanted to kill him right there." Angry tears spilled onto his cheeks. "Dear God, he's lying. Please, he's gotta be lying. Father, You take up for Shannon and avenge her."

For a long time Chuck drove, unaware of distance or direction. His pulse throbbed in his neck, and his grip on the steering wheel never relaxed in spite of the extra driving. He had to calm down before he faced Bobbi. He knew she was pacing by now, worrying, or even worse, she'd be expecting Shannon to be with him because of the delay.

He couldn't face her. This was so much deeper than fury and heartsickness. This was retribution for things he had done. Payback in kind. Things . . . things Bobbi didn't know, things he never even told Phil Shannon. And his daughter was paying for his sin. He'd rather have a curse.

Bobbi met him in the entry hall. "What did you find out? Where is she?"

"He wouldn't tell me anything. I'm sorry."

She dropped her eyes, bit her bottom lip, then scuffed back toward the kitchen, her shoulders drooping.

He couldn't tell her the rest of it. Not now. Give her something to cling to. He jogged to catch her. "Honey, he's not our only option."

She dropped into one of the kitchen chairs and rubbed her temples. "You know what? I'm tired. I'm tired of people telling me how sorry they are."

"And I would have given anything not to come home empty-handed." He pulled a chair over close to hers, and as soon as he touched her hand the floodgates opened. He lay over on the table and shook with sobs. He could hear Bobbi call his name. He could feel her hand on his back, a gentle kiss on his neck and a whisper in his ear. He didn't deserve her compassion, but he didn't have the strength to pull away from her.

"Calm down," she whispered. "It's not you. I'm sorry. I didn't mean it . . ."

"No . . . Bobbi . . . there's . . . we need to talk."

"I'm listening."

He nodded then pushed back from the table and staggered to the kitchen sink to splash water in his face. He yanked a paper towel from the roll then forced himself to face his wife. "You said Shannon was ashamed to come home."

"That's what she told Katelyn." Then Bobbi raised a hand to her mouth and tears brimmed in her eyes. "That boy."

Chuck could only nod. "But . . . Bobbi . . . this . . . When I was in college, there was a girl, and God help me, I don't even remember her name. Cute girl, and . . . just a good person. Went to church. We went out a couple of times."

"All that's in the past. I don't care—"

"Bobbi, I stole that girl's virginity! She gave me a boundary, and I violated it."

"Chuck, what are you saying? Did that boy . . . ? Because if he hurt Shannon . . ."

He shook his head. "Shannon was emotionally compromised, Bobbi. That's where it starts, and that's my fault. She was hurt and angry at me. And now it's payback time for what I did to that girl, and to her father."

"Not that idiotic curse again!"

"Not exactly, but—"

"There's no connection. The only curse you're living with is guilt and bad memories."

He shook his head. "It's all coming back. I intentionally . . . She told me 'no,' and I . . . and now Shannon's paying for it."

Bobbi slipped her arms around his neck, held him while tears silently trailed down both their cheeks. "It's been paid for," she whispered at last.

Chuck blew out a long, deep breath and raised his head. She was right. She had a gift for finding redemption, tracing the hand of God back to His heart. Even in the midst of her own maelstrom, she could find the anchor he needed. He squeezed her hand and gently kissed her. "Thank you."

They sat in silence for several long minutes, then she leaned back and gazed across the room at nothing in particular. "I've been thinking . . . I'm going to take my retirement."

"Retirement? But Bobbi—"

"I don't feel like teaching. The thoughts of trying to get everything ready . . . I just can't."

"I understand you don't feel like teaching right now, but by August all that may change."

"Is Shannon coming home before August?"

"Surely—"

"But we don't know."

"No."

"Then I'm retiring."

CHAPTER 10
LANGUOR

Thursday, July 10

Bobbi had already used a day's worth of energy showering, but she still had to get dressed and get moving for a ten thirty appointment. Shannon was officially a missing person now. However, that meant most folks expected her to get on with her life. As if there could be a normal, natural routine without her daughter.

In the four weeks since she'd lost Brad, the chance for justice faded daily. Detective Ramirez gave Chuck details of all their efforts, the dozens of people they had interviewed, but in a neighborhood where distrust of the police ran high, he didn't get much. He held out hope that Brad's character and reputation would be enough to get someone to step forward with some crucial piece of information. Translation—they had no chance of finding and catching Brad's killer.

When her second attempt to button her blouse left her shirttails uneven again, she gave up and pulled a sleeveless cotton sweater from her drawer. This appointment wasn't critical. It was just a mammogram. Easily rescheduled. But then Chuck would give her that look—the disapproving but worried one—and start hovering.

He gave her that look this morning when she put him off about their anniversary. Thirty-eight years, and he wanted to go celebrate. Celebrate. Now. Honestly.

The clock on her nightstand showed five after ten. If she was going, she had to leave now. *Get it over with.* She checked her hair one last time, then turned out the light and headed downstairs.

Jack stood in the entry hall, waiting for her. "Mom, I'd like to take you to lunch today for your anniversary."

"Thanks, but I'm not in the mood for celebrating."

"Okay then, can I take you out to lunch because I don't have to go to work today?"

"Jack . . ."

"I need to talk to you. Please?"

"But I've got this appointment."

"Fine," he said. "I'll drive you, then we'll go eat."

"You're determined, aren't you?"

"Yep, besides that, all the women at the mammogram place will think I'm cute." Jack grinned and adjusted his Cardinals hat.

"They'll be absolutely right about that." At least Jack finally sounded like his old self again. Maybe there was hope. She fished her keys from her purse. "Here. We'll take my car." She couldn't ride in Brad's car.

"You have to get these every year?" Jack unlocked the passenger side door of her car.

"Since I was thirty." Bobbi slumped in the seat. "Because of my mother."

"She was really young, wasn't she?"

"Diagnosed at thirty-nine, and she lived another . . . almost three years."

Jack pushed her door closed, then rounded the car and got in. "Well, I'm glad you stay on top of it."

"Yeah," Bobbi muttered.

Once the test was finished, she found Jack in a corner of the waiting area with a magazine. "You're something else," she said, tapping his knee.

"What? It was a *Sports Illustrated*, and I'm all caught up on spring training camps now."

"Spring training was three months ago, wasn't it?"

"Yep." He grinned and laid the magazine on the table beside him. "So where do you want to go?"

"Oh no. Any young man who endures the humiliation of the imaging center should at least get to choose the restaurant." Choices paralyzed her.

"I feel like spaghetti. Want to go for Italian?"

"Always."

"And it wasn't that bad." He held the door for her and unlocked her car door before walking around to the driver's side.

"Even so, you must have something major to discuss."

"At the restaurant. I can't talk and drive at the same time." He grinned again, and his eyes twinkled.

Maybe lunch with Jack was just what she needed. Maybe for an hour or so, she could lay everything else aside and just soak in his energy. When he turned toward Antonio's, her favorite restaurant, he watched her until she smiled.

He checked his watch. "It's not too early for you to eat, is it?"

"No, this is fine. We won't have to wait for a table." Jack held the door for her, then when they reached the table, he steadied her chair so she could sit. "I must be hungry. Everything smells wonderful."

"Joel and I used to say they should make perfumes that smell like food. Guys would be much more responsive to pot roast than some dumb flowers."

Bobbi shook her head. "Now I know why you don't have a girlfriend." She flipped the menu open and held it at arm's length. "I don't know why I even look. I can't resist the manicotti." She laid the menu to the side, then looked across the table at him. "You seem happier than you've been in several weeks."

"I don't know about that," he said. "I guess I'm just confident that you can help me."

"Don't bank on it." He had his hopes pinned on her, and there was no way she could come through for him. She sipped her water to buy some time. If she had any wise words, she'd use them on herself. He sat across the table looking like he'd had his hands smacked for reaching in the cookie jar. Great. She took another gulp of her water and dove in. "So you're still struggling with Brad and Shannon?"

He sat up and scooted his chair closer to the table. "I keep praying, and reading, trying to find some kind of answer, but there's nothing. So why won't God answer me unless I've done something wrong?" He dropped his eyes. "Just like Shannon said."

"You and your dad." Before she could say any more, the waiter returned with their drinks and salads. Bobbi opened a package of sweetener and poured it into her tea, stirring it slowly. "Shannon validated your fears, so you're buying everything she says. Your dad's the same way. She told him this was all a curse he brought on us, and he swallowed every bit of it. It's a lie."

She tasted her tea, decided it was sweet enough, then laid the spoon beside the glass. "I want you to get this, Jack. Brad is not dead because of anything you did or didn't do. Brad's gone because we live in a sinful, fallen world, full of sinful people who behave in terrible, evil ways."

She watched him blink and nod. He needed to hear more, but she wasn't certain she could go on. Three or four sentences had been her absolute limit. "That's the only way I can make it make sense to me. Maybe it will be easier when someone is finally arrested for it."

She took a long drink from her tea. "I wish I knew what God was thinking when He let it happen."

"You're mad at God?"

Was she? Maybe. Probably. Yes. "I can't believe that there wasn't any other way for Him to accomplish His purposes than to take my son. He didn't have to do this."

Now that she'd opened the door, the rest of the indictment spilled out. "Your aorta is three centimeters, just this big," she said, indicating the width of her two fingers. "Anywhere else on his body, and Brad would have lived. It was such an implausible shot—" She gulped her tea and pushed the threatening emotion back down. "But that's not helping you."

"It helps more than you know. At least I'm not the only one who thought that."

"It's not a good way to think." The church answer. The mother answer. Paste on a happy face and tell everyone you're blessed. She sighed and tried to come up with something that would help him. "Jack, the times I've felt like God wasn't listening to me happened for one of two reasons. I wasn't listening to Him, or He'd already told me the answer and I was ignoring it because I didn't want to do what He'd said."

"When? I didn't think you ever had to struggle with doing what God said."

Poor, deluded boy. "Believe it."

The waiter brought their food, and Jack watched until he was out of sight, then he turned back to her. "I'm sorry. It was with my mom, wasn't it?"

She pulled her plate closer and stabbed at the pasta. "Sweetheart, I don't know if it's really appropriate for me to discuss your mother."

"So how much older do I have to be?"

She sighed and laid her fork down. Sure, why not tell him exactly what she thought of his mother? Shatter him. Alienate him. Let him blame himself for all of that, too.

"Your mother . . ." She pulled her napkin from her lap and dabbed at the corners of her mouth, stalling. "When your mother came back, all that pain, it churned right back to the surface." She pushed at her food, avoiding Jack's eyes. The same eyes Tracy had. "Truth is, I was terrified. I was afraid for my family."

"Afraid of my mom?"

Bobbi raised her eyes long enough to nod. "Donna, Donna Shannon told me it was because I'd never forgiven her for the affair. I was sure she didn't want it, and wasn't convinced she deserved it."

"But you did it." No trace of recrimination in his voice, he was encouraging her.

"The morning you were baptized, that's when I talked to her."

"And she was dead the next week," Jack said quietly. "Do you think it made a difference to her?"

"Who knows? Your mother was so guarded. She wouldn't let anyone get close to her, and she wouldn't open up to anybody. She was the most tragic person I have ever known. There was help and healing all around her, but she completely rejected it."

His silence convicted her. She'd overstepped. Mercifully, he changed the subject. "Dad said you were gonna retire."

"I turned the paperwork in a couple of weeks ago. They'll approve it at the next board meeting." Don't try to explain it or justify it. Leave it there.

"I don't blame you," he said. "I haven't told Dad yet, but I'm not sure about going back to school this fall."

At last. What he really wanted to talk about. "Why wouldn't you?"

"I'm not sure what I'm supposed to do. I don't even know if religion is the right major anymore."

"Because Brad's gone?"

He nodded. "I was going to follow him and work at the mission. I had it all mapped out."

She had to give him something to go on, something to work toward. "Sweetheart, why don't you ask Brad?"

"What?"

"You have his notebooks and his Bible. He wrestled with going to law school or seminary. Maybe he wrote down the process, or something that crystallized it all for him. Maybe that will help you."

Jack leaned back and grinned, the twinkle returned to his eyes. "Mom, you are brilliant."

Friday, July 11

Bobbi sat at the kitchen table, sipping a cup of coffee. The morning paper lay beside the placemat, still unread. When Chuck came in a moment later, he smiled at her, then poured himself a cup of her coffee. That meant he had some proposition he expected her to go along with. He wanted her to see they were on the same team. They were drinking the same coffee after all.

"I made reservations for seven," he said, as he slid into the chair across from her. He'd left his suit jacket off and rolled up his sleeves. Casual, no pressure. Surely, after all these years, he understood she was on to him.

"Chuck, I love you. I am extremely blessed to be married to you, but I'm in no mood to celebrate our anniversary right now. We can go out when Shannon comes home."

"You can't put your life on hold this way."

"Nor can I go on with some stupid routine and pretend that everything is normal."

"I'm not asking you to pretend anything." Chuck gulped coffee. She'd stung him with the insinuation that their anniversary was part of a stupid routine. "So we're staying home tonight?"

"You can do what you want." Bobbi pulled the newspaper close and made a pretense of reading it.

"Great, it's settled then. Seven o'clock."

"Chuck—"

"No, we've been under emotional siege for a month now. We need a break."

Before Bobbi could protest further, the phone rang, and she reached for it.

"Mom," Joel said. "I think we've decided to grill out Sunday after church for Ryan's birthday. Will that work for you?"

Ryan's sixteenth birthday, and she completely forgot. "Umm . . . yeah, Sunday's fine."

"You sure?"

"It just slipped up on me, that's all. What can I bring?" *What can I have Chuck pick up that can be dumped in a serving dish so it looks homemade?*

"Dad and Jack."

"Seriously, Joel."

"I'm very serious. We'll take care of everything. Just come."

Bobbi frowned and rolled her eyes. "What do you want Dad to bring, then?"

"Ummm, Dad can bring a salad or something, but you better not help him."

"You are incorrigible."

"Yes, I am. Oh, happy anniversary. You guys going out?"

"Under protest, yes."

"Why don't you want to go out?"

"Aside from the obvious?"

"Mom," Joel said gently, "punishing yourself isn't going to bring Shannon home sooner."

"I'm not punishing myself."

"Are you punishing Dad, then?"

Tired of defending herself, tired of being admonished for her grief, she snapped. "When you have kids of your own, maybe you'll understand." In the heart-squeezing silence that followed, she realized how deeply she'd cut Joel. "I'm so sorry. That's not what I meant at all."

"We'll try to eat about one."

"Joel, please—"

"We'll talk later, Mom. I have to go now."

Bobbi laid down the phone and buried her face in her hands. She felt a touch on her arm. "He knows you didn't mean it," Chuck said.

"He practically hung up on me," she said, raising her head. "What a spiteful, cruel thing to say. Is that who I am now?"

"No," he said, taking her in his arms. "It was a slip. You would never hurt Joel or any of us."

"Never say never."

"Bobbi . . ."

"I've seen too many things here lately that I never dreamed would happen. It's like all of a sudden I don't understand the rules or the boundaries anymore."

"You'll get your bearings back."

She shook her head. "I feel like a monumental failure."

"Honey, we've been through this. Shannon . . . It was because of me. I came down too hard on her."

"No, she left because I never taught her how to cope."

"But she'll come home because you taught her what real love is, what family is all about."

Bobbi leaned back in her chair and took a long drink of her coffee. "Chuck, I want to get Ryan a car for his birthday."

"What?"

"My grandson is turning sixteen. I want to get him a car."

"We never got our kids cars when they turned sixteen."

"Grandchildren are different."

"You're setting a ridiculously high standard for our future grandchildren."

"Do you realize how old we will be before any other grandchildren hit sixteen? This may be our only chance."

"You're serious."

"Completely."

"You're not going to want to buy somebody a car every time you think you've hurt someone's feelings, are you?" Chuck asked, raising his eyebrow.

"There's no question that I hurt Joel's feelings. Can't we buy a decent, used, high school kid kind of car out of that money market account?"

"Yeah, but Bobbi, you never do anything impulsive. Is there something else going on?"

Prove to Joel that she really did think of Ryan as theirs. Deflect attention from herself. Do one thing right. "No, I just really want to do something special for him. He's a wonderful young man, and I don't think he realizes that."

"I'll talk to Joel first."

Bobbi rolled her eyes. "That'll ruin the surprise."

"Even so," Chuck said.

"I want to go car shopping before dinner this evening."

Chuck pushed his office door open, but before he could set down his briefcase, his phone rang. Christine waved for him to pick up, which meant it wasn't work-related.

"Dad, what's going on with Mom?" Joel asked without saying hello.

"Nothing. I mean everything's still wearing on her." He held the phone and wriggled out of his suit jacket. "But I don't think it's anything major."

"Did you hear what she said?"

"I was right there."

"That's not like her. It worries me a little."

Chuck dropped into his chair, swiveling it to face the back wall of his office. "Then this is gonna sound really bad."

"What? There's more?"

"She wants to buy Ryan a car for his birthday. Like today, before we go out to dinner."

"You can't get him a car. That's too much."

"It's the only thing she's shown any initiative with or interest in lately."

"Again, that's not like her. She's depressed again, isn't she?"

"Probably, but I think she's got reason to be."

"Is she suicidal?"

"No! That's crazy." Completely. She wasn't. Couldn't be.

"How did she pitch the idea of getting the car?"

"She wanted to do something special for Ryan, and we may not get the chance to do anything like this for our other grandchildren."

"See, that fatalism? That's exactly what I mean."

"I'm as concerned about her as I've ever been, but do the math. If you had a baby today, I'd be almost eighty before he could drive. She has a point."

"Maybe," Joel mumbled.

"This is important to her. I think we need to let her do it."

"On one condition," Joel said. "Well, two conditions. One, you don't get anything extravagant, and two, if she does anything else like this, anything out of character, you get her under a doctor's care for depression."

"Joel—"

"I'm serious," Joel said with a childlike urgency in his voice. "I've lost a brother, my sister's left home, and I can't . . . I don't want my mother stolen away by grief and depression."

CHAPTER 11
FORMALITY

Just three hours, that's all, Bobbi coached herself as she smoothed foundation across her cheeks. Three hours tonight, and three hours on Sunday. Focusing on Ryan's car would get her through.

She finished putting on her makeup, touched up her hair and dutifully put in the earrings Chuck bought her for a past anniversary. She checked herself in the mirror. Convincing enough. Unless she tried to smile. Three hours.

She picked up her purse and walked over to switch on the bedside lamp. Her devotional book lay on the nightstand, untouched since the night before Brad's death.

Great Is Thy Faithfulness, the cover announced. It's great. Just not great enough. It had lapses. The devotional books never mentioned that, though. They had no solace for those moments when God turned His back, or closed His eyes. Where were the quick and easy answers for that?

She heard the front door open, which meant Chuck was home. She took the book from its spot, and on her way out of the bedroom, she dropped it in the wastebasket.

Chuck caught her on the staircase and kissed her lightly. "You look fabulous. You sure you want to be seen with me?"

"Not really. Want to stay home?"

He frowned and slipped his hand around hers. "I think this will be good for you. Besides, we're going car shopping, remember?"

"Oh, I have Joel's permission?"

"He said nothing extravagant."

"Let's go, then," Bobbi said. The sooner she went, the sooner she'd get it over with.

Car shopping proved simpler than she envisioned. They went to the Toyota dealer she always bought from and quickly narrowed down her choices. Chuck never protested they could get a better deal somewhere else. He gave her positive, constructive comments but let her make the decision. After a few quick signatures, the dealer promised to have the Rav4 detailed before Chuck picked it up tomorrow afternoon. Mission accomplished. But dinner still loomed.

In the car, she made a show of flipping through the dealer's paperwork before she stuffed it deep in her purse. When Chuck pulled into a restaurant she didn't recognize, everything tensed, her neck, her shoulders, but especially her stomach. For a moment, she wondered if throwing up would get her a trip home.

Oliver's Twist was a new grill featuring live music on the weekends. Chuck opened her car door, walked her across the lot, then held the restaurant's door for her. Inside the dimly lit foyer, loud music greeted them and wait staff in brightly patterned shirts and wireless mikes charged back and forth.

"Oh, we're way too old for this place," Bobbi protested.

"Nonsense."

Chuck took her hand and pulled her to the host's stand. A moment later, the smiling young man led them to their table. He took their drink orders, then disappeared. Chuck reached across the table for her hand. "Thank you."

"For what?"

"For giving me that hand in marriage years ago, and for coming to dinner. I know you didn't want to go out tonight, but you did it. That means a lot to me."

"I learned a long time ago that you don't listen to me when I say no."

A pianist, a guitarist and a drummer took their places on the small stage across the room from them. Once set, the guitarist began to sing a soft ballad. "Not your typical lounge lizards," Bobbi said, nodding toward the band.

"May I?" Chuck asked.

"May you what?"

"May I have this dance?"

"We'll look ridiculous."

"No, we won't. It will be very touching and romantic. I'll get all the other husbands in trouble."

"At least your motives are pure," Bobbi said. "Not tonight."

"When was the last time we got to dance?"

"Christmas party."

"That was months ago."

Bobbi pulled her hand away from his and leaned across the table. "I don't want to be here. Don't push it."

Chuck slumped back in his chair and sighed. "What can I do? How can I bring you out of this?"

"You can't. You can't bring Brad back, and you can't bring Shannon home."

"Then how can I help you carry it?"

"I don't think you can. I doubt anybody can."

Sunday, July 13

From the kitchen window, Joel saw his parents roll up in a shiny, silver Rav4, and a moment later, Jack pulled in behind them in his father's Impala. "Here they are, Abby. She did good."

He stepped back so Abby could look out the window. "It's perfect for him," she said. "I still can't believe your mother."

"Me, either." He followed Abby to the front door, pausing at the steps. "Ryan! Your grandparents are here!"

"Which ones?"

"My parents, and Jack."

The teenager tromped down the stairs and strode to the front door, a step ahead of Joel and Abby. "You guys get a new car?" Ryan asked as he held the door open for them.

Joel watched his mother carefully, but she played it very cool. "We bought a car," she said. "What do you think?"

"It's nice. Doesn't look much like a grandparent's car, though."

"That's what I thought, too." She hooked his arm and steered him toward the car. "I want you to see the stereo."

Ryan lowered his voice. "Nobody calls it that anymore."

"Seriously?"

"Sound system," he said with an insider's nod.

She opened the driver's side door for Ryan, as the rest of them crowded in closer. "Have a seat." Ryan carefully eased into the driver's seat. He gripped the steering wheel, then adjusted the rearview mirror.

Joel slipped an arm around Abby's shoulder. "Won't be long, Buddy, till you're behind the wheel."

"Of Mom's car," he muttered. "Nothing like this."

"So this car is cool?" Joel's mother asked, without the slightest hint of a smile, without any sparkle in her eyes.

"Way."

"Cool enough for a sixteen-year-old grandson?"

"What?" Ryan asked. Joel grinned as Ryan sputtered. "You're not . . . Are you . . . No way!"

She handed him the keys. "Happy birthday, sweetheart."

"For real?" Ryan cradled the keys and looked up at Joel for confirmation. "Can I take it for a drive?"

"You already know how to drive?" his mother asked. At least her surprise seemed genuine.

"Mom, you know how it is with guys and cars," Joel admitted.

"Don't you at least need an adult in the car?" Abby asked.

"Jack counts! Come on!"

"Don't wreck it the first day," Joel called. Ryan shook his head as Jack climbed in the car. "Abby, we're ruined. We'll never top this."

When the car disappeared around the corner, Abby motioned to Joel's parents. "Let's get you folks inside where it's air conditioned." She swung the front door open. "You coming?" she called to Joel.

"I want to wait for Ryan. You know, give him the standard lecture."

"Of course," Abby said. "Should've guessed."

Joel shuffled over and sat down on the porch step to wait. His mother seemed fine just now, like normal. Was he the one overreacting? Clearly, she was able to get out, shop and choose an ideal car, three or four years old, cheap to maintain, and great gas mileage. Maybe they were all underestimating her.

After a few minutes, Joel spotted the Rav4 maneuvering carefully down their street back to its original spot in front of the house. Ryan clambered out of the car, grinning broadly. "Can you believe this?" he said, patting the car's roof.

"No, I can't," Joel said. "She never did anything like that with us, did she, Jack?"

Jack locked his passenger door and shuffled to the porch, faking dejection. "Now we know who she likes best."

"Give us a minute, okay?" Joel asked.

"Sure." Jack continued his shuffle through the front door. "I'll get first shot at the food this way."

"I don't think I could eat right now anyway," Ryan said.

As soon as Jack shut the door, Joel said, "You know you cannot tell your other grandparents about this."

"No kidding."

"Ryan, your grandmother needs you right now."

"Me? Why me?"

"She's lost a lot in the last month or so. She needs to feel connected, you know?" Ryan nodded. "I want you to make sure you spend some time with her today, just you and her."

"After this, I'd go move in with her!"

As his mother began clearing dishes from the table, Ryan watched his grandmother until she made eye contact with him. "Can I take you for a drive?"

"I thought you'd never ask." She smiled and followed him outside. He made sure to hold the door for her, and to close the passenger door once she settled in the seat. He wiped his palms on his shorts before adjusting the rearview mirror, then he pulled away from the curb.

"Sweetheart, relax. Driving instructors don't drive this carefully."

"I don't want my car taken away on the very first day."

"I don't think you have to worry."

He wound his way through residential neighborhoods, avoiding the busier streets.

"Have you learned to parallel park yet?"

"I've tried it a couple of times."

"Let's head over to the library. The parking lot should be empty, and it's a good place to practice. That's where your dad learned." When he turned into the lot, she pointed to the curb. "Let me out and I'll be the corner of the parked car."

He put the car in park, then twisted around to face her. "Can I ask you something first?"

"Always."

"Why'd you do this?"

"What?"

Ryan shook his head at her pretend innocence. "The car."

She reached over and squeezed his hand. "Because I love you, because you're very special, and I'm not sure you understand that."

"I know you love me."

"But not the rest of it."

She had him, but without the standard "you shouldn't feel like that" undertone. Maybe he could risk saying a little more. "Well, my mom and dad . . . They aren't . . ." How could he get it across? "I just don't feel like I fit in, you know."

"No, I don't. Explain it to me."

He blew out a long, slow breath and debated going with his first instinct, saying "forget it" and changing the subject. His dad said she needed to feel connected, though, and shutting down a conversation was probably not the way to do that.

"All you guys, well, Dad and Jack and Uncle Brad . . . They were all big-time jocks and straight-A students. . . . You have this wonderful, perfect family, except for me."

"Ryan, you *are* my wonderful, perfect family. We aren't some ridiculous, false standard you have to measure up to. Sweetheart, this family is a gift that God gave you, and you are a beautiful addition. Don't ever think you don't fit in or you're not as good as anybody else."

"That's hard," Ryan said. "It's pretty ingrained."

"Then ingrain this one. Jesus Christ was the son of a teenage mother, and everybody knew He wasn't His father's natural son. That didn't matter to Him or His dad, right?"

"Maybe not."

"You're your father's son, and you're my grandson, regardless of what your birth certificate says." She dug her billfold from her purse and opened it to his school picture. "Look at this one."

"I'd rather not," he mumbled.

"Let me make my point." She shoved him gently and flipped back to a family photo. "Now look at this picture."

"So?"

"Who looks more like me? You or Jack?"

He took the billfold from her and flipped the pictures back and forth, comparing them. "Um, I do, I guess."

"You guess? We have the same eyes! I couldn't have mail-ordered a more perfect grandson."

Ryan handed the billfold back to her. "Since you're my grandmother, then it's about time I came up with a name for you."

"Yeah, I've noticed," she said with a smile. "I don't think you've ever called me anything."

Ryan felt his face flush. She'd caught him. "It has to be cool, special, but still kind of grandmother-ish. . . . What about Nan?"

"Nan?"

"Much hipper than Nana, plus I'm way too old for that."

"And I'm not old enough," she said. "I love it."

"What do you think about Pop?"

"For Chuck? It's perfect." She opened her door and swung her feet around to the pavement. "Thank you. That was a very special gift."

"What?"

"The drive, the conversation and the names."

"Thank you," Ryan said. "You blew me away."

"Pop had a little to do with it. He signed the check."

"You have lifetime guaranteed grass mowing." He raised his right hand to back up his promise.

"If Jack ever moves out, I'll be sure and call you. Now let's see you park this baby."

Joel paced on the front porch waiting for Ryan to return with his mother. He had no worries about the teenager or his driving, but catching his mother alone had been his one goal for the day, and he was running out of opportunities. Brad always teased him for being a mama's boy, but he knew he wouldn't get a decent night's sleep until they cleared the air over that snarky comment from Friday's phone conversation.

His dad clung to the belief that she wasn't depressed, at least not clinically, and she seemed good today. She was quiet at lunch, a little tired maybe, but those gentle smiles for Ryan had to be genuine. Unless it was all a show. Unless she saved every ounce of energy she had to fake her way through the afternoon. Surely not . . .

Joel watched as Ryan pulled up to the house again. As soon as he parked the car, the teenager got out and trotted around to open his grandmother's door. "Her hair didn't turn white," Joel called. "That's a good sign."

"Dad." Ryan rolled his eyes. "I'm going to go tell Pop thanks." He kissed his grandmother's cheek and high-fived Joel on his way in the house.

"Who's Pop?" Joel asked as his mother made her way up the sidewalk.

"Dad," she said. "I'm Nan. We're official now." She stepped up on the porch. "Can I apologize to you?"

"No. There's no need." It wasn't about the apology.

"I don't believe you."

"I don't believe you when you say you're just fine."

She sat down on the edge of the porch, and Joel took a seat beside her. "I'll tell the truth if you will," she offered.

"Fair enough," Joel said. "It was a cheap shot, but it was totally out of character, so I didn't put too much stock into it after the initial hurt."

"I'm not sure what's in character and what's not, right now. I've been short with your dad. I raised my voice at Shannon the night before she left. I can't think straight. . . ." She stared out across the street, energy draining by the moment. "I'm afraid this is what insanity feels like."

"Mom—"

"No, this isn't right. I know it isn't, but I can't fix it."

"It's not insanity." Joel dropped his head and stole a glance at her. "It's grief, Mom. You've got to let yourself grieve and stop stuffing it. The longer you keep it in, the more it's going to build and leak out as anger or something else." She turned her head away from him and gazed down the street. "Are you sleeping?"

"About one out of three nights."

"That makes it worse. Can I talk you into seeing a doctor?"

She shook her head. "Give me some time."

"How much?" Joel glanced at his watch with an exaggerated motion, and she gave him a half smile.

"I've never done this before. I'm not sure."

Thursday, July 24

Chuck sipped his coffee and tried to will Bobbi to talk to him. Instead, she sat an arm's length away, staring into her coffee cup without ever engaging. The hall clock chimed nine o'clock. He could stay a few more minutes.

He finished off his coffee and stood to rinse the cup before putting it in the dishwasher. "You have plans for today?"

"Not really." She never had plans, just a succession of empty days. She never went out, never picked up the phone, even when Rita called. When he challenged her about it, she claimed she was leaving the line open for Shannon.

"I should be home a little early." No matter what was on his calendar, he was leaving at three.

"I think Jack is working ten to six." As if she weren't worth coming home to.

"You want to get some dinner somewhere?"

"We'll see." She took a sip of her coffee.

"I need you to help me out at the grocery store. Can you do that much?"

"This evening or tomorrow?" The first dodge.

"Whichever is better for you."

"Let me think about it." And the second dodge.

"You can let me know tonight. You need anything before I go?"

"I don't think so. Thanks." She wouldn't let him do anything for her, and he'd run out of ideas. Next week would mark a month since Shannon left home. If Bobbi didn't show some signs of life over the weekend, she was seeing a doctor, even if he had to drag her.

Chuck leaned down to kiss her, and at least she tilted her head toward him. "I love you," he said, and she nodded.

"I wish that was enough," Bobbi said barely above a whisper.

And he was supposed to pick up his briefcase and leave after that. "Bobbi, we have to—" The phone rang. In frustration, he yanked it from its cradle. "Molinskys."

"Bobbi Molinsky, please." It was a calm, measured man's voice.

"It's for you." He held the receiver out, and she snatched it from him with an icy glare.

"This is Bobbi . . . I see . . . Today?" The ice melted. "We'll be there." She handed the phone back to him.

"Who was it?"

"It was Dr. Karsten. He wants to discuss my mammogram. He said I should bring you."

CHAPTER 12
DIAGNOSIS

"That's bad, isn't it?" Chuck pulled out one of the kitchen chairs and sat down before his knees buckled under him.

"Maybe. Let's keep it quiet until we know more."

"Are you going to be all right? I can stay here with you."

"That's not necessary. I'll meet you at the doctor's office."

"I'd feel better if I could drive you."

Bobbi sighed and finished off her coffee. "Can you be home about two thirty, then?"

"Of course."

"Are you okay? You look a little pale."

Pale? He was trying to focus on her words to keep from passing out. "I'm a little worried."

"How could it be any worse than what we've already been through?"

It was after ten o'clock by the time Chuck dragged himself to his office. He dropped his briefcase on the floor and swiveled his chair around, giving him as much privacy as he could get with glass walls. Resting his elbows on his knees, he buried his face in his hands. Breast cancer. What would this do to Bobbi and to his sons? And Shannon? How could he get the information to Shannon? Bobbi said to keep it quiet. Did that mean she didn't want him to call anybody?

He wasn't sure he could make it the entire day without telling somebody.

"Chuck?"

He spun his chair around to see Christine at his door. "I don't think you've ever called me Chuck before."

"You didn't hear me the first three times when I said 'Mr. Molinsky.' You need me to pray?"

"That obvious?"

"You didn't speak to me when you came in."

"I'm sorry," Chuck said. "Bobbi . . . her doctor wants to see her about her mammogram, and he said I should be there."

"I'm so sorry." She blinked several times, then pointed at his briefcase. "You're not going to get anything done today."

"I know. Bobbi . . . she wanted . . . I don't have anyplace else to go. Besides, if I'm going to draw a paycheck, I should at least show up once in a while."

Christine looked back at her desk. She probably thought he wouldn't see her wipe her eyes. "Maybe it's not cancer."

"Her mother died at forty-two from it. That's what scares me."

Christine nodded and pressed her lips together. "She sees the doctor today?"

"At three. She wants me to keep it quiet until we know more."

"I'll pray very quietly." She smiled gently and eased his door closed.

Chuck leaned up to his desk and picked up the picture of Bobbi from their trip to Maui almost twenty years ago. He lightly traced her smile, the shy, self-conscious one, the one he'd give anything to see again. The picture blurred, and he quickly rubbed his eyes.

Even if it's cancer, it's treatable, right? Weren't there women on television who had lived ten or twenty years after breast cancer?

He carefully placed the picture back in its spot at the corner of his desk blotter. This was just another test, a little more refining God needed to do with them, that's all. They'd make it through this, just like Shannon was going to come home.

Chuck sighed and leaned back in his chair. *God, help me believe that.*

Chuck arrived home at two thirty as promised, and Bobbi stood in the foyer waiting for him. She was smartly dressed in slacks and a green patterned blouse that always looked good on her. Her makeup was done, and every hair lay perfectly. He coughed to hide his surprise, but seeing her gave him the lift he needed. Maybe the threat of cancer would bring her back. He took her hand and leaned in to kiss her cheek. "You look terrific."

"It'll be easier for Dr. Karsten to tell me if he thinks I can take it."

"Can you?"

"It's just one more thing. Hardly noticeable." A hopeless resignation soaked her words.

"It's not necessarily cancer."

She gave him a quick frown, enough for him to understand she wasn't arguing, but he was wrong. "I was thinking . . . I had the high white count when I spent the night in the hospital. I'm sure it's connected."

"I forgot all about that." Dizzy and nauseous once again, the only thing running through his mind was the memory of the day his dad was diagnosed with lymphoma. Jim Molinsky spent two years growing weaker and sicker before it finally killed him. He couldn't watch Bobbi go through that.

Bobbi checked her hair in the hall mirror, then she picked up her purse. "I guess I'm ready."

He wasn't. How could he prepare himself to sit in a doctor's office and hear him say the word "cancer"? As he drove, he held tightly to Bobbi's hand, more for his own comfort than hers, letting go only long enough to back into a parking spot.

"Can we pray before we go in?" Bobbi nodded and closed her eyes. Chuck reached over to hold both her hands in his. He took a deep breath and let it out slowly before speaking. "Dear God, I'm begging You, please don't make Bobbi go through this. Let it be something else besides cancer. If this is what You're laying before us, though, You're going to have to show me what to do. I don't think I have the strength for this."

Before he let go of her hands, she looked him in the eyes. "Chuck, I'm so sorry."

"What on earth for?"

"This is going to be much harder on you than it is on me."

Chuck hadn't settled in the overstuffed waiting room chair before a nurse summoned them back to Dr. Karsten's office. Bobbi walked a few steps ahead of him in the narrow hallway, her steps confident. The nurse opened a door for them. "He'll be right in," she said.

The office was smaller than Chuck expected, with only a desk, a table, a bookcase and a couple of extra chairs. One for the patient, and one for the husband. He followed Bobbi in, then tripped on his way to the chair next to hers. He sat down hard and mumbled, "The guy couldn't get a bigger office?"

"He's probably never in it," Bobbi said.

So it was like a movie set, a room just for delivering bad news. And he was going to sit here in this fake little room and hear this guy say the woman he loved had . . . cancer.

Chuck flinched when Dr. Karsten came in and Bobbi took his hand. Slightly built, the doctor hadn't aged much since delivering Shannon, and still sported a trim mustache and goatee. He shook hands with Bobbi and Chuck and sat down, dropping a folder on his desk. He never smiled.

"Bobbi, you have a small mass on the right side." He pulled a sheet from the folder and turned it so Bobbi could see it. Chuck leaned over to see and tried to follow as the doctor pointed to shadows on scans, then drew circles and arrows and scribbled meaningless numbers in the margins. "With your history, I think we need to get a biopsy."

"It's cancer."

"I don't know for sure. We won't know without more testing—"

"I had some blood work about six weeks ago that showed an elevated white count. We attributed it to some other things and didn't follow up on it. Is it related?"

He sat in silence for several minutes, staring at the folder in front of him, then he folded his hands. "I hate this part of my job," he said quietly. "Can you go for a biopsy tomorrow?"

"If you say so," Bobbi answered.

"Wait," Chuck said. "Tomorrow? So you think it is cancer?"

"Mr. Molinsky, everything changes when you give someone that diagnosis. I don't want to be premature."

"Look, if you're wrong, we'll praise God for a miracle, but I need to know what I'm . . . I mean, we're, what we're up against."

Dr. Karsten looked at Bobbi, then fixed his eyes on Chuck. "All right then, candidly speaking, I will be very surprised if it's not cancer."

Bobbi took his hand again before they left the doctor's office, before he had a chance to wipe it on his slacks. "You want me to drive home?" she asked.

"No. It's just, he was right. Something changes once you hear a doctor say the word 'cancer.'" He opened her car door, then closed it for her once she was inside. Everything changes. He rounded the car almost afraid to take his eyes off her. "I'm taking off tomorrow."

"For the biopsy? You don't have to."

"Bobbi, honestly, it's not just for your sake."

She laid her hand, warm, soft, reassuring, on his. "I've never seen you like this."

"You've never been threatened with death before."

"You'll handle this, too. I promise."

"So can we tell the kids and Rita?"

"I'd rather not."

"I can't keep this a secret. We have to tell them."

Bobbi sighed and turned away from him, gazing across the parking lot. "I don't want everyone to make a big fuss. Can you at least tell them that much?"

"Not fuss . . . ? Honey, your family loves you, and they're going to want to be there for you."

"This is not going to make any sense to you, but right now, a lot of hovering will make things worse for me." She squeezed his hand. "I need some space to sort all this out."

Space he understood, but she was asking him for isolation.

Bobbi brewed a cup of Indonesian coffee and retreated to the solitude of the study. Chuck allowed that solitude only because she promised to call Rita. She closed her eyes and savored the warmth of the coffee as it diffused through her body. The biopsy tomorrow was a formality. She knew it was cancer. She could feel it. The risk, the fear had always been in the back of her mind, but after she passed fifty, she thought she had escaped.

So she hadn't escaped, but coming on top of everything else, the diagnosis was robbed of its impact. Last year, it would have devastated them. But coming now—cancer? Of course. What else could it be?

Taking another drink to steel her nerves, she reached for the phone and dialed her sister's number.

Rita answered on the second ring. "Hey, baby, how are you?"

"I'm not sure."

"What's that supposed to mean?"

There was no easy way. "I have a biopsy tomorrow. It will likely confirm that I have breast cancer."

Not a sound.

"Rita? Are you still there?"

"I need to sit down," she said weakly. "Give me a minute."

"Sure."

"Canc . . . How? I don't understand."

"I know."

"Do you need me? I can be there in a couple of minutes."

"I should ask you the same question."

"Yeah, I guess I wouldn't be much help. You're sure about this? That it's cancer?"

"I'm sure."

"A lot has changed since Mama had it."

"I know."

"Have you told Joel and Jack?"

"Chuck's calling Joel, and we'll tell Jack tonight when he gets home."

"Shannon. When word of this gets to Shannon . . . she'll come home."

Shannon wasn't coming home. Bobbi didn't have the energy for that kind of hope. "Listen, I want to keep this kind of quiet for now."

"I can't tell anybody?"

"Just family for now. Please?"

"Afraid somebody's going to pray for you? Is that it?" Rita asked bluntly.

"What?"

"You don't want anybody to help you through this?"

"You sound like Chuck."

"Baby, you've been through hard times before, and you know that cutting yourself off from everybody, especially your family, is not the answer. That's what Daddy did, and that's what brought you to a crisis point after Chuck's affair."

"Rita—"

"This is why you have a family. Is Chuck going with you tomorrow?"

"Yes."

"When will you get the results back?"

"I don't know. A few days I guess."

"I'm making your dinner tomorrow. You can let me know if you want to eat at home or here with us."

"That's not necessary."

"Yes, it is," Rita said. "You don't realize how much help you need right now."

"This is exactly what I was trying to avoid."

"Then I'm on the right track."

Chuck collapsed on the sofa in the family room and rubbed his temples, trying in vain to make the pounding stop. Cancer. And she took the news like it was nothing more than having to wait for a table at Antonio's. No big deal. Expected.

She sat two rooms away, processing the diagnosis on her own, leaving him with empty fear. He needed her strength, her calm. He needed her to explain where that resolve came from, and to describe how she was going to fight and win. He needed to feel that bond, that connection . . . but she needed space.

He reached for the phone and called Joel's cell.

"Dad, can you believe I am actually in my car, on my way home at four thirty? That's almost like normal people hours."

"You're driving right now? I want you to pull over for a minute."

"Dad, what's wrong? Is it Shannon?"

"No . . . just . . . please."

"All right, I'm in a parking lot. What is going on?"

"Your mom's having a biopsy tomorrow. The doctor's fairly certain it's breast cancer."

"Wha . . . ? Cancer? Mom?"

"We just came from the doctor's office."

"How is she?" Hardly anyone else would have caught the waver in Joel's voice, but Chuck was fighting that same battle to maintain control.

"Good. I mean, we're trying to, uh, grasp it all. Mom . . . she wanted to keep this kind of quiet for now, just family."

"Why doesn't she want anybody to know?"

"She said it would make things harder for her, that she needed 'space' to deal with it."

"Space? She needs space? I don't know if I'd give it to her. Listen to her closely over the next few weeks or so."

"Did anybody ever tell you that you were paranoid?"

"All the time, but it's not paranoia if you're right."

"You want a cup of coffee?" Bobbi asked Jack, as she filled the pot with water. After enduring Chuck's glances at her throughout dinner, she wanted to explain to Jack about the doctor's appointment here in the kitchen, where it was safe and private. Chuck protested when she asked to do it alone, but she wanted to keep things low-key and not worry Jack. Chuck finally gave in.

"Sure." Jack slid into a kitchen chair. "Is it American?"

"It's Turkish, I think." Bobbi turned the bag around to check. "Yep."

"Just about a half cup, then."

"Wimp," Bobbi teased.

"I know, I know. I've always been a mama's boy."

"Those are the best kind." Bobbi pushed the button on the coffeemaker and leaned against the counter. "Joel was a mama's boy, too."

"Not Brad?"

"No, Brad was Daddy's boy from day one. We weren't close until after the ServMed summer. When he was little, he would have gladly traded me for a puppy and not batted an eye."

Jack leaned back and crossed his arms across his chest, arching his eyebrow in mock disbelief. "Mom . . ."

"Listen, your dad was not the same man with you and Shannon as he was with Brad and Joel. With the boys, he was totally disengaged. I think it was his way of punishing me for staying home. Since I wanted to raise them, then I could have it. I had to be the enforcer."

"He never disciplined Brad and Joel?"

"I didn't say that. He'd lose his temper and lay down the rules, then I had to be the one to make sure the boys followed them. They never realized how hard I was working, trying to keep them out of trouble with him. I was the bad guy all the time."

"Moms get a bum rap that way."

"Yes, don't do that to your wife."

"I won't." Jack put his left hand on his heart and raised his right hand. "Promise."

The coffeemaker hissed as it finished, so Bobbi poured a cup for herself, and a half cup for Jack, then took a seat across the table from him. She stared at the reflection of the overhead light on the shiny black surface of the coffee.

"You might as well tell me," Jack said quietly.

She managed the slightest smile before she raised her eyes to his. "I had a doctor's appointment today."

"This is going to be bad, isn't it?"

"Maybe. My doctor thinks I may have breast cancer, and he's sending me for a biopsy."

"It's bad," Jack said softly.

For just a split second, Bobbi pictured the six-year-old Jack saying those words, with his knees drawn tightly to his body. "So what's going to happen?"

"I'll have the test. It will confirm the diagnosis, then they'll probably want me to see an oncologist."

"Are you going to have to have chemotherapy and all that?"

"I don't know yet." She took a long sip. So far he was taking the news better than any of them.

"This is survivable, isn't it?"

"It can be, yes."

"So this is just something else we have to go through?"

"Apparently."

"It doesn't seem fair," Jack said.

"Fair" left a long time ago . . .

Jack lay on his bed staring at the ceiling. Cancer. His mom had cancer. He lost his brother, his sister left and now his mother had cancer. Or could have. It wasn't absolutely certain. His mom was extraordinarily calm, so he wouldn't worry either. Brad wouldn't worry. He was cool, with rock solid faith, just like his mother.

She had to come through this. Brad would say it meant God was gonna do something miraculous, giving them all some amazing story to tell about how He worked on their behalf. That had to be it. He couldn't let his mind even drift toward the alternative. He couldn't lose his mother again.

He shook his head and sat up. Don't fall into that hole. Get the brain going somewhere else. "What do you think, Brad?" He reached over to his desk for one of Brad's notebooks, and opened to the spot where he'd left off reading.

A prayer. An outline for a lesson or something on Jesus raising Lazarus from the dead. A gut-wrenching confession over snapping at a guy he worked with. "Good grief, ease up on yourself, man." On the next page, Jack saw his own name and smiled.

The little guy's here for something bigger,
more than just connecting with Dad.

But what? Then as Brad started law school, the entries lost their spark. He complained about not sleeping, about God not answering him, about empty study times.

I don't understand. Everything feels wrong,
like I'm in a foreign country, where nothing makes

sense. Everyone else is zipping along, but my wheels fell off. How do I get back on track?

Is this even the right track?

Exactly. Brad nailed the way he felt. And . . . he was going to explain how he got out of it. Jack grinned and flipped the page. He scanned the page, promising to go back and read it all later, until the word 'seminary' jumped out at him. This was it.

> *John twenty-one, toward the end after all the "Peter, do you love me" stuff. Jesus says, "Peter, I know you blew it, but I still want you. I still have a job for you. Now, I'm not gonna sugarcoat this. You take this job and it's going to cost you your life. But I promise you, it'll be worth it." So then Peter looks at John and asks Jesus, "What about this guy? What's he gonna do?" Jesus answers him, "Don't you worry about anybody else, and what they're doing . . . <u>you follow Me." That's it!!</u> I can't look around at what my dad did, or what my grandpa did. I have to follow what He's calling <u>me</u> to do. He's calling <u>me</u> to seminary, to ministry, to minister to the people in this neighborhood.*
>
> *Now if I can just tell my dad.*

"Oh Brad," Jack said, "that's perfect. That's exactly it. I wanted to follow you, but Jesus wants me to follow Him." He reread the entry. "'You take this job and it's going to cost you your life.' Brad, did you know? You couldn't have . . . But it did cost you . . . your life."

He lay back on the bed with the notebook across his chest. "God, You did it. You answered my question. It's not the mission, and doing what Brad did. If I really want to follow Brad's lead, I've got to break out of what I think my 'duty' is. Brad couldn't stay in law school because that wasn't where You wanted him. I can't work at the mission all my life because that's not where You want me. Next questions. Where do You want me to go, and what's it gonna cost? Is Mom part of that, or Shannon?"

CHAPTER 13
IMPARTATION

Friday, July 25

Chuck watched himself in the mirror as he tied his necktie. Bobbi balked when he mentioned taking the day off. Maybe it would help her if she believed he was going on into work after all. He couldn't focus on anything but the coming battle, though.

He lay awake most of the night, listening to her breathe, wondering where she would find the strength for this fight. Where would he? His life had become a runaway mine car, careening out of control, deeper into darkness, and he couldn't seem to find any way to bolster his wavering faith.

He took his cell phone from the dresser and called Christine.

"Mr. Molinsky, this is a bad sign," she said.

"Bobbi's got a biopsy this morning."

"So soon?"

"The doctor is almost certain it's cancer. The biopsy will confirm that and give us a clearer picture of exactly what she's dealing with." Before Christine could ask him any more questions, he said, "I need you to clear my calendar."

"Mr. Molinsky," she said, the gentleness in her voice calming him like a mother's hug. "I don't want to sound like I'm minimizing things, but I know God is doing something. I keep praying He'll show you what that is real soon."

"That's all I'm holding onto right now." He snapped his phone shut and dropped it in the front pocket of his slacks. If God didn't have a purpose in all this, there was no room left for hope.

As soon as he stepped out of his bedroom, he smelled bacon. Who was making bacon? It wasn't Jack, his door was still closed. Surely Bobbi wasn't . . . But she was. He found her standing over a skillet frying eggs.

She smiled at him. "Pick your jaw up so you can eat."

"I don't understand."

"I don't either, but I felt like making us breakfast."

"I'm not going to argue with that." Chuck kissed her cheek. He hadn't had bacon or anything fried since his trip to the emergency room. She engineered this to lift his spirits, to encourage him. That settled it. He had to get his act together now. She needed to focus on her own issues. "Did you sleep?"

"Fairly well. You?"

Chuck shook his head. "I had a lot on my mind."

She set two plates of eggs and bacon on the table. "Coffee or milk?"

"Milk today," Chuck said, taking a seat at the table. Bobbi poured him a glass of milk, then set the margarine and a jar of peach preserves on the table. She brought her coffee over and took the seat next to him. He held out his hand, and she slipped hers inside. "Lord, thank You for today, for this meal and for the little reassurances You give."

Bobbi closed the front door behind her, leaning against it for just a moment, gathering the strength to move. The breakfast, the low-key biopsy and a quick lunch accomplished exactly what she needed them to. Chuck, renewed and reassured, went on in to work.

Following her routine, she checked the phone on the console table for messages from Shannon, and like every day for the past month, there were none. No missed calls even. Tomorrow, she'd start calling down the list of Shannon's friends again. Tomorrow.

Tonight, Rita and Gavin were coming, and she needed some time alone, time to find something inside to draw from to get her through the evening. She brewed a cup of coffee, the Turkish blend again, and headed for her favorite spot, the love seat in the study. She slid off her shoes and settled in her corner. Chuck always sat on the left, and she always sat on the right. Always. That much was still predictable.

She felt a twinge of pain when she leaned against the armrest. The anesthesia was wearing off. Great. She shifted around and lay against the armrest, then she took a long drink from her coffee. Breast cancer would be predictable. That was oddly comforting. No more shocks or surprises, just a straightforward course of action. That should make it easier on everyone.

"Mom?" Jack called from the entry hall.

Bobbi hadn't even heard the door open. "In here."

"I smelled coffee. I knew you had to be here somewhere. How did things go?" He pulled the desk chair around and straddled it.

"Okay, I guess. We'll find out in a week or so."

"Find out what?"

"Exactly what type of cancer it is, and what happens next."

"Dad went to work?"

"Yes. I told him he's going to have to cut his own pay if he didn't." Jack nodded, then his eyes wandered around the study. "What's on your mind, Jack?"

"I don't know if I should say."

"Why wouldn't you?"

"I didn't want you to think I wasn't concerned about you. Mine's pretty minor compared to cancer."

"I would love to talk about something else," Bobbi said. She pushed herself up to sit on the love seat.

"Well then, I think I might go to law school." He looked just like Chuck when he grinned.

Bobbi smiled broadly. "Really?"

"That's not funny, is it? 'Cause I'm serious about it."

"Just ironic. Brad gave up law school for seminary, and here you are giving up seminary for law school."

"Well, I'm not entirely sure I'm giving up seminary, exactly."

"You're going to do both?"

"Maybe."

"Then what?"

"Religious freedom advocacy law," Jack said with a nod of his head at the end.

"How long have you been thinking about this?"

"How long have I been at work?" He checked his watch.

"This just all came together, then?"

"Yeah, it was crazy. I didn't sleep last night."

"I'm sorry. I shouldn't have told you about the cancer."

"Yes, you should have, but it's a lot to think about. Anyway, I was reading Brad's notebooks, which was a brilliant idea, by the way."

"You're welcome."

"He had this entry after he read at the end of John where Jesus tells Peter not to worry about what anybody else is called to do. That's what settled him on seminary. It was like a lightning bolt, Mom." He slammed his fist into his open palm. "I can't follow Brad any more than he could follow Dad and Grandpa Jim. It's not what I'm supposed to do. Then I kinda slept on it."

"And woke up to law school?"

"Yep, I reckon lawyerin's in my blood," Jack drawled. Bobbi rolled her eyes at him. "I couldn't get it out of my head today. That has to be it. What do you think Dad will say?"

"He'll be thrilled. He could use some good news."

"Yeah," Jack said. He drummed his hands on the desk. "I'm gonna go do some research online and see what I'm in for."

"Aunt Rita's bringing dinner tonight about six."

"Outstanding!" Jack said as he stood up. He kissed Bobbi on the cheek and headed up to his room, taking the stairs two at a time.

Bobbi set her coffee cup on the desk and closed her eyes for a moment. Jack was back. Just to see him excited and animated, with something to shoot for, was priceless. He could lift her spirits in a way that no one else could. Maybe God knew that a long time ago when He brought Jack to them. Maybe God knew in the middle of all these disasters how much she would need Jack.

Promptly at six o'clock, the Molinskys' doorbell rang. Bobbi roused herself from the love seat, but before she could slip on her shoes and answer the door, she heard Jack tromp down the stairs. "My favorite aunt," he said.

"I'm your only aunt, and you're not getting any samples." Rita jabbed him in the ribs with her elbow as she passed, all the while carrying a deep dish with potholders.

"That cuts deep," Jack said.

"I've seen it all before. Joel was the worst."

"Is there more to bring in?"

"Gavin may need a hand." Jack trotted outside to help.

"It smells wonderful," Bobbi said. "Roast?"

"Actually it's stew," Rita said. "Just the thing you want in the middle of summer when it's ninety-five degrees outside."

"That's why we have air conditioning. Come on back." She led Rita back to the kitchen, where she set the dish on the counter. "Chuck set the dining room table, so we can have a real dinner."

"Gavin's bringing the bread and a cobbler."

"Blackberry?"

"Yes."

"Thank you. Chuck and the ki—, and Jack have been deprived this summer. I don't think they've had decent dessert in months."

"I'm glad you finally let me do something."

"I know," Bobbi said, dropping her eyes.

"So you rested?"

"Yeah, I spent the afternoon on the love seat. Anesthesia wipes me out."

"There's more than just anesthesia at work," Rita muttered.

Before Bobbi could defend herself, Gavin and Jack came in the kitchen with Chuck close behind. Everyone pitched in, and they got the food and the drinks to the table quickly and settled in for the meal. Gavin and Rita managed to keep the conversation moving, steering it toward lighthearted subjects like Cardinals baseball and the recent Heatley family reunion. Bobbi didn't say much, but she worked to stay engaged.

Rita brewed a pot of coffee before serving the cobbler. Then with the dessert finished, she cleared the table and loaded the dishwasher. "I didn't know I was getting a full service meal," Bobbi said, following her sister into the kitchen.

"It's the least I could do." Rita quickly wiped the countertop and began wrapping up the leftover bread. "You seem amazingly calm. Is that for real?"

"I'm coping."

Rita turned and faced her. "You're lying."

"Rita, not now." Not this fight. It took all her energy to convince Chuck she was okay. But Rita wouldn't relent.

"I think you were already drowning and somebody just threw you an anchor."

Bobbi folded her arms across her chest, taking care not to touch the incision spot. How could she respond without telling a shameless lie?

"I suspected as much," Rita said quietly. "You can't fight this cancer unless you are mentally and emotionally prepared."

"I understand that."

"Then what can I do to help you?"

She couldn't make them understand—that question didn't have an answer anymore. "Chuck asked me the same thing."

"And you won't answer him, either. So you're not going to church, and I'll bet you haven't touched your Bible in the last month."

"I think I'm beyond simple platitudes."

"You can't shut yourself off from the only one who can fix it."

"Fix it! God caused this. There's nothing for Him to fix."

"God is not like that. You know this. You've seen it yourself." Rita pointed at her in a rebuke Bobbi wouldn't tolerate from anyone else. "You are so consumed by what you feel, you've lost sight of what you know is true."

Before Bobbi could answer, Gavin came in the kitchen. "Rita, are you ready to go?"

"Yeah, we're finished." Her eyes lingered on Bobbi's an instant too long before she punched the start button on the dishwasher. "I'll leave the rest of the cobbler."

"Thanks," Bobbi said without making eye contact. Gavin hugged her before following Rita out of the kitchen. Once they were gone, Bobbi got a cup and emptied the coffeepot into it. None of them could see. They had no idea how much she hurt. Brad was snatched away in the prime of his life. She couldn't just pick up and go on. It wasn't that simple.

And Shannon. As much as she loved Shannon, it hadn't been enough. Her daughter chose God-only-knows-what over home and family. If Shannon would just let them know she was okay . . .

Bobbi sighed and took a long drink from her coffee. She always felt like raising her children was her mission in life, but with two gone and the other two grown, was cancer a sign that she'd done her job? She finished off her coffee and even though it was just after eight o'clock, she headed up to bed.

"I can't thank you guys enough," Chuck said as he walked Gavin and Rita out to their car. "That was almost miraculous. Bobbi took part in the conversation and seemed to enjoy herself. It's been weeks since I've seen her like that."

"You're welcome," Rita said. She glanced at Gavin, then looked Chuck in the eyes. "I know you want to believe that, that Bobbi is coming around, that the grief is lifting, but it's not."

"But she got up this morning and made breakfast."

"Even so. Whether she's pretending for your benefit or whether you just don't want to see what's there, she is teetering on the edge."

Tears formed in Chuck's eyes. Rita was right, completely, unequivocally right. He leaned over the hood of the Heatleys' car. "I don't know what else to do for her. Am I supposed to make her talk to me? Or drag her to a doctor? Hospitalize her against her will? I'm out of ideas."

"What about Jack?" Gavin asked. "Could he get through to her?"

"Jack doesn't try to get through to her. That's why she still talks to him."

"Bobbi is a remarkable woman of deep, tested faith," Gavin said. "God will let her wrestle until she's exhausted, then He'll show Himself."

"I hope you're right," Chuck said, turning back toward the house.

"He's always right," Rita said, then she smiled. "I hate that."

As the Heatleys pulled away, Chuck walked slowly back toward the house, pausing just before he stepped inside. He raised his eyes to the limitless expanse of sky, softly lit by the fading sunlight. "Lord, You can intervene just any time now."

He walked inside and took the stairs two at a time, then pushed the bedroom door open. Bobbi lay on the bed, covers pulled just up to her knees. He walked over and stretched the blanket over her. She breathed deeply but didn't stir. The bottle of prescription painkillers sat on the nightstand. Chuck opened it and counted the pills. Six. The same six they left the pharmacy with. She hadn't taken any.

Ashamed for even suspecting her, he recapped the bottle and put it back on the nightstand. Bobbi had had a long, difficult day. She'd get back on track soon.

He headed downstairs to clean up the kitchen, but Rita had taken care of everything, so he wandered into the study. The study was the best room in the house, and the love seat was the best piece of furniture he and Bobbi ever bought. On the opposite side of the house from the family room and the television, it was a refuge for them individually and as a couple. He switched on the floor lamp and dropped onto the love seat.

On the bookshelf sat a small plaque someone had given him. *"For I know the plans that I have for you,"* declares the LORD, *"plans for welfare and not for calamity to give you a future and a hope."* He leaned his head back and rubbed his eyes.

"It sure doesn't look that way right now, God. All I can see is calamity."

He sighed and bowed his head. *Wherever Shannon is tonight, keep her safe. Let her know we love her, and that we want her home, that she can come home. At least, Father, let us hear from her. That would help Bobbi out so much just to know something.*

"Dad? You got a minute?" Jack stood just inside the doorway of the study.

"Yeah, come on in." Chuck sat up a little straighter on the love seat, and Jack pulled the desk chair over. "What's up?"

"Well, you know I've been kinda lost since Brad died, not really sure what I was supposed to do next?"

"You found something?"

"You're gonna ruin the story," Jack said with mock aggravation. "I had lunch with Mom a couple of weeks ago, and she said I should read through Brad's notebooks to see how he decided to drop out of law school and go to seminary." Jack slapped his thighs and grinned. "I think I want to go to law school, Dad."

"Are you serious?" Chuck asked, breaking into a wide smile himself.

"Yeah, but I think I still want to go to seminary, too. I'd like to defend religious freedoms. You know, fight for kids' rights to say prayers at graduation and stuff like that."

"We need lawyers like that. I think that's a tremendous decision."

"Mom said you'd be happy."

"She's pretty sharp. You know I can probably get you a better summer job than the sporting goods store."

"At your place? I'm not qualified."

"What's your last name?" Chuck asked, and Jack smiled. "See, you're qualified."

"Thanks." He stood up and slid the chair back under the desk. "I won't keep you. I just wanted to let you know."

"You're not keeping me."

"Well, truth is, the Cards are on. I'm gonna pop some popcorn and watch the rest of the game. You wanna watch, too?"

"I'll be right there." Jack nodded and headed for the kitchen. Once he was gone, Chuck pointed to the ceiling. "Hope. Thank you."

On the other side of town, Shannon Molinsky locked her apartment door, dropped her purse on the floor and collapsed on her sofa, exhausted. This was her fourth fourteen-hour day in a row.

She volunteered for as many overtime shifts as she could get, not really for the extra money, although that came in very handy. She needed to fill the empty hours. That's when the homesickness became almost unbearable, but she couldn't stand the thoughts of facing her mother and admitting what she'd done, seeing the quiet disappointment in her mother's eyes. Rebelling against her dad had been bad enough, but the other . . .

No, staying invisible was the best plan for now. No one she knew would be staying at a hotel here in town, especially one with a casino. Even if the guests saw her, they didn't acknowledge her presence. She had dropped off the face of the earth.

So far, she hadn't figured out how to get word to her family without tipping them off about where to find her. If her dad knew where she was, he'd be down here in two seconds to take her home. She sighed deeply. Sometimes, that's what she wanted more than anything.

CHAPTER 14
PRONOUNCEMENT

EIGHT WEEKS LATER
Saturday, September 20

Chuck slouched on the sofa in the family room, remote in hand, trying to concentrate on the Missouri Tigers game. Bobbi was around somewhere, the kitchen or the study he guessed, but if he tried to get close, she would slip away to a different room.

When the biopsy confirmed her cancer, they shuttled through a revolving door of doctors, tests and follow-ups. Then she decided she wanted a second opinion. It wasn't that she didn't trust the oncologist Dr. Karsten had recommended, she said, she simply wanted to be sure they had all the information on all the options available to them. He suspected it was a stall tactic. With the next chosen oncologist out of town, she had another week.

Since Jack had returned to college, she had merely haunted their house, an apparition who passed through the hallways in silence. Chuck began working from home, alternating mornings and afternoons at the office just to be near her. He cooked for her, cajoled her to eat and handled the laundry. To shield her from the endless no's, he picked up the routine of calling Shannon's friends each week.

He asked her, begged her, to tell him what he could do to snap her out of this, and each time she'd press her lips together and drop her eyes but never utter a word.

Missouri scored a touchdown, and he closed his eyes. Wonder if he could convince Bobbi to ride over to Columbia to see Jack tomorrow? He heard a rustle and opened one eye. Bobbi! Sitting in the easy chair across from him.

"How much time is left?" she asked.

"Oh, about a quarter and a half. Why?"

"I thought we might drive out to the lake after the game."

Chuck couldn't click off the television quickly enough. "Look at that. Game's over."

"Let me get my shoes." She left, found her shoes and met Chuck in the entry hall.

"What brought this on?" he asked.

"Seemed like the right day for it."

Chuck held the door for his wife and locked up behind her. The afternoon sun shone brightly, the sky was deep blue and the leaves were just starting to change colors. A perfect fall day. Once out on two-lane roads, he rolled the car windows down so they could smell the fresh air.

Dixson Lake had always been one of their favorite spots. Their first date had been a picnic by the lake. They got engaged there on a moonlit night under the stars. Bobbi chose the lake each time she told him he was going to be a daddy. Years ago, when they were separated, Bobbi began the healing process for her and for them there on the boat ramp on Thanksgiving afternoon. Maybe that's what she had in mind.

She made casual conversation on the drive out, asking him about work, about the baseball standings, and relaying Rita's plans for Gavin's upcoming birthday. He was tempted to pull over and stare at her. He wanted to touch her and prove to himself that she was real.

"I'll just park at the boat ramp," he said, "unless you wanna try somewhere else."

"We can get to the trails from there, can't we?"

"Yeah, two or three of them start here." He pulled into a parking place. Several other vehicles were there, many with trailers, evidence of how many people were taking advantage of the beautiful Saturday afternoon.

"It's more crowded than I expected," she said as she got out of the car.

"Is that bad?"

"Well . . ."

"You want to go to the other side of the lake?"

"No, this is fine."

Chuck locked the car, and taking his wife's hand, they started on one of the hiking trails. She had a plan. He couldn't read her mind, but every step was confident, purposeful. "How many times do you think we've been here?" he asked.

"Counting before we got married? Three or four dozen, I guess."

"There were a lot of years we never made it out."

"The workaholic years?"

Chuck scowled. "I've outgrown all that."

"Yes, you have. You've come quite a long way in these thirty-eight years."

"What are you trying to say?"

"Just that." She pointed a short distance up the trail. "There's a bench."

"Tired already?"

"Not exactly." She took a seat on the end of the bench and waited for Chuck to sit beside her.

"Bobbi, is something going on?"

She turned slightly so she could face him and took his hands. After a long, slow breath, she raised her head and looked him in the eyes. "Chuck, I'm not going to treat my cancer."

Not treat . . . "What are you talking about?"

"I cancelled my doctor's appointment. I'm not having surgery. I'm not taking chemotherapy or radiation. I'm just not."

Chuck sat for a long moment, as the smothering heaviness of her words settled on him. His brain dragged itself from "not treating" to the inevitable. . . . Misfire. He tried again. *If she doesn't treat . . . And she's said she's not going to. She's "just not." So she's . . .* She brought him out here to tell him . . .

"I thought when you wanted to come out here—" He jerked his hands away from hers and began to pace. "You can't . . . You have to treat your cancer."

"It progresses very slowly."

He stopped and stared at her. It progresses . . . And she said it like . . . like "I made chicken for dinner." Like dying— Like it didn't matter. *I'm not treating, but hey, it progresses slowly.* "Is that supposed to make it easier?" He shook his head. "This . . . this is insane, Bobbi. I need to get you some help."

"I'm not crazy." She blinked slowly and arched her eyebrow. Her eyes, those beautiful, deep brown eyes, fixed on him with cold indifference.

"Yes, you are!" he shot back. "Rational, thinking people fight back. You haven't been thinking straight since Brad died."

"I can't stand it anymore," she said quietly. Her voice tightened, and she pounded her knees with her fists in slow strokes. "I hurt every minute of every day, and it never, ever lets up."

And she couldn't tell him this? She couldn't vent this pain and frustration, even at him? She had to choose not to treat . . . He sat down with her, his knee touching hers, and he gripped her hands. "Bobbi . . . sweetheart . . . We can find somebody to help you get through that, but you have to treat—"

"Chuck." She let a long, deep breath go, and pulled her hands back, like she didn't want that intimacy. "Everything happens for a reason. The timing of this cancer isn't a coincidence. God is giving me a way out."

Again she used the most calm, rational voice, as if she was trying to explain to a six-year-old why he should wear a hat outside. And he exploded.

"Bobbi, that is the STUPIDEST thing I've ever heard! God doesn't arrange . . ." *Say it. Call it what it is.* "He doesn't arrange suicides!"

"I have a right to refuse treatment."

"You're not in any condition to make that decision."

"All right, take me to court. Have me declared incompetent."

Incompetent . . . ? That would make him as irrational as she was. "I'm not going to take you to court."

"Then respect my decision." As if that settled it.

"NO! I cannot be a part of this!"

"You don't have to be. You don't have to go along with it or agree with me. I didn't expect you to."

"What exactly did you expect? You've obviously thought about this for a while. Surely you had some idea."

"I can't make you understand."

"You haven't tried. You haven't talked to me in weeks. You won't let me hold you, or cry with you. Do you know how that hurts me? What a failure I feel like?" He slumped back on the bench.

"Let's go home."

"See, you're doing it again. You're shutting down, cutting me off." He leaned back and sighed. "You've cut yourself off from everyone you love." Then he straightened up. "Or is that the problem? You don't love us anymore?"

She sat in silence, tearing him apart with the long, slow blink of her eyes. She was slamming the door again. He had to keep her talking even if that meant making her mad. "Or do you think we don't love you? What do you need me to do to show you that I love you and that I need you?"

"Nothing."

Her kids. Chuck's last hope to reach her. "Do you know what this is going to do to Jack? He . . . he just got his bearings back. He'll drop out of school. Don't you remember what it was like to hold that little boy in the hospital when his mother died?"

"He's not six anymore."

"He will never get over this!" He jumped up from the bench again. "You will destroy him. You're going to keep him from fulfilling what God's given him to do."

"Now you sound crazy," she muttered. Maybe she was listening.

"And Shannon. What's going to happen when she gets home? 'Sorry, Shannon. Your mother's dead. You weren't worth waiting for.'"

Bobbi stood up and pushed past Chuck, walking briskly back up the path. "I'm going home."

He found the button. "You hadn't thought about that, had you?" He took a few quick steps to catch up with her. "Or is this all some warped plan to get her home?"

She spun around to face him and growled, "Shannon is not coming home! You need to face that."

Anger, thank God. Some life. Some emotion. He goaded her on. "Like you have? Is this how you face things? Throw up your hands and say, 'I quit'?"

"Quit? You think I've quit?"

"That's what it looks like."

"Quitting I could fix." The emotion evaporated, leaving lifeless indifference. "I haven't quit. I failed. Shannon left the first chance she had over NOTHING!" She jabbed her index finger at her own chest. "I didn't teach her anything. I . . . am . . . a failure." She turned away from him and started back up the trail. "If you want a ride home, I'm leaving now."

He caught up with her in two long strides and took her by the arm. "Bobbi, this isn't over. You can't end this here."

She pulled her arm away. "We can talk about it from now on. You can line up Joel or Rita or whoever else you can think of to try and change my mind, but it's a waste of time. A waste." She pulled her car keys from the pocket of her jeans. "My decision's been made."

"You brought your keys?"

"I figured you'd be like this and I'd have to drive home."

He got in the passenger side and slammed his door shut. He saw her glance his way, the corner of her mouth dipping in the slightest show of disapproval. Disapproval. For slamming the car door. She figured. She knew. She played him, coldly calculating his every response. No compassion, just a betrayal of his confidence and his love for her.

How could she . . . ?

He squeezed his eyes closed and gripped the door handle until his fingers went numb, but he was not going to shed even one tear in front of her. Oh no. She didn't deserve that victory. How could she plot and plan this? How could she sit at the table and drink coffee with him with this running through her mind?

He opened his eyes and saw the first gas station on the outskirts of town. "Pull in there," he said.

"Why?"

"So I don't have to jump out of a moving car."

She eased the Impala into a spot away from the building. "Should I wait?"

"Should you?" He slammed the door again and stalked inside, into the men's room, and locked the door. The tiny restroom was too small to pace, so he held on to the wall sink, wishing he could pull it away from its fixtures and sling it to the parking lot.

Instead, he turned on the cold water and splashed his face, then ran his cold fingers across the back of his neck, hoping to shock the throb in his head and make it stop. If only he could make it all stop. What was she thinking? How could she twist reality to the point that not treating her cancer seemed like the logical answer? How could she deceive him?

When he reached to turn off the water, his eyes landed on his wedding ring. She had given it to him twice. Once at their wedding and again after they reconciled. After his affair. After he betrayed her. He slumped against the cinderblock wall. He knew exactly how betrayal happened. He knew how self-absorbed and callous a heart could become when it was consumed with filling its voids at any cost.

The road back had taken such intense focus, such commitment, and meant such pain for both of them as they learned to trust each other, love each other again, anew. But he had poured all his energy into winning her back.

She wasn't interested in winning anything right now. She needed far more help than he could give her. Before he trudged back out to face her again he dug his cell phone from the front pocket of his jeans and dialed Joel.

Abby quickly answered. "Hi, Dad!"

"Is Joel home? I need to talk to him."

"Has something else happened? You sound absolutely wrung out."

So he wasn't doing such a good job of hiding it. "No, I just need to discuss some things with him."

"He's at the hospital. You can call his cell, but he may not pick up. I can have him call you when he gets home."

"I'll catch him tomorrow."

"It's Mom, isn't it?" Abby asked gently.

"Are all women mind readers?"

"I just know how much you love her, how hard things are on you right now. Joel would be the same way."

"That's why I wanted to talk to him. It'll keep though."

"You sure?"

"Tomorrow's fine." He clicked off the phone and stuffed it back in his pocket, then he shuffled outside to the car.

"Are you all right?" Bobbi asked.

"You don't care."

"Is this how it's going to be now?" She backed out of the spot and wheeled the car through the lot and back out on the road.

"What do you want, Bobbi? You don't want to confide in me. You seem irritated that I love you. I'm at a loss here."

"I want you to accept—"

"Your death wish?"

"Accept the way things are. Stop trying to change . . . stop feeding me empty hope."

But he wasn't. He rarely mentioned Shannon in front of Bobbi, even when he prayed. This was a smokescreen, and he only knew one way to get her out from behind it. "You know, driving the car into one of these light poles would kill you a lot quicker than cancer would."

She never moved her eyes from the road.

"But then people would know, wouldn't they? There's no shame in dying from breast cancer—"

"I cannot believe you're mocking me."

"I'm trying to understand how you arrived at your decision."

"No, you're moving down your list of negotiation techniques. Anger. Grief. The condescending lecture. The kids. Now it's the old standby, sarcasm. It's not going to work either."

"I'm not playing some game, trying to win an argument. This is your *life*, our life together."

She jerked the car into their driveway and jammed it into park. "And what you refuse to see is that I have no life anymore."

He reached for her hand, but she slipped out of the car. He caught her as she stopped to unlock the front door. "Do you know how it kills me to hear you talk like this?"

"That feeling . . . that powerlessness . . . how unbearable it is for these few minutes? Imagine living there." She spoke with a quiet urgency. "I go by Shannon's room every single day. I sit in the same kitchen where she and Brad ate breakfast. Her car sits out in the driveway. Their pictures are all over the house." She waved a hand in a wide arc. "I can't escape it." After a lingering glance, she dropped her eyes and left him standing on the porch.

"You're not supposed to escape it! You're supposed to go through it!" he called, but it was no use. The conversation was over. He dropped to the porch step and buried his face in his hands, reeling from so many levels of hurt. She hadn't trusted him enough to tell him that this was building inside her. How could she even consider a slow death over living out her years with him? It was as if her pain was the only pain that counted. Did she think he didn't hurt? That no one else grieved over Shannon and Brad? Just because he went on to work every day didn't mean that Shannon wasn't on his mind. It was his fault she left, after all.

"I gotta get out of here," he muttered. He found Bobbi on the love seat in the study just as expected. "I'm going for a drive." She nodded without turning around. "Will you be here when I get back?"

"What's that supposed to mean?"

"Are you going to commit suicide in the next hour or so?"

"That's uncalled for."

"What is called for in this situation? This is new territory for me."

She didn't respond.

"I'll be back later." Chuck slammed the front door behind him. He knew leaving her alone was the wrong thing to do, but he couldn't help her right now. He was beginning to wonder if anyone could.

He drove without engaging, staying in the center lane, rolling through each intersection just like the car in front of him. She had to know how much he needed her and depended on her. Of course she was disheartened. They all were. But not treating her cancer . . .

Suddenly, the screech of tires and the blast of a car horn jolted him back to the present. Instinctively, he wrenched the car to the right then hit his brakes, barely missing a small pickup truck. The other driver shouted and flipped an obscene gesture Chuck's way before speeding through the intersection. Chuck eased to the side of the road until his hands quit shaking. He needed to find someplace to go. His office maybe. He was halfway there already. No, he needed advice. He needed to unload all this so he didn't carry it back home to Bobbi.

Rita and Gavin would know what to do.

"Chuck? What's wrong?" Rita asked, opening the door wide to let him in.

"I need to talk to you and Gavin."

Rita closed the door behind him and guided him into their living room. She took a step back toward their kitchen and called Gavin, then she turned back to Chuck. "Can I get you something? Coffee or a Coke, maybe?"

Chuck shook his head and dropped on the sofa.

Rita took a seat in the armchair closest to him. "It's Bobbi, isn't it?"

"She, uh . . ." He dropped his eyes to the carpet and felt the fear and grief push aside the anger he'd vented all afternoon. The tears were going to come, wanted or not. "She told me she's not going to treat her cancer." He raised his head and looked Rita in the eyes. "I'm going to lose her."

"Chuck, no." Rita moved over to the sofa and slipped an arm around his shoulder.

She cried with him while he sobbed in fear and frustration. He knew she understood though. He could feel the burden shifting, his head clearing. He took a deep breath and rubbed his eyes. "Thanks. I needed that."

When he raised his head, he saw Gavin had slipped into the living room and sat in the armchair. "Shannon or Bobbi?"

"Bobbi's decided not to treat her cancer."

"Did she tell you why? How she came to that decision?"

"It makes perfect sense to her," Chuck said. "She believes God's giving her a way to escape her pain."

"You challenged her, I'm sure."

"But I handled it all wrong. I got angry."

"That may not be a bad thing. Did she argue with you?"

"Some. She said she had a right to refuse treatment. Didn't seem to care what it would do to Jack or Shannon or the rest of us. Then she said Shannon leaving was her fault because she never taught Shannon any coping skills and I needed to quit feeding her empty hope."

"She wants to be left alone."

"Completely."

"And warned you not to try to change her mind?"

"She said I could line up you guys or Joel or anybody else I could think of, but it wouldn't do any good."

Gavin nodded then crossed his legs. "She knows she's in trouble. She wants you to get her some help."

"Then why doesn't she say that! Why drive me out to the lake and tell me she wants to die?"

"Because she knows that's not right either. She doesn't have the strength to figure it out, so if she shocks you into action, you'll solve it and save the day."

"If I knew what to do, Gavin, I would have done it a long time ago." The throb in his head returned, and he tried rubbing his temple.

"Let's start small. What do I say to her when I get home? Am I supposed to go along with her or what?"

"I'd be very dispassionate about it," Gavin said. "Have her start planning her funeral."

"Absolutely not!" Rita said sharply. "You'll push her to suicide."

"No, it will make her face the very real implications of what she's decided."

"I don't think I can do that," Chuck said.

"All right," Gavin said, "if that's too extreme, what if you put her on a suicide watch? We can divide up the time and stay with her during the day while you're at work."

A suicide watch. He got a rise out of her when he asked if she'd be there when he got back. There was some appeal to keeping her fighting. Just then, Chuck's cell phone rang. "It's Joel," he said as he answered it. "You're not driving, are you?"

"Not again," Joel said. "What?"

"Your mother's decided not to treat her cancer."

"Why? What treatment options are they giving her? Does she understand it's not anything like when her mother had it? Let me talk to her."

"It's not that." Chuck knew that "take charge, let me fix it" attitude all too well, but he also knew how close Joel and Bobbi were. "She, uh, she doesn't want to treat . . . because she'd rather let it kill her."

"That's insane," Joel whispered. "She said that? That she'd rather let it kill her?"

"She said God was giving her a way to escape the pain she lives with day after day."

"Dad . . . I thought after Ryan's birthday . . . I thought she was doing better. How was she when she told you?"

"Very straightforward, matter-of-fact. Said her mind was made up."

"She's relieved."

"In a way, I guess. What am I going to do with her? She told me she had a right to refuse treatment. I said she wasn't in any condition to make that decision, and she said, 'take me to court.'"

"Draw up the papers. I'll sign 'em."

"Joel!"

"Okay, maybe not. You haven't called Jack yet, have you?"

"No. I thought I'd make her tell him to his face. Let her see what it does to him."

"Oh, that's good. What about Aunt Rita?"

"I'm at their house. Gavin says to put her on a suicide watch and keep someone with her at all times."

"She'll go ballistic."

"Good! I'd like to see some life out of her." Chuck took a deep breath and sighed. "How do I get her back? She's lost her will to fight this. She's given up on Shannon ever coming home. This suicide watch thing, that's a band-aid." He held the phone against his chest. "You guys, too," he said to Rita and Gavin. "How do we get her back?"

"She has to do it," Joel said. "It has to be her own revelation. Do you think she'd read anything?"

"I doubt it. She told Rita reading her Bible makes it worse."

"She knows she's wrong," Joel said. "She's knows she shouldn't be shutting God out."

"So what do you suggest?"

"Surround her. Watch the preacher channels on television. Do your Bible study in the kitchen where she can see you, and make sure the car radio is on Christian stations."

"And hope something clicks?"

"Exactly. God's Word never returns void, and it always accomplishes His purposes."

"Joel, you just might be brilliant," Chuck said.

"It's not me. I'll swing by and see Mom on my way home."

"Tomorrow would be better. She hates hovering, and I'm already gonna be in trouble for telling you."

"Hang in there, Dad. Everybody's praying. Something's got to give."

"I know," Chuck sighed. "I love you, Joel." He snapped the phone closed and pushed it back in his pocket. "He says surround her with God. Preachers on TV and radio. Read and study in front of her."

"I like it," Gavin said.

Rita nodded. "Then I'll be there at nine tomorrow, but Chuck . . ." She glanced at Gavin, then crossed her arms tightly across her chest. "I mean, far be it from me to argue with you and Gavin, and now Joel, but I think it all hinges on Shannon. Bobbi was just beginning to heal after Brad's death, then Shannon left. You said she's given up hope that Shannon's coming home. That's what brought her to despair. Shannon may be the only one who can draw her back."

"Then I have to find Shannon," Chuck said.

CHAPTER 15
CANDOR

Chuck pulled into his driveway as the last light of day faded behind him. His house was dark except for a soft glow from the study. Bobbi. He hadn't felt so much riding on a conversation with his wife since she discovered his affair. And he blew that one.

He opened the front door as quietly as he could and locked it back carefully. Bobbi sat in her corner of the love seat, sipping a cup of coffee, exactly where he'd left her.

Not wanting to startle her, he spoke quietly. "Bobbi? Can we talk?"

She never turned around, but she set her cup on the desk beside her. "Do you think we can be civil?"

"Can you forgive me for raising my voice?" He shuffled across the room, silently coaching himself to keep his voice low and controlled. If he came across frantic or desperate, she'd tune him out.

"I asked for it." She drew her legs closer to make room for him on the love seat, but he pulled the desk chair around instead. She frowned at him. "So who did you rat me out to?"

"Rita and Gavin and Joel." Chuck leaned forward in his chair and looked into those beautiful brown eyes, now drained of all their energy. He had to make this about her. "Bobbi, you've thrown up a wall between us. I can't take what you say at face value anymore."

"You think I'm lying to you?"

"You're keeping things from me, and yes, I believe you've been misleading me." He took a deep breath. "Right now, I don't trust you to be by yourself."

"And you just left me for three hours?" she huffed. "Do you know how ridiculous—"

"This is not negotiable. Somebody's going to be here with you around the clock. Unless you decide to go to church with me in the morning, Rita will be here at nine o'clock."

"You're treating me like a nutcase!"

"No, I love you and I have an obligation to protect you. If that means protecting you from yourself, so be it."

Her eyes darkened with tight fury. "I don't need protection." She swung her feet down off the love seat and stood up. "I want to be left alone."

She tried to sidestep his chair, but he caught her by the arm and spun her around to face him. "Oh no. You're not walking out on me." The genuine shock, or maybe fear, in her eyes burned through him and he dropped his hand. Anger was the last thing he wanted her to see. He'd lost it with Shannon and she left. He stepped back and wiped a hand across his mouth. "I'm sorry," he whispered. "Bobbi, I would give my own life, right now, if I could take your anguish away, but I can't."

Fear and failure threatened to choke off the words before he could get them out. "I have loved you from the moment I laid eyes on you, and I love you more every single day. I can't sit by and watch you die a thousand deaths when it doesn't have to be this way."

He reached for her hand, but she held it close, glaring at him. "I'm gonna fight this, and if it means I have to fight you, I will."

Sunday, September 21

Rita rang the doorbell at Chuck and Bobbi's and paced. *Be calm and detached,* Gavin said. *Bobbi doesn't need you to solve this today. Just be there for her.* Right. It would take every ounce of restraint she'd ever mustered to keep from going in there, shaking Bobbi, and screaming, "Have you lost your mind?"

She knew when Bobbi was diagnosed that something was . . . off, but she reasoned it away. What right did she have to dictate how Bobbi should respond to the waves of heartache? If she and Gavin had to face what God asked of Bobbi and Chuck . . . she would have collapsed long ago. Not Bobbi. Bobbi was like tempered steel. She would find her anchor. Some way, somehow. Because if she didn't . . .

The front door swung open. "Rita, thanks," Chuck said. "Bobbi's back in the kitchen."

"How is she?"

"Barely speaking to me for having you come over."

"Did you sleep?"

He shook his head. "Sleep? What's that?"

"I'll get lunch together for you."

"Thanks. For everything." He picked up his Bible from the table and headed out. "I hope you can get through to her."

Rita watched Chuck drive away, and apprehension seized her. What if she said the wrong thing? What if she made things worse? Everyone knew how often her mouth got her in trouble. Calm and detached, she coached. She sighed and walked back toward the kitchen. She couldn't do calm and detached.

Bobbi sat at the kitchen table with a cup of coffee. The morning paper, still in its plastic bag, lay within easy reach. "I hope he's paying you the standard rate for sitters."

In spite of the bitter edge in Bobbi's voice, Rita joined her at the table. "Have you had breakfast?"

"Yes, and I took a shower, too. I'm not quite as pathetic as you guys think."

"I don't think you're pathetic. You're heartbroken. I don't know how you've kept going this long." Bobbi dropped her head but didn't respond. "And you're not the only one. Chuck's wearing himself out trying to keep up appearances."

"Chuck . . . He wants to fix everything." She absently straightened the fringe on the placemat. "Things are so hard for him."

"Then how can you even *think* of not treating your cancer?" She said it. Now she had to keep pressing. "This will kill him."

"No." She jerked her head up and made eye contact with Rita for the first time. "No, Chuck is very strong, and God will be there for him."

"But He's not there for you? You know that's not true."

Bobbi folded her hands and pressed her lips into a tight, thin line. Nobody was going to change her mind on this one. Rita pushed away from the table and got a cup from the cabinet, buying herself some time to think.

The conversation couldn't be about Bobbi. She was far too prepared to fight that battle. Rita had to shift the focus to get Bobbi to soften up, to drop her guard, to listen to reason. Shift to what, though?

On the windowsill by the sink sat a salt and pepper shaker set, a little black kitten for the pepper and a white kitten for the salt. The shakers belonged to their mother and sat on their kitchen table when they were growing up. Of course. Mama.

"Do you remember what it was like with Mama? When she got sick?"

Bobbi relaxed and let a deep breath go. "I can remember looking up the word 'cancer' in the dictionary. The big dictionary by the telephone table. And I remember 'canary' was on the same page." She dropped her eyes and picked at the placemat again. "One of the definitions said something about evil that spreads. I couldn't understand how Mama could have evil inside her."

"She was livid that she had been diagnosed with cancer." Rita emptied the pot of coffee into her cup. "She had things to do and girls to raise." She rinsed out the coffee pot and turned it upside down in the dish drainer. "She said God might have given her cancer, but she didn't have to take it. She fought it with everything she had."

"Didn't she go to Chicago a couple of times?"

Rita nodded and took her seat again. "She heard about a doctor up there who had tried something new, and had some success. She lived at the library. She read everything, every bit of research. She changed her diet, took vitamins. Anything that held the slightest promise, she was all over it." Rita shook her head. "She and Daddy went to Mass every morning, and oh, how they prayed. Mrs. Robbins, who lived across the street—"

"With that hateful little dog."

Rita smiled not just from the memory of the yapping dog. Bobbi was engaged. "Mrs. Robbins brought over some oil and anointed Mama, and then prayed over her, in tongues. Without a doubt the weirdest thing I ever saw, but Mama wasn't gonna discount anything. Everything was worth a shot."

"See, I never knew all that was going on. By the time they told me . . . she . . . the fight was over." Bobbi stared past Rita, maybe at the little kittens on the windowsill. "She threw up a lot, didn't she?"

"All the time. She was so weak, and then she was in so much pain. At the end, it had spread to her liver. She barely knew where she was the day we got married, she was on so much morphine." Rita took a long drink from her coffee, struggling with her own memories. "She begged Gavin to marry me before she died. Honestly, I don't think he was quite ready yet, but how could he deny a dying woman's last wish?"

"Always a gentleman." Bobbi's shoulders relaxed, and her voice had softened. Maybe she was listening.

"Baby, please, I'm begging you . . . You can treat this now, and next year, it'll be a distant memory. This is a terrible way to die. I've seen it. Don't make me go through it again. This is my worst nightmare."

"You'd be surprised how much worse your worst nightmare can get."

"Is that what you think God is doing? Showing you what a nightmare really is?"

"I don't know what God is doing."

"Waiting."

"Waiting? For what?"

"For you to give up."

"I'm already there," Bobbi said.

"No, I think you're in a battle for control. You think not treating your cancer puts you back in the driver's seat. You had no say with Brad or with Shannon, and you've finally found something you think you can control."

"This doesn't feel like control, I promise. It feels like insanity."

"God's not the author of that." Rita leaned back in her chair. It was time to leave Bobbi alone and let her digest the conversation, let her remember. "I could quote a lot of Bible verses to you, but you know them. You know what you should do, and you know what's waiting on the other side of this dark time. If I could bring you out of this I would, but only you can do that." She stood and pushed in her chair, waiting for a response that never came. "I'm going to throw in some laundry."

Chuck pulled out of the church parking lot and headed for home. He couldn't remember any of the songs or the announcements and the sermon was a blur. At least he hadn't fallen asleep in the service. Glen pulled him aside afterwards to ask about Bobbi, and Chuck told him about the visit to the lake.

"Stop trying to fix this on your own," Glen said. "Shannon told you this was all your fault, and you haven't gotten over it. Bobbi's not getting better, you think it's your fault and it's killing you. I can see it on your face."

He couldn't argue with Glen. He felt guilty leaving Bobbi just for the morning. The verses Glen scribbled on the business card he carried in his shirt pocket would likely add to that guilt. Maybe he'd wait until tomorrow to look them up.

He pushed open the front door and took a quick glance at the empty study. He strode back to the kitchen where Rita stood over a large pot on the stove. "Where's Bobbi? What happened?"

"She said she was going to take a nap." She put a lid on the pot and turned the heat down.

"You check on her?"

"Not in the last three minutes. I think we can trust her."

He sighed. "I'm overreacting, I know."

"No, you're not." She pulled the coffee pot off the warmer. "I made her some fresh coffee. You want a cup?"

"No thanks. Is that chili?"

"That's what you had to work with."

"It's better than my skills could produce, I'm sure." Chuck collapsed into one of the kitchen chairs. Rita poured a cup of coffee and joined him at the table. "Did she talk to you any?" he asked.

"I did most of the talking, but she seemed to listen. Especially when we talked about Mama."

"That's good. Listening is a major step."

Rita sipped the coffee, hedging.

"What? Is it about me?"

"She feels abandoned . . ."

"How . . . ?"

Rita raised a hand. "By God, not you." Her eyes began to tear up. "If it weren't for you, she'd already be dead." She wiped her eyes and stared into her cup. "I told her that her decision was an attempt to regain control. She had no power to stop Brad's death or to stop Shannon from leaving, so at least she's going to have a say about her own life and death. She didn't answer me, so maybe I hit on something."

Chuck nodded. Could there be some hope?

"You know, talking about Mama . . . The thoughts of Bobbi going through that . . ." She shook her head slowly.

"She'll go for treatment. She has to."

"I promised my mother that I would take care of her, and the last time I saw Daddy, that's all he wanted to talk about."

"She's an adult now. You're not responsible for her anymore."

She smiled slightly. "I guess you expect me to believe you don't feel responsible for her, either."

"I'm her husband," Chuck said, returning the smile. "That's different."

"Of course it is." She glanced up at the clock. "I'd better go. Gavin needs to eat."

"Take him some of the chili."

She shook her head. "You may need it this week." She rinsed out her coffee cup and put it in the dishwasher, then Chuck followed her to the front door. Before she opened the door, she stopped and faced him. "I want you to know . . . I don't believe there's anyone on earth who loves Bobbi like you do." She hugged him gently and turned the door handle. "We pray for you as much as for Bobbi. Call me if you need me tomorrow."

Chuck watched her drive away, then closed the front door. Rita understood. He did love Bobbi more than anyone ever had. She earned permission to discuss cancer treatment with Bobbi by connecting with her, not dictating to her. He'd do it Rita's way.

He heard a rustle behind him and turned to find Bobbi coming down the stairs. "Hey," he said, reaching for Bobbi's hand. "Were you able to rest?"

She hesitated, frowned, then took his hand. "I slept a little."

"Rita made some chili for lunch."

"Maybe later."

Chuck frowned and nodded. The wall between them remained just as high and just as impenetrable.

She shifted and blinked, avoiding his eyes. "I'll, uh, I'll sit with you while you eat."

"That would be great," Chuck said, and he led her back to the kitchen. She let him take her hand, and she was going to sit with him. Rita worked a miracle. Did he dare hope for more from her? "You want tea?"

"Just a glass of water."

Chuck quickly got everything together and sat at the kitchen table with her. "Would you bless the food?" She couldn't refuse to say table grace. That would make her look like a hardened, hopeless case.

"I'm not eating."

"I know. But would you? Please?"

Bobbi shifted in her chair, and without ever looking up at him, she mumbled, "Sure, okay." She bowed her head and closed her eyes. "Dear Lord, thank You for this food. Thank You for Rita and for her care of us, and thank You for Chuck. In Jesus' name, amen." Chuck smiled at her as he started to eat. It wasn't much, but it was a start. A good start. And he made the short list.

After taking a few bites in silence, he opted to push his luck. "Glen asked if he could stop by and see you."

"What'd you tell him?"

"I said it would make you mad."

"Great. I hate to imagine what Glen thinks about me now."

"But I was right."

"And that matters, doesn't it?"

He pushed the spoon deep in the bowl and wiped his mouth with his napkin. "If you want to bait me, or criticize me, to vent whatever you've stored up, have at it. I'll even fight back if that makes you feel better."

"Chuck—"

"No, I want to hear what you're thinking, what you're wrestling with. I promise I won't try to change your mind, or talk you out of anything."

"You won't lecture me?"

"Promise."

"What did Rita tell you?"

"Not much. Just that you talked some about your mother."

"She didn't tell you I was a control freak?"

"She mentioned her theory."

"She's wrong."

"Okay." Determined not to push her, he reached for his spoon.

"You think I don't pray? That I'm not listening to anything from anybody? I heard everything you said yesterday."

God, please . . . give us that breakthrough . . .

She fixed her eyes on her glass and wiped the condensation away with her thumb. "Last night . . . while you were gone . . . I sat there in the study. And I replayed every word you said. Every word I said." She took a long drink from her water.

He knew she was stalling, so he leaned back in his chair, trying to appear relaxed, nonthreatening, whatever it took to keep her talking.

"And I got the phone. I held it in my hands and I begged God to let Shannon call." She raised her eyes to his. "I prayed that if I was wrong . . . If He'd let Shannon call . . . I'd be at the doctor's first thing Monday morning."

"And she didn't call."

She shook her head slowly. "What am I supposed to think, Chuck? What's He trying to tell me?"

"Bobbi, that's the reason you need to talk to Glen. He could give you an answer."

"I don't want to talk to Glen. I want to talk to you."

He had to fight back the impulse to take her in his arms. She wanted to talk. To him. Hallelujah! He pushed the chili to the side and folded his hands on the table in front of him, faking calm reserve the best he could. "I, uh, I don't know how much help I can be."

She almost smiled. "You've been more help than you know. Just letting me say . . . all those things. Being strong enough to hear them. I can't tell you how much . . ." Her voice trailed off, and she twisted the water glass on the place mat. "He's through with me."

Chuck wanted to shoot back, "No He's not! That's ridiculous!" Instead he nodded. "Do you feel like God's giving you permission not to treat your cancer? That He's okay with that?"

"I asked Him to tell me otherwise, and He didn't."

"Would you change your mind if He said something different?"

"If?"

"When."

"We'll see."

"How's Mom?" Joel asked as soon as his father opened the front door, skipping the hello.

"I'm guardedly optimistic." He stepped aside to let Joel in. "She talked to Rita a little bit, then she sat with me while I ate lunch."

"She'll get there." Joel nodded. "You look tired. You should find a football game to sleep through."

"Maybe so." His father's eyes darted to the wedding picture hanging in the entryway. "Listen . . . I . . . your mother . . . medically speaking, how much danger is she in by putting off treatment this way?"

"This is not my field—"

"I trust you. Just tell me."

Give the man some hope, some reassurance. "It sounds like they found it early, so depending on how quickly she decides to go for treatment, it may not set her back very much. It may just change her treatment options or the duration of the treatment. But again, I don't know a whole lot about breast cancer. You'd have to ask her doctor."

"That's good enough. I want . . . I'm trying to respect her, to be patient, but I don't want her . . ."

"It's okay, Dad. I think you're handling it just right. So is she around?"

"Out on the deck."

Joel strode back through the house and opened the back door carefully. He stepped out and before he could close the door, his mother spoke. "Is it your turn?"

"My turn for what?"

"To sit with me. Dad says I can't be left alone." She sat in a chair in the corner of the deck where she could look out across the back yard. A paperback lay face down on the deck beside her.

"No, I just came to visit," Joel said, leaning down to kiss his mother's cheek. He pulled a deck chair closer to hers and sat down. For a long moment neither of them spoke. "What can I do?" he asked.

"I don't think this can be fixed."

"You know, there are easier ways to die than breast cancer." She didn't answer but gazed at a fixed spot somewhere off in the distance. "And you wouldn't have to wait two or three years."

She sighed deeply and slowly turned to look at him. "Joel, I don't want to die, I just don't want to live. Does that make any sense?"

"It makes a lot of sense," Joel said gently. "Mom, I know you hurt in ways the rest of us can never understand, but letting yourself die isn't going to take your pain away. It'll just transfer it."

"To?"

"To Dad and me and Jack . . . and Shannon."

"Shannon doesn't care," she shot back.

In that quick snap, she revealed all he needed to know, but he played dumb. "What makes you say that?"

"Oh, I don't know," she said with harsh sarcasm. "Not calling for three months, maybe."

"You're just like her."

"Excuse me?"

"You're both hurting, except you collapsed and don't have the will to go on. She exploded and ran."

"Why did it have to come to that? Why didn't she say something, come to me, before she cut herself off from everyone, everyone who loves her and needs her?"

Joel leaned forward, never moving his eyes from his mother's, watching as the question drained into conviction. "She's got too much stubborn pride," he said.

She recovered quickly. "Joel, you're so charming, I hardly know I've been insulted." She scowled and raised an eyebrow.

"I'm not trying to insult you." No wonder his dad looked like he'd gone ten rounds with a prizefighter. Just when he thought he'd scored some points with her, she threw up another wall. "Shannon . . .

she's not going to come home until she's ready to face all that pain. The pain she feels . . . and the pain she caused."

His mother nodded. She knew he was right. In spite of her protests and jabs, she knew.

"Mom, for you to heal, you have to do the very same thing. Face the pain you feel and the pain you caused."

"I can't," she whispered. "It's too much. I can't."

"No, you can't, not alone. You've got to get back in church. Tonight."

"Joel—"

"I don't want to hear it. I'll drive you myself if I have to, but you have got to go."

"Give me another week."

Joel shook his head. "You sound just like that lawyer you live with, always negotiating. You won't do it if you put it off. You'll back out."

"No, you have my word. Next week, I promise."

Chapter 16
Parting

Monday, September 22

Chuck waved to Christine as he strode past her desk. "I need to see Chad."

"Of course. Is everything all right?"

"It will be." He closed his office door behind him and hung his suit jacket on the coat rack like he did every morning. Today, though, he set his briefcase on his desk, snapped it open and began emptying it. He never looked up, knowing Christine would be at his door as soon as she realized what he was doing.

He pulled the large file drawer on his desk open and slid the folders from his briefcase inside. Next he fished his key ring from his pocket, unhooked the firm's keys and laid them in the desk drawer.

"Chuck? Christine said . . . What's going on?" Chad stepped into the office and closed the door behind him.

Chuck glanced past him. Christine was watching. "Chad, I need you to take over here."

"Temporarily, right?"

Chuck frowned but didn't respond. "I've got to take care of my wife and I have to find my daughter and those two things are going to take all my time and energy."

"I'll do whatever you need me to," Chad said, "but what happened? What changed?"

Chuck gripped the desk and sighed. No matter how many times he said it, it never got easier. "Bobbi told me Saturday afternoon she's not going to treat her cancer. She thinks . . . She's kinda lost her will to go on."

"Over the cancer?"

"Over Shannon mostly, but I don't think she got over Brad's death, either."

"This doesn't sound like her."

"No," Chuck said quietly. "In any case, I can't keep working while she's drowning like this. I'm going to put out a memo that you're the man now."

Chad shoved his hands in the pockets of his slacks. "I hate that it has to be this way."

"That's why I trust you. Make sure you give yourself a raise."

"I can't do that."

"Call Christine in then. She'll do it."

He opened Chuck's door and waved to Christine. She laid aside a stack of papers and walked gingerly across the lobby to Chuck's office. "I don't want to hear this, do I?" she asked Chad as he held the door for her. He shook his head and closed the door behind her.

"Christine, Chad is responsible for the day-to-day operations of the firm. Make sure his base is commensurate with those additional responsibilities."

"No," Christine whispered. "Not like this. You can't . . ."

"I'm ordering my priorities," Chuck said. "Right now my wife needs me far more than my clients do."

"You'll be back?" she asked.

He dropped his eyes without answering her and went back to his desk. "Everything is in the desk, Chad, including my keys."

"Mr. Molinsky . . ."

Chuck had to ignore her. He couldn't afford to discuss or debate his decision, and he certainly couldn't watch her cry. He carefully placed the photographs from his desk into his briefcase, taking a lingering look at the one of Bobbi and him. Lastly, he picked up the desk clock his father had given him when he joined the firm, and laid it gently in the briefcase, then snapped it closed. "Just box up the rest of my stuff. I'll get it later."

He rounded his desk and reached out his hand to shake Chad's. He reluctantly returned Chuck's handshake. Chuck then gave Christine a long hug. "Thank you for everything. You really are the best."

She wiped away tears as he let go. "You can still call and boss me around," she said, trying to smile.

"That's Chad's job now."

"Keep us posted," Chad said. Chuck nodded, draped his suit jacket over his arm, then walked out of his office and out of the building.

"I feel sick," Christine said.

"He'll be back," Chad said. "Don't take him off the payroll or make any other changes. This isn't the end."

Sunday, September 28

Bobbi sighed as she watched the neighborhoods flash by. The drive to Preston Road Community Church passed entirely too quickly. They'd be there in minutes. She massaged her icy fingers and tried not to draw Chuck's attention.

He'd been home with her all week, but he hadn't smothered her. He spent his days in the study on the telephone and on the Internet, trying to get a lead on Shannon. He hadn't had any luck. However, Bobbi knew *he* wouldn't give up. She loved that about him. He never lost hope.

Chuck eased into a parking place and turned off the car. "You okay? You look a little pale."

"I feel sick."

"You sure you want to go?"

"No, but I don't want to face Joel either." She unbuckled her seatbelt and reached for the door handle.

"You want to pray first?"

"I'll be okay." She opened the door and got out.

Chuck caught up with her in a couple of quick steps and surprised her when he took her hand. "Yes, you *will* be okay. This won't last forever. It just seems like it right now."

What did he know?

They slipped into the sanctuary just as the worship service was beginning, grabbing a seat on the far aisle, close to the back. Immediately, tension and guilt spiked inside her, but as the service progressed, warm security and a sense of belonging enveloped her. She wished she could throw it off like a blanket. She didn't want to feel comforted and welcomed. She wanted confirmation of the cold, hard rejection in God's heart.

Glen Dillard stepped up to the podium and opened his Bible. Thankfully, he didn't mention her name, didn't even glance her direction. He read an e-mail joke, then he began his sermon.

"Last week we had a cliffhanger. We left the Israelites trapped, with the Red Sea in front of them and the greatest army in the world bearing down on them from the rear. It appeared that their choices were death, or death. Let's pick up in Exodus chapter fourteen and we'll just read a couple of verses. Start at verse thirteen." He paused a moment as people leafed through their Bibles.

Bobbi purposely left her Bible at home, but Chuck held his out for her to read. She conveniently forgot her reading glasses as well, so the words were a blur. She shook her head and pointed to her eyes. He nodded and offered his glasses to her. She shook her head again. Chuck had the vision of a near-sighted bat. Wearing his glasses would give her a bigger headache than she already had. She settled back, hoping her mind would quickly drift to something else as Glen read.

> And Moses said to the people, "Do not be afraid. Stand still, and see the salvation of the LORD, which He will accomplish for you today. For the Egyptians whom you see today, you shall see again no more forever. The LORD will fight for you, and you shall hold your peace." And the LORD said to Moses, "Why do you cry to Me? Tell the children of Israel to go forward."

"There were four things Moses and God told these people to do, and we're going to look at each of them," Glen began. "First, Moses told them not to be afraid. What were they afraid of? Just the Egyptians . . . and drowning. Look at where they stood. Egypt, their past, was behind them, gaining on them, threatening them. What was in front of them—the future, walking by faith with this Moses guy, following Jehovah—didn't look too promising either. Maybe that's where you are. Your past threatens you. It follows you, ready to attack, ready to drag you back to bondage."

Bobbi folded her arms and almost smiled. Her past was not her problem. The sermon wasn't for her. She was going to escape.

"But in some ways, that's better than the unknown," Glen continued. "It may be better than following Jehovah, who, even if you know Him, you're pretty sure you don't understand Him. Especially now. Especially in this lose-lose situation."

Bobbi's stomach knotted around the words "lose-lose." Glen didn't . . . he couldn't know how she felt. Unless Chuck told him. She could imagine the two of them scripting a message for her. She rolled her eyes Chuck's direction, but he sat innocently engaged in the sermon. Innocent. Glen said this was a continuation from last week. Also innocent. Not conspiracy between Chuck and Glen. No, it was God, and He was after her.

He could chase all He wanted. She wasn't moving. She didn't trust Him right now. Like Glen said, she didn't understand God anymore. She always believed He didn't act randomly or capriciously. That just wasn't His character. So how could Brad's death possibly work for any good and God's glory? No one could answer that one.

Besides, God is the sovereign Lord. He can do what He wants and she had to accept it. Isn't that what Job concluded?

She saw Glen check his notes and raise a hand, counting off his points. He was wrapping up.

"Israel was told not to be afraid of the past or the future," he said. "They were told to stand still and not make things worse by trying to do things on their own. Finally, Moses told them to look for God's deliverance. God was going to do something incredible and He didn't want them to miss it. God was going to rescue them from peril, defeat their enemies and bring them to the other side."

He leaned away from the podium and grinned. "Now, parting the Red Sea is kind of hard to miss. Think, though. Are you missing your deliverance? See, that's one reason you have to stand still. Where is your deliverance coming from? What avenue is God using to pull you out of your situation?"

Bobbi dropped her eyes. *He's not. He's not rescuing me.*

"Maybe you're thinking, 'God delivers those other people, but He's sure not doing anything for me.'"

Bobbi stiffened, refusing to move, refusing to give any signal that she even heard Glen's words.

"Let me tell you something you can take to the bank. God would not have brought you here if He could not finish the job." Glen tapped the podium loudly, emphasizing the last few words. "You think God was caught off-guard when the Egyptian army showed up? You think He hadn't thought out how He was going to get this whole nation across the water?" Glen shook his head. "You think your circumstances are a surprise to God? Or maybe He's having to rethink things before He intervenes?"

He's not going to. He's had months, and things keep getting worse.

Glen leaned on the podium and spoke quietly. "Here's the thing. God said, 'Move forward.' That's what got this miracle going. Israel trusted God's character, His faithfulness. They believed God would do what He said He would, and they moved forward." He closed his Bible. "What's keeping you from moving forward? Are you afraid it's going to be worse than it already has been?" He paused and looked out over the congregation.

That was twice. Two times Glen Dillard read her thoughts. At least he made eye contact with people across the aisle and not with her.

"Does bondage sound better than possibly drowning? Don't be afraid. You're not going to drown. I know some of you—it's taking everything you've got just to hold the line. Aren't you tired? Stand still. Let God do the work." He stepped out from behind the podium. "Or perhaps you're wondering where God is. He's deserted you. At least it seems that way. Keep watching. You'll see Him do great things. Now move forward. Let's pray."

Bobbi bowed her head and let herself breathe. Glen made it sound ridiculously simple. Just have faith. Just trust God. Please.

The invitation music started and Chuck slipped his hand around hers, steadying her as she stood. It wasn't that simple. She had to resolve how a good, loving, heavenly Father could snatch her son away. She had to settle that before she dared ask Him to bring Shannon home.

After the last prayer, Chuck mercifully led her toward the nearest door, doing his best to shield her from everyone. They were about to step outside to the parking lot and freedom when Glen called to them. She took a deep breath and tried to smile as Glen shook her hand.

"Bobbi, you've taken a huge step today. I'm glad you came. I know it was very hard."

He knew? He had no idea.

"Can we get together and talk? The four of us? You and Chuck and Laurie and me?"

"I'm not ready for that."

"When you are ready, I want you to know that no matter what you're wrestling with, whatever questions or thoughts you've had, I would be honored if you would trust me and Laurie enough to let us walk through this with you."

"I trust you."

"Then what's holding you back?"

"I don't know," she lied. "Give me a little more time."

ONE MONTH LATER
Saturday, October 25

Bobbi stood at the back door and watched the steady rain fall just as it had done all day yesterday. The pelting stripped the trees in the back yard of their leaves, reducing them to bare limbs. She held her cup of coffee close to her lips, trying to wring some consolation from the aroma, from the warmth.

This morning, after a month of supervision, Chuck finally left her alone. Not because things had changed. Nothing ever changed. Jack came home from college last night, so for his sake, she got to pretend that she wasn't under constant supervision, that she wasn't bribed or dragged to church every week, that his dad still went in to work every morning. Until this afternoon.

Chuck flatly refused to tell Jack anything, leaving it all in her lap. He made it clear she had one chance to explain everything to Jack alone. Otherwise he'd sit in on the conversation. Jack would never hear her if that happened.

Jack was a sensitive kid. He would understand why she couldn't go on like this. He felt the same way not so long ago. He would grasp why she didn't trust God with her health, or with Shannon . . . not after what He did to Brad. How could she call on a God who twisted every prayer she'd ever uttered for her son into that one unspeakable answer? How could she trust that He was good, that

He loved her, that He was working everything to His glory? She couldn't.

The hall clock chimed eleven. Chuck and Jack would be home from the cemetery soon. This past Monday marked thirteen years since Jack's mother died, and visiting her gravesite was his primary reason for coming home. He alone remained singularly devoted to Tracy Ravenna. He never whitewashed the woman's flaws, but he loved her fiercely in spite of them.

She sipped her coffee, but it was shame that warmed her. Forty-seven years ago today, her own mother had lost her battle with cancer. She passed that day in the waiting room at University Hospital with Gavin, while Rita and her father spent the last moments with her mother. She never got to tell her mother she loved her. She never got to say good-bye.

That's the way it was with Brad. And then again with Shannon.

Hearing the front door open, Bobbi brushed a tear away quickly, took a deep breath and prepared to fake her way through lunch.

Chuck dropped the last of the lunch dishes in the dishwasher, then made some sorry excuse about needing something from the home improvement store, and he disappeared. He expected the conversation to be over by the time he returned. Bobbi wiped her sweaty palms on her jeans and found Jack in the family room, trying to decide which football game to watch.

"Jack, can I talk to you for a few minutes?"

"Sure." He turned the television off and scooted over to make room for her on the sofa. "I've been wanting to talk to you, too."

"What about?" Yes, she was stalling.

"Things seem weird. Like there's something going on. Like between you and Dad." There was a hint of panic in his eyes.

"Not exactly."

"Not exactly?"

She shifted and took a deep breath gathering what little resolve she had. "Sweetheart, after thinking about things very carefully" —she flipped up the corner of the afghan—"I've decided . . ." *Look him in the eye. You have to look him in the eye.* "I'm not going to treat my cancer."

"What do you mean not treat it?"

His painfully earnest questions were worse than Chuck's angry protests. She couldn't stay with her script if he made her explain every statement. "I mean," she said, then her throat seemed clogged. She coughed and slowly raised her eyes back to his. "I mean, I'm not having surgery, and I'm not taking chemotherapy or radiation."

"But won't the cancer kill you if you don't do those things?" His eyes begged her to say any other word than the one she intended to speak.

"Yes."

For an agonizing minute, he didn't move except to blink slowly. Then he asked softly, "You want to die?"

"Yes."

"Why?" he whispered.

For a hundred thousand reasons that made no sense to anyone but her. "It's too much, Jack. I hurt every minute of every day. I've lost my son, and my daughter—"

"What about Joel?" he snapped. "What about me? I'm not worth living for?"

"It's not about you—"

He jumped to his feet, towering over her. "Yes, it is! I'm your son!" He snatched up the remote control and slammed it on the sofa. "Or at least I thought I was." He turned away and paced over to the television and gripped the top of the entertainment center. "Is Dad okay with this?"

"Things are a little strained between us."

"Strained? I bet they're strained," Jack said sarcastically. "I'm surprised he hasn't brought the hospital to you."

If it were possible, Chuck would.

Jack shook his head, his jaw clenching, his neck flushing the way Chuck's did. "It makes sense now. He stood there and cried today. . . . I've never seen him cry like that. He wasn't crying over her. It was over you."

"Sweetheart, I can't expect you to understand—"

"Don't call me that!"

The words, the rejection in them, bit her. Jack didn't grasp what she was trying to get across. It was like tearing Chuck's heart out again, and the only way she survived that was with stone-cold anger.

"How can you do this to me?"

"No, it's God doing this to you. He's the one running things. He's the one who took my kids and He's the one who gave me this disease—"

"That's a cop-out! He doesn't work that way, and you know it."

"I can't get rid of this hurt, Jack. My only option is to shorten the time I have to deal with it."

"Your only option?" Jack stood and walked across the room, staring at the ceiling. "That was a real exhaustive search, I bet."

"Excuse me?" In the thirteen years Jack had lived with them, he had never been disrespectful.

"What else have you tried? Who have you gone to for help?"

Bobbi stared at him, her own jaw clenching.

"That's what I thought." Jack shook his head. "You know, you're just like my mother." He jabbed a finger at her as he spoke, his voice rising in intensity. "You're choosing to be angry and bitter. You're nursing it. There's help all around you, and you refuse to accept it!"

He shook his head again and said quietly, "You do what you want. I don't need a mother."

Jack stormed out of the family room leaving Bobbi shell-shocked, and moments later, she heard his bedroom door slam.

This was all wrong. She didn't mean . . . He took it wrong . . . She had to explain . . . She rushed upstairs and from the hallway outside his room, she could hear movement and shuffling. "Jack? What are you doing?"

"Packing."

Dear God, no. Not him, too. "Why? Where are you going?"

"I'm going back to school. For good."

"You're upset with me, but please don't do this to your dad—" She flinched when he jerked the door open.

"Me? What you're doing to him is way worse. You have no room to talk to me about taking other people's feelings into consideration." He went back to throwing his clothes into his gym bag. "I see where Shannon gets it. She got it in her head that everything was my fault and that was the end of it. No reasoning with her."

"Sweetheart—"

He whipped around to face her, his eyes, Tracy's eyes, blazing. "I said don't call me that," he growled, jabbing his finger at her again. "You know, your pain, your feelings are more important to you than anything else in your life right now. That makes 'em your god." He flipped his gym bag around and yanked the zipper closed. "Well, I'm not worshipping at that altar. Tell Dad I'll call him when I get there." He pushed past her and was down the stairs and out the door before she could react.

"Ja—" She rushed to the window in time to see his car screaming away from the house. "Jack . . . don't . . ." Chuck would never forgive her. She couldn't blame him. She steadied herself against Jack's dresser, as her next breath worked to force itself into her lungs. It was this place. She was going to smother if she didn't get out. Now.

Holding the wall, then the banister, she staggered downstairs, dug her keys from her purse and left. She drove through the rain, jamming the accelerator to the floor. At the first red light she hoped she shut the front door. Was the light at Danbury and Wright green? It must've been. She didn't remember stopping and she didn't hit anybody.

She had no idea how many streets she'd been on, or what route she had taken when she found herself drawn to the cemetery, to Brad's gravesite. She hadn't been there since they buried him. She rolled slowly down the narrow cemetery road and parked her car. She could see his marker just a few yards down.

Ignoring the rain, without an umbrella or even a jacket, she got out and walked down the grass row to the place where they had laid her son to rest. She reached down and lightly touched the cool granite, tracing the letters. BRADLEY JAMES MOLINSKY.

They named him after Chuck's parents. Bradley was Ann's maiden name, and Chuck's father was Jim. They liked Bradley James because they were afraid he might end up being called Jimmy. Brad was a good, solid, masculine name, Chuck said.

Tears began to slip down Bobbi's cheeks, almost unnoticed in the rain. "How could You do this to me?" She startled herself when she said it out loud. She looked up into the sky and shouted with a guttural primal voice she didn't recognize. "How could You take him? What good did this accomplish? I've done everything You've told me to." Bobbi began counting on her fingers, pointing and accusing. "I raised my children. I love my husband. I forgave him after he cheated on me because You told me to. I forgave Tracy because You told me to. We raised Jack, and I love him just like my own son! Doesn't that mean anything? Doesn't that count?" She grabbed up a small rock and with a grunt heaved it into the sky, stumbling to keep her balance.

"You could have stopped it, but You didn't and my son was murdered!"

She wanted more rocks. And she wanted to punch and kick and thrash and scream, but she couldn't see for the tears. She pressed her palms tight against her eyes and that's when she heard it.

"*Bobbi, My Son was murdered, too.*"

CHAPTER 17
INSIGHT

Jack jerked his car from lane to lane, trying to get to the interstate as quickly as possible. He gripped the steering wheel with his right hand so he could wipe away the steady stream of tears with his left. The windshield wipers squeaked with every stroke, providing the only break in the heavy silence.

She . . . How could she not treat her cancer? Of all the . . . And then his dad couldn't relay that information? Three dozen phone calls and it somehow slipped his mind? And Joel's? He slammed a hand against the steering wheel. How could . . . How could they stand for this?

Realizing at the last minute the traffic light had turned red, he screeched to a halt. "I gotta get my head straight. I can't drive like this." He pulled over into a parking lot and turned off his car.

Things were just starting to feel normal again, but here she was, giving up. She's the one who got him back on track. "God, what does she need? What will make her see past the pain?" He closed his eyes as his own angry words echoed in his head. Here she was, opening up, trying to explain the deep, soul-killing hurt she was carrying . . . She needed compassion and sympathy. He was an idiot. He shouldn't have talked to her like that. He shouldn't have, under any circumstances, walked out.

Going back home would be the easy part. What could he possibly say to her? Would she even speak to him? Then he'd have to tell his dad. He needed some wisdom. And he'd need his umbrella. He reached under his seat and pulled out an umbrella and tossed it on the passenger seat. He smiled and shook his head. She bought the umbrella and insisted he carry it. He started his car and drove straight to the cemetery, to Brad's gravesite.

He'd visited Brad's grave so many times, he could almost drive there with his eyes closed. Right, left, right, sweeping left, then over a small hill and a quick left. As soon as he topped the hill, he spotted his mother's car. Surely not. What would she be doing here? Then when he made his left turn, he saw her leaning against, almost sitting on, the headstone, her face buried in her hands. When Jack parked his car behind hers, she never looked up.

"She's gonna catch pneumonia," he muttered. He left his car running to keep it warm for her, then grabbed the umbrella and got out. He flipped the collar of his jacket up to guard against the cold rain. The saturated grass squished under his foot with each step.

His mother hadn't heard him. She stood there, shivering, soaked through, water dripping from her elbows and her bangs. He eased in behind her, shielding her with the umbrella. "Mom," he said gently, "let's go home."

She raised her head slowly and pushed her hair back away from her face. "You came back."

"I never should have left. I'm sorry." Jack threw his arms around her, trying his best to keep the umbrella upright. He twisted out of his jacket and threw it around her shoulders, then pulling her close, he guided her toward his car.

He felt her stiffen. "I can drive, Jack. I'm okay."

"But my car is warm."

"But I have leather seats. Yours will get soaked."

"Ask me how much I care about that right now." He opened the passenger door and held the umbrella over her while she got in.

She settled slowly as if every muscle ached, then slipped her arms into his jacket sleeves. "Something wrong?"

"Why don't you call your dad and tell him he can come home," she said.

Jack leaned in to kiss her cheek. "I love you, Mom."

"I can tell. I love you, too."

Jack shut her door and walked around to the driver's side. He paused just an instant before he opened the door, glancing up at the sky. "I still need that wisdom."

His mother didn't speak on the way home, except to nod when he asked if she was warm enough. Of course she was lying. She hugged herself tightly, shivering whenever she thought he wasn't looking. "Well, I'm freezing," he said, then turned the blower up full blast. A few moments later, she relaxed and leaned back in the passenger seat.

When they turned on to Danbury Court, he had to smile when he saw his dad's car in the driveway. Apparently his dad was a lot closer than the home improvement store when he called. Jack hit the button on the garage door opener and pulled into his mother's spot. Almost as soon as Jack got out of the car, his dad stepped into the garage from the kitchen with a heavy blanket draped across his arm.

Jack nodded. "She's freezing and exhausted, and if she doesn't get sick from this, I'll be surprised."

"I'll take care of her."

"You want me to put some coffee on?"

"Thanks, thanks for everything, Jack."

Jack smiled and waved to his mother, then went inside to start a pot of coffee as promised. Just as the coffeemaker finished, his dad came into the kitchen.

"She's taking a hot shower, so between that and the coffee, we should get her warmed up. She didn't say much, though. What happened?"

"It was bad," Jack said. "I kinda let her have it." He leaned against the counter and crossed his arms. "I need to apologize to her." Jack recounted the conversation, admitting everything he'd said. "I'm sorry, Dad. I shouldn't have talked to her that way."

"You don't have to apologize. You may have said just what she needed to hear."

"Maybe." Jack frowned. "Dad, so, speaking of things people need to hear, how come you didn't tell me about any of this? I mean, this has been going on for months. I was almost as mad at you as I was at her."

His dad dropped his eyes and shoved his hands into the front pockets of his jeans. "I failed her. Nothing was getting through. Nobody could reach her. I thought . . . I hoped . . . if she saw with her own eyes how much it hurt you, she might, you know, reconsider." He looked past Jack and blinked back a tear. "I had no right to use you that way."

"You're a little hard on yourself."

"I think so, too," his mother said, startling both of them as she breezed into the kitchen. "Coffee, perfect." She got a mug from the cabinet and poured a full cup. "Thank you, whoever brewed it."

"It was Jack," his dad said.

"Thank you, swee—" Her eyes darted away from his. "Thank you."

"Mom—"

"No, I understand. I understand what it's like to hurt, and to try to distance yourself from whoever you think caused it." She sipped her coffee. "Believe me, I get it."

He slouched against the counter so he could look her in the eye. "Mom, can we go back and start over? Just forget this whole stupid afternoon ever happened?"

She shook her head, but he could see the slightest smile. "No, because I learned some very important things today."

"Like how your son is an inconsiderate jerk, who rants like a crazy man and totally ignores your feelings?"

"No, I learned my son is not a kid anymore. He's a very wise young man who's not afraid to speak the truth, no matter what the risk." She laid her hand on his and squeezed gently. "I am very proud of him."

"Well, he would be very pleased to have you call him 'sweetheart' again."

She smiled broadly and set her mug on the counter then hugged Jack tightly. "You don't know what it did for me when you came back. Everything changed."

"So you're going to the doctor?"

She pressed her lips together and took a step back away from him. "Will you grant me the grace to come to that decision in my own time?"

"Why would you want to wait?"

"I need to get some other things settled first."

"Like what?" his dad asked with sharp frustration.

"I've damaged my relationship with God. I've got to fix that, and I don't feel like I can focus on anything else."

"Bobbi, you have to see the doctor. No more excuses."

"I know I don't deserve any time or consideration from you guys after what I've put you through. Grace is unmerited favor. Please?"

"No. Honey, you don't comprehend how irrational you've been these last few months. You haven't been open with me or anybody else. Now you're asking me to support you in your decision to postpone treatment just because you say things have changed. I'm not sure I trust you."

She glanced at Jack, then reached for his dad's hand. "Can we rebuild our faith together? Chuck, I had a prayer answered today. Do you have any idea how long it's been since that's happened?"

"When I came back?" Jack asked.

She nodded as tears began to slip down her cheeks. His dad pulled her into his arms and whispered, "Let it go, Bobbi. Let it all go."

Bobbi sat on the love seat in the study, wrapped in an afghan, nestled against Chuck. "We really should go get my car before they lock the gates at the cemetery."

"Jack said he'd take care of it while he was picking up the sandwiches," Chuck said.

"How is Jack going to take care of it?"

"I have no idea, but he said he would, so I'm not moving and neither are you." He kissed her gently and wrapped his hand around hers.

"Can I apologize to you?"

He shook his head. "There's enough fault to go around."

She closed her eyes, listening to the rhythm of his heartbeat. Strong and steady. "I'm beginning to realize how much I've missed you."

"I've been right here."

"In spite of everything I did to push you away. You're pretty terrific."

"So what changed this afternoon, besides Jack coming back?"

She sat up and twisted so she could face him. "He knows, Chuck. God knows what it's like to have a son murdered. He knows the frustration and the injustice . . . and the emptiness." A sideways glance at Brad's picture sitting on the desk caused her to tear up. "For months, I've felt like God did this *to* me. That He could have prevented Brad's death, and for whatever reason, He just didn't." She wiped her eyes quickly with the heel of her hand. "I didn't understand what God was doing and after a while, I didn't want to."

"So you cut yourself off from God?"

"I was acting like a three-year-old. 'If that's the way you're gonna be, I'm not gonna play anymore.' Jack, he called me on it. Did he tell you?"

"A little."

"He said my pain had become my god. So, when I ended up at the cemetery this afternoon, I unloaded everything. I said all the things I've harbored in my heart, and if God chose to strike me dead for it . . . then I would come out ahead."

"Bobbi—"

She raised a hand to cut him off. "Chuck, I'd lost Brad and Shannon. I drove Jack away. I figured it was only a matter of time before I lost you and Joel, too. So I prayed. I told God if there was anything salvageable in my life, He had to show me, because I couldn't see it."

"And Jack showed up."

"It wasn't ten minutes later."

"Honey, if you've gotten this confirmation, why are you holding out on treating your cancer? It's like you want to keep the death option open."

She shook her head. "It's like when we were separated. My head was way ahead of my heart when it came to reconciling with you, and we both had to wait for my heart to catch up. Intellectually, I know God is right and I'm wrong, but I don't have the faith to say, 'I'll take whatever You give me.' I'm pretty sure I can get there, though, if I have some time and some guidance."

"So you feel like God cheated on you?"

"I felt betrayed, yes."

"What can I do to help you?"

"Be patient with me a little longer."

Shannon paced in her apartment, checking her watch with each pass. Her dad gave her that watch when she graduated from high school this spring. That first Saturday, furious at her father, she almost sold the watch. Now she'd give up her right arm before she'd part with it.

The knock at her apartment door startled her. With a hand on the deadbolt, she leaned against the door. "Who's there?"

"Tommy. I called about your television."

"Right." Shannon unlocked the deadbolt and opened the door just wide enough for the guy to squeeze through. "It's right here."

He picked up the remote and began scrolling through the channels and the menu on her TV. "What's wrong with it? Why are you selling it?" The stale smell of cigarette smoke swirled around him. At least Shannon hoped it was just cigarette smoke. "Is it stolen?"

"Good grief, no. I've got the receipt for it. There's nothing wrong with it. I've only had it four months, but I'm in a tight spot, and I need some cash."

"Gotta support your habit?"

You'd know about that, wouldn't you? "Rent's due."

He crossed his arms across his broad chest, showing off his dragon tattoo. "You know, a girl like you . . . you could make some quick cash—"

"Do you want the television or not?"

"Three hundred?"

"I paid five for it, so yeah, I think it's more than fair."

"I'll give you two."

"Excuse me? I just said I paid five hundred dollars for it. It's practically brand new!"

"I heard you say you're desperate for cash. Two hundred dollars. Unless you want to negotiate." He blinked slowly and grinned. "You know?"

Her hands went icy cold, as she realized how stupid she was for letting this jerk in her apartment. He stood between her and the door and outweighed her by at least a hundred pounds. Losing a hundred bucks on the TV was a small price to pay if it meant he would just go away. "Fine. Two hundred dollars."

Tommy pulled a huge wad of cash from his front pocket. He peeled off two one–hundred-dollar bills and handed them to her, then he stuffed the remote in his back pocket and jerked the set's power cord from the wall.

He balanced the set on his knee as he fumbled to get her door open, but Shannon stood rooted to her spot. Maybe he'd drop the TV. As soon as the door closed behind him, she rushed over and locked the door once again and burst into tears.

She slid down the door to the floor, held her face in her hands and sobbed. What she wouldn't give to cry on her daddy's shoulder, or to hear he mother say, "Shhh, baby, it's okay. Everything is okay." Instead, she was alone in a rat hole.

Really taught my dad a lesson, didn't I? Taught him the boys listen, but not me. Showed him how one of his own can turn her back on every good thing he'd ever given her, humiliate him and ruin her life in the process. Yep, I sure showed him.

And with her savings exhausted, she had seven days to come up with the rest of the rent money.

Sunday, October 26

Chuck sat at the kitchen table enjoying a cup of coffee with his wife. He'd given up trying to read the paper, because he couldn't take his eyes off her. Her spark, her energy, her very life had returned, and he felt a thousand pounds lighter.

She set her cup on the table. "So, how much notice do you think I have to give Glen?"

"For what?" Chuck asked.

"I want to talk to him about . . . things. I need some insight."

"About fifteen seconds." Chuck reached for the phone. "I'll see if he and Laurie are free for lunch."

"That's fairly nonthreatening."

Chuck rolled his eyes at her. "Glen Dillard's about as threatening as my grandmother."

"I never knew your grandmother." She arched her eyebrow and he nearly melted when she smiled. Chuck punched their pastor's number in and waited for him to pick up.

"Do you all always get up this early on Sunday?" Glen asked.

"For Bobbi, this is sleeping in," Chuck said. "Listen, are you free for lunch? You and Laurie?"

"You mean with you and Bobbi?" Glen's voice dropped to a near whisper. "Thank You, Jesus."

"So that's a yes."

"I'd cancel church to talk to Bobbi. You name the place and we'll be there."

"We hadn't thought that far ahead."

"So what happened? What changed her mind?"

"Probably someplace out of the way," Chuck said, glancing at Bobbi.

"She's right there, isn't she?"

"That sounds good," Chuck said.

"You can tell me later, then. Let's eat at Rico's so you don't have to lie to your wife anymore."

"All right, Glen. Thanks a lot." Chuck hung the phone back in its cradle. "Rico's after church."

"What about Jack?"

"What about him?"

"Is he invited or not?"

"That's up to you, I guess."

"I want him there. I don't want to keep things from him or you or anybody else." She finished off her cup of coffee. "Now that I have the grace of a second chance."

Bobbi flipped a menu open and tried to find the right spot to hold it to bring the print in focus, while Chuck stood behind her chair watching the door. "What sounds good, Jack?"

"Meatloaf," Jack answered with a grin. "They have the best!" Bobbi dropped her jaw. "Except for yours," he quickly added, "and Aunt Rita's."

Bobbi winked at him. "Theirs probably is better than mine. I think that's what I'll have, too."

"Hey, there's Glen." Chuck waved, then waited to shake Glen's and Laurie's hands before he took his seat. "You got here pretty fast," he said.

Glen held the chair for Laurie, and then took his place beside her. "I'll probably have folks lined up outside my office tonight."

"I'm sorry," Bobbi said. "We should have—"

Glen pointed a finger and gave her a teasing smile. "Ma'am, we will get off on the absolute wrong note. This is the most important item on my agenda this afternoon. Everybody else is just gonna have to understand that." They made small talk long enough to order lunch, then Glen took a long drink from his tea. "Bobbi, you've put me off for weeks, then you wanted to meet out of the blue. What changed?"

"Everything," Bobbi admitted. She recounted the conversation with Jack and her time at the cemetery the previous day. "I know I'm wrong, and I'm ready to get back to where I should be, but I need some help making peace with Brad's death before I can even think about Shannon."

"What's the biggest frustration, the biggest hurt?" Glen asked.

"It just . . . it's so senseless. He was so gifted. He had a wonderful heart. He could have done so much more good . . ."

"So much lost potential," Laurie said with a gentle understanding.

"Exactly," Bobbi said. "There was so much that could have been."

"When we lost our babies, I could not get that thought out of my head, and I knew Glen and I would be good parents. It made no sense."

"So how did you get through it?" Bobbi asked.

"Part of it was a realization that God equipped us to do a wide range of things, but this was the path He was asking us to follow. Maybe it's that way with Brad. With his talents, he could have accomplished any number of things for God, but giving his life this way was the one God chose for him."

"But why?"

"You probably won't get a decent answer to that until you can ask God Himself," Glen said.

"So in the meantime?"

"Two things. Are you reading?"

"I will. What's your suggestion?"

"God is still the same God He was five months ago, and His plan is still proceeding on schedule. I want you to read about His character, Psalms or the prophets. You'll find something."

Bobbi scowled. "The psalms or the prophets or something? That's it?"

"See, he's no help," Chuck teased.

Glen waved at Chuck to be still, then he turned back to Bobbi. "Second, ask God to show you the good things that He's doing. I promise you it's there, and you'll be able to let go of this if you can see Brad's death wasn't wasted."

She knew Glen was right, but everything in her screamed his death was a waste. She dropped her head and blinked back tears, then she felt Chuck's hand on hers. "That's a tall order."

"I know it is," Glen said. "It'll take awhile."

"Got any hints about those good things?"

"You're sitting across the table from one of them." Glen nodded at Jack.

"Me? How do you figure that?" Jack asked.

"You are completely focused, self-assured," Glen said. "You've got a purpose I don't think you would have ever found otherwise."

"He's become a man almost before my eyes," Bobbi agreed. "I owe him quite a bit." She squeezed Jack's arm and he blushed.

"Bobbi, did you get to see Brad before he died?" Laurie asked.

"No, he was in surgery when we got there—" No more words would come, and Chuck squeezed her hand. "No, I didn't get to see him."

"I think it's a lot harder when you don't get to say good-bye."

"That's the thing I remember most about when my mother died," Bobbi said. "I was too young to go in the intensive care unit, so I never got to tell her good-bye."

"Shannon slipped away, too, didn't she?"

"Yeah, she did," Bobbi said.

"It may not help, but one of the things Glen and I held onto was the story of David, when his and Bathsheba's son died. He said, 'I will go to him. He can't come to me.' Bobbi, I'll see my babies again. I didn't have to tell them good-bye. They're waiting for me, and I'll spend eternity with them."

"The question is, will I see Shannon again before heaven?"

CHAPTER 18
RESUMPTION

Monday, November 10

Chuck had to take a step backward to keep his balance when Christine threw her arms around his neck. "Mr. Molinsky! You're back!" she squealed. When Chuck's face flushed, Christine quickly let go and widened the distance between them. "And Mrs. Molinsky is better?"

"We're getting there. She hasn't gone back to the doctor yet, but she's had a breakthrough. She's spending a lot of time studying, trying to sort out all of this."

"But you feel good enough about it to come back to work."

"Yes and no. I'm here, but I'm not ready to get back to work yet. I'm still trying to track down Shannon. I think it's easier on Bobbi if she can't see me searching and not finding anything."

"You haven't heard from her even?"

"Not a word since the twenty-ninth of June."

"Let us help you," Christine said. "I don't know anyone here who wouldn't drop everything to work on this."

"Isn't that a little unethical?" Chuck protested.

"What good is it to be in charge of everything if you can't take advantage of it once in a while?" She winked at him and headed back to her desk. "Bring me a list of phone numbers to call as soon as you get settled."

"Thank you," Chuck said. "Thanks for praying, too." He unlocked his office and turned on the lights. Even the ink pens on his desk were untouched in the seven weeks he'd been gone. He turned on his computer and pulled a folder from his briefcase. He spread out the pages of handwritten notes, phone numbers, lists, hand-drawn maps and printouts from Internet searches.

Hours of work, with nothing to show for it, not a lead, not even a sighting. He picked up the top sheet and walked back out to Christine's desk. "I don't have a magic formula," he said. "I'm assuming she's still in St. Louis, she's using her real name, and she has a job somewhere, so I've been calling every business in the phone book asking for her. I'm on *K*." He handed the sheet to Christine. "Of course, if I'm wrong on any of those assumptions, I'm sunk."

"Oh, Mr. Molinsky."

"I know. It's very tedious and discouraging. I'm open to better ideas."

"No one has talked to her? She hasn't contacted any of her friends?"

"There was a punk that helped her leave, and her cousin spoke to her the morning after she left. Those are the only contacts we know of."

"You've talked to them, right?" Chuck nodded. Christine swiveled around to her computer and began typing. "What's the punk's name?"

"Dylan Snider, but he's not going to help."

"Maybe not directly," Christine said quietly as she continued to type.

"What are you doing?"

"ZIP is a social site, like Facebook or MySpace. Kids have pages where they leave each other messages, pictures and so forth. It's mostly silly stuff. However, you'd be amazed at how much information they'll give up."

"You spy on your girls?"

"It's not spying," Christine said with a smile. "I am an informed parent." She stopped typing and frowned. "How do you spell his name? I can't find him."

"S-n-i-d-e-r."

"Here we go." Christine pointed to the screen as Dylan's ZIP page popped up.

Chuck pulled out his glasses and leaned over Christine's shoulder. "He's a predator. . . . Everything's about girls. . . . What's that little thing with the number beside the girls' names?"

"You probably don't want to know," Christine said.

"Scroll down the list," Chuck said. "I want to see if . . . I mean, I hope she's not." Christine silently clicked down the page past Brittneys, Taylors, Morgans, Jessicas and Emilys. Until she found Shannon.

With Shannon's name, however, there was a series of grainy photographs, just revealing enough to prove he hadn't lied about his conquest. The caption under the picture read, "Oh yes, I did! Wes, you owe me $50."

Chuck gripped the back of Christine's chair to keep his legs from buckling under him. His daughter, his baby girl . . . And this little . . . using her . . . bragging to his friends . . .

"Mr. Molinsky, I never dreamed . . . I should have let you do this in private. I am so sorry."

"He . . ." Angry tears blurred his vision, and he used his remaining strength to wipe his eyes. "He told me . . . I didn't want to believe him." With another deep breath, he thought he could take a few steps without stumbling. "I'll be in my office," he said.

Christine wanted to cry with him. He had worked so hard to make up for his infidelity and it never seemed to be enough. She watched him slump into his desk chair and bury his face in his hands. "Dear God," she prayed quietly. "Can You give these people a break? Just this once?"

Bobbi walked through her empty house, unsure what to tackle first now that she was finally "allowed" to be home alone. "When in doubt, make more coffee," she muttered to herself. She pulled a bag of Indonesian dry roast from her cabinet and brewed a single cup.

Holding the cup in her hands, she said a quick prayer for Chuck on his first day back at work. He hated to leave her, he said, and she had gotten very accustomed to him being there. More than once, she prodded him to go ahead and take his retirement. Things were undone, he said, and he couldn't leave just yet.

Long-term limbo she could identify with. She had been following Glen's recommendation, spending most of her days reading and studying, but answers, or even hints, had yet to materialize. Maybe God was checking to see how serious she was about finding an answer. Maybe there was no answer to be found.

No, she didn't believe that. God was waiting again. Waiting for her. But why? She vented all her anger over Brad. She was going to church, reading, healing. "All right, Lord. It's not anger. What is it?" She closed her eyes, sipped her coffee and then she knew. Shannon. God wanted her hopelessness, but He was asking her to face it and own it before He would take it.

Facing it wasn't the problem. Hopelessness insinuated itself into every facet of her existence—her decisions, her emotions, her relationships all reflected that despondency. Untangling herself from it, impossible as it seemed now, was her only real option. And it had to begin in Shannon's room.

She stood at the bottom of the stairs, wavering between taking that first step and waiting another day, when a slicing chill worked its way from her hands to her spine until it crept across her jawline. *Take the first step, Bobbi. I'll take the rest of them.*

She blew out a deep breath, grasped the railing and pulled herself up to the first step, then the second, each one coming a little more easily until she reached the door to Shannon's bedroom. She hadn't crossed the threshold since that last Saturday in June.

She grasped the doorframe to steady herself and with a trembling hand, she turned the knob and pushed the door open. She stepped in carefully, surveying the room. Nothing had been moved since that Saturday morning. She opened Shannon's closet and inhaled deeply. It was stale yet familiar, almost comforting, like coming home after a trip. Bobbi lightly touched each shirt, each pair of pants still hanging inside. Shannon left in the summer . . . did she have winter clothes? Was she warm enough?

Shannon was a smart girl. If she could pull off running away, then she was more than capable of getting a decent winter coat. Bobbi eased the closet door closed again and skimmed her hand across the desk as she passed. The note lay not far from its original spot. Bobbi spent every sleepless night visualizing that note. She passed her hand by without touching it.

The bed was uncharacteristically well made, and Bobbi smiled. She gave up the battle for a made bed years ago. "What's the point?" Shannon said. "Nobody's gonna see it but me!" But Shannon made the bed before she left. "Mom, I reject everything you've ever taught me, but I'll submit to your authority on bed making before I go."

Bobbi sat down on the bed and pulled the spread back. Taking Shannon's pillow in her arms, she hugged it to herself. The scent of Shannon's shampoo and her favorite perfume clung to the fabric as if she'd slept there just last night. "You know what it's like to have a daughter who leaves home, don't You?" Bobbi said to ceiling. "And I've been that daughter." She squeezed the pillow once more, then she laid it back in its place and lovingly remade the bed.

She lingered in the doorway, giving God one last chance to say something, do something . . . anything. "Lord, here's the thing. You knew where I was the whole time. I don't know where she is. I don't know if she's okay. That's what's killing me. I don't know." Tears choked off her words.

But I do.

"You underestimate yourself, Bobbi. You'll find your answers, and the rest of us will stand back and marvel how God brought you through one more time." Rita winked and sipped her coffee.

"Just once, I'd like to be in the 'marveling' group," Bobbi said. *Just once.*

Rita glanced at the kitchen clock. "I'd better get out of here."

"Don't rush. Chuck won't be home on time his first day back."

"I'm glad he went back to work. I think you needed that vote of confidence."

"If you guys are so confident, then how come you conveniently showed up so I wouldn't be alone today?"

"Habit."

Bobbi rolled her eyes. "Chuck didn't 'suggest' you stop by?"

Rita put a hand over her heart. "I haven't talked to Chuck in days. But honestly, you are much better. Things are almost back to normal."

Normal. Bobbi shook her head. "I'll learn how to cope, but things will never be what they were."

"No, you're right. I'm sorry."

"That's not what I . . ." She closed her eyes and tried to go back to that moment, standing in Shannon's bedroom when she felt the arms of Almighty God enfold and reassure her that He knew, that He had Shannon in the palm of His hand, that there was a plan and purpose to all of it. "Do you think Shannon is okay?"

"I do."

"How . . . what makes you so sure?"

"I know her mother."

"Not good enough," Bobbi said. "I need more evidence."

"All right, this sounds twisted, but the fact that she hasn't come home tells me she's doing okay."

"You're right. That is twisted."

"Bobbi, Shannon is just a little spoiled, just a little stubborn, and as long as things are clicking along for her, then it looks like she's right, and she's done the right thing. She'll be home as soon as it all falls apart."

"And in the meantime?"

Rita smiled. "You pray for her to be miserable."

"Does Gavin know you pray for people's misery?"

"Are you kidding? He helps me. Of course, he doesn't frame it exactly like that. He says things like, 'God, bring her to the point of surrender.'"

"You've been praying for me a lot lately, haven't you?"

"Actually, yes. And I'm seeing some answers."

"Some?"

"Have you made a doctor's appointment yet?"

"No."

"Then it's just 'some.' Will you tell me what on earth you're waiting on?"

"It's hard to explain."

"I hope you're this difficult with Chuck," Rita huffed.

"She is." Chuck swept into the kitchen. He paused an instant to kiss Bobbi, then got a glass from the cabinet.

"You're home much earlier than I expected," she said. "What's wrong?"

"I don't know," he muttered. "Everything. Nothing."

"This time I am leaving." Rita stood and pushed her chair in. "Gavin's home tonight if you need him, Chuck."

"Thanks." Chuck emptied a can of Diet Coke into his glass, then slumped into the chair across from Bobbi. As soon as Rita closed the front door, he looked up at Bobbi. "That punk . . . He took pictures."

"Pictures? What . . . ?"

"Of Shannon. They're on the Internet."

"Shannon? With that boy?"

"Yeah. Her first night away from home and she spent it with that . . . that Snider kid. Mocking us."

"That's ridiculous."

"Bobbi, I saw the pictures with my own eyes."

"I don't care what you saw—"

"See, I debated whether I should even tell you—"

"And that is exactly the same kind of knee-jerk reaction that escalated things in the first place."

He pushed back from the table, unbuttoned the top button of his dress shirt and tugged at the knot on his necktie. When he spoke, his voice was low, almost patronizing. "She rejected everything we've taught her, our values, our authority, and God's moral law, Bobbi. It was calculated—"

"You don't know that!"

"The boy couldn't have taken the pictures if Shannon wasn't..."

"Consenting. I understand that, but you don't know that she did it in defiance. When we first found out about this months ago, you said yourself she was emotionally compromised."

"But her brain was engaged."

"Just like yours was? With Tracy?" She instantly regretted the words, but it was too late.

With shock and shame in his eyes, he said quietly, "I asked for that, I guess."

"No, it was a cheap shot. I'm sorry." Bobbi reached across the table for his hand. "Chuck, you and I have both been where she is now. Defiant, callous and self-righteous." She squeezed his hand. "And isolated, afraid and miserable. I don't care what she's done, we need to get her home."

"I'm doing everything I can. Rita's been calling Shannon's friends for me—"

"She never mentioned that."

"She has been. Relentlessly. Christine's putting notices on Facebook and those other sites. I don't even remember all of them. Chad and some of the others called a bunch of places today, but we're not getting anywhere." He frowned and picked up his glass and gulped half the contents. "What if I rent a billboard? Tell her everything's okay. It's okay to come home."

"I think it's a beautiful idea. Do you know what that will cost?"

He shook his head. "Thousands of dollars, I expect."

"What if she's not in St. Louis anymore?"

"I'm assuming she'd want to stick where things are familiar. So what do you think?"

"Rent the billboard. Rent a hundred if you have to."

He kissed her hand. "I probably should warn you, we may be entering into some legal action, too."

"We are?"

"Yes, we advised Mr. Dylan Snider to remove the photos of Shannon from his ZIP page in twenty-four hours unless he could produce a signed consent form agreeing to the use of her likeness."

"Or?"

"I don't know. Something really bad. Chad wrote the thing for me."

"Can you do that?"

"Eventually yes, but it'll be a lot easier if he just goes along with it. We named his parents, too, even though he's nineteen."

"I thought they were 'unengaged' as far as parenting went."

"They are, but I'm guessing they don't want their names in the paper, and they don't want to risk paying the settlement over a couple of pictures."

"I hope you're right."

"That would be nice for a change."

That evening after Bobbi had gone to bed, Chuck sat alone at the desk in the study. Those pictures. That boy and his leering grin, his hands where only a husband's hands should be, crudely bragging about being with his only daughter. Chuck would carry those images to his grave.

It wasn't just the pictures but what they had touched off inside him—waves of grief, powerlessness and a profound sense of failure. He failed to shield his daughter. He failed God Himself. He immediately assumed the worst about Shannon, her actions, her motives and her intentions.

Where was all that grace he claimed to believe in? Maybe that was why there was no mother in the story of the prodigal son. Shannon's actions didn't seem to matter to Bobbi. She unconditionally loved and accepted Shannon. Did he?

He always thought he was a good father. But he thought he was a good husband until Phil Shannon told him he didn't love Bobbi. Phil challenged him to learn how to love sacrificially. Now Bobbi blasted him for seeing only Shannon's actions.

God, what do I need to do? How do I change this?

He leaned back in the chair, closed his eyes for a moment, and he could visualize the page in his Bible with Psalm 37. "Do not fret because of evildoers . . . for they shall soon be cut down like grass."

Easier said than done.

He rolled his chair over and grabbed his Bible from the table by the love seat, and quickly found the well-worn page for Psalm 37. Without his glasses, focusing took more effort and he caught himself skimming the familiar passage. 'Rest,' 'wait patiently,' 'He shall bring it to pass.'

After what that . . . after what he did to Shannon, You want me to just let it go?

He got his glasses out of his shirt pocket to reread the chapter. "Their sword shall enter their own heart."

You wanna spell it out a little plainer maybe? He huffed and laid the Bible aside. *God, this goes against everything inside me.* But that was the point. Doing things his way heaped the disasters one upon the other.

"All right, God, Dylan Snider . . . You can have him. Now, You have to help me live that way, because I know when I wake up tomorrow, it's gonna be right there again." He sighed and pulled the Bible closer. "Now what about Shannon?"

He read through the psalm, quietly mumbling the words to himself. "'The steps of a good man are ordered by the LORD, and He delights in his way. Though he fall, he shall not be utterly cast down; for the LORD upholds him with His hand.'" He shook his head. "The story of my life."

Though he fall . . . Not just the story of his life. Shannon's. Shannon fell just like he did, but God was going to uphold her, support her and defend her. Like a father.

And that was exactly what he would do, too.

CHAPTER 19
COMMENCEMENT

Tuesday, November 11

A little after nine, Chuck strode into the lobby of Benton, Davis & Molinsky with renewed purpose, ready to slay dragons on Shannon's behalf. Before he spoke to Christine, he glanced across to his office and stopped dead in his tracks. "Christine, why is there a homeless man in my office?" He never took his eyes off the man.

"He's not homeless," she said, "and he wants very much to talk to you."

"You couldn't have warned me?"

"I called. I got your voice mail."

He frowned and pulled his cell phone from his pocket. "Dead battery," he grumbled. "Of course. Who else is in the building? Is Chad here?"

Christine smiled broadly. "Mr. Molinsky, are you afraid to go talk to that man?" she teased.

"Of course not," Chuck said, although he wasn't sure he meant it. "I was just mentally taking roll."

"You'll be glad you talked to him. I promise."

"Who is he?"

"Go," she said. "He's an answer to prayers."

What could this old guy possibly know about Shannon? When he pushed his office door open, the old man in the chair stood, smoothed his baggy pants and held out a callused hand.

"She told me to wait in here, Mr. Molinsky. I hope that's all right."

His voice was raspy and soft, and what hair he had lay in gray wisps across his head. Several days' worth of stubble grew on his narrow face. His clothes, while ill-fitting and wrinkled, were clean, and he smelled of cheap aftershave.

Chuck set his briefcase down and shook hands with the man. "What can I do for you, Mr. . . . ?"

"Reynolds. Edward Henry Reynolds. I understand you knew my daughter."

Chuck knew his jaw dropped, and he wouldn't make a gracious recovery from this one. Edward Henry Reynolds, Tracy's father . . . here, in his office. Jack *had* seen his grandfather the night Brad was killed.

"Mr. Reynolds . . . this is . . . this is quite a surprise." Chuck leaned against his desk, hoping it looked casual and not like his knees were ready to give out. "You'll have to forgive me. I'm a little stunned."

"I apologize for that, but I was afraid you might not see me if I called ahead. You understand, I hope." He was painfully polite, just like Tracy, and just like Jack. "But you see, I have something for you."

"Mr. Reynolds, you don't have to . . ."

"I saw who shot your boy, Mr. Molinsky. I know who it was, and I'm on my way to the police after I talk to you."

"I gotta sit down." Chuck steadied himself against his desk as he pulled a chair close and eased into it. An eyewitness. For Brad. This would blow his case open. Before his excitement could build, guilt strangled it. He'd let Brad down. With Bobbi and Shannon consuming his attention and his energy, he hadn't followed up with the detectives in weeks. But God . . . God answered a prayer he'd forgotten to pray. "You saw it?"

"Yes sir. I'd just left that mission he ran and was on my way back to my room." He shifted in his chair and cleared his throat. "Those boys are two-bit hoods trying to impress somebody. Don't have any idea how deep in they were."

"Which boys? The killers?"

"Yes sir. They thought they could get in good with their boss if they could pull off something daring. Prove they were fearless." He shook his head. "They better hope the law finds 'em before that gang boss does."

"I don't understand."

"Murder's bad for business. Brings the cops out, makes the neighborhood jumpy."

"You mean drug trafficking."

"At least. Depending on how energetic they are, they probably keep hookers or run numbers or what have you."

Dear God, please . . . Shannon can't be mixed up in anything like that. "So, Mr. Reynolds—"

"Just Ed. Don't deserve that kind of respect, especially from someone like yourself."

Someone like . . . Was that sarcasm? "Mr. Reynolds, I mean Ed, why didn't you come forward before now? The police canvassed the neighborhood."

"With my . . . history, I don't make a very credible witness. It took me awhile to get a name to go with the face."

"Mr. Reynolds, would you excuse me just a second?" Chuck stood and walked to his office door. "Can I bring you back a cup of coffee?"

"No sir, thank you."

Ed had a name, the name of Brad's killer. Chuck quickly crossed the lobby to Christine's desk. "You know who he is?"

"Yes, he told me when he got here. Jack is holding on line two."

"How'd you know to call Jack?"

"Years of practice." Christine handed Chuck the receiver.

"Dad, what's going on? What's wrong?"

Chuck wished he could see Jack's face and ease his panicked confusion. "Your grandfather, Jack. He's sitting in my office."

"I'll be there in two hours," he said, and the line went dead.

"Jack, wait—" It was too late. Calling back would be useless. Chuck handed the phone back to Christine. "That man in my office served almost thirty years in prison for beating his wife to death. Tracy was mortally terrified of him. Why weren't you?"

She tilted her head to look toward Chuck's office. "Does he look like he's here to hurt anybody?"

"Looks can deceive."

"They can, but I think he's looking for peace, maybe even forgiveness from Tracy, through Jack."

"Maybe." The prosecutor, John Dailey, never believed Reynolds, though. What if it was a setup? What if he was lying, luring Jack here? Chuck's brain refused to chase that rabbit. Just as well. "Call Bobbi for me and tell her what's going on. I'll call her as soon as I can, but he says he knows who shot Brad. He's going to the police. We may get a break."

Christine's eyes brimmed with tears. "That's exactly what I've been praying for, Mr. Molinsky. Exactly."

"Don't stop. You may be the one turning this all around."

"Oh, I doubt that."

"I don't." Chuck walked back to his office, trying to impose some coherent order on the thousands of questions forming in his mind, chief among them, why, exactly, was the old man here? What did he want?

"Thank you for your patience, Mr. Reynolds." He took his seat again. "There's a reward for information leading to the arrest of my son's killer. Are you aware of that?"

"I don't want money. Nah, your boy deserves justice."

"You knew Brad?"

"I heard him once. He was a good man." He shifted in the chair and rubbed his hands on his pants. "That, uh, that boy that worked for him that night . . . He said his name was Jack."

"Jack? That's my son."

He nodded slowly and pressed his lips together. "I see. I was hoping . . . well, I knew, uh, I knew Teresa worked for you, and I thought, I thought maybe you might know what happened to her Jack."

"What do you want with him? Redemption?"

He smiled but seemed embarrassed by it, as if someone had told him he had no right or reason to smile. "That's the sweetest word in the world, Mr. Molinsky. You ever look it up in the dictionary? Taking something corrupt, worthless and giving it value . . . I been redeemed. Jesus Christ did that."

"You were saved in prison?"

"Yes sir. Hardly anyone believed me, though." He looked away in shame. "I'd lied about it three or four times to try and get paroled. You can only cry 'wolf' so many times, you know."

A fake conversion or two would explain John Dailey's misgivings.

"You see, sir, I've spent near thirteen years, trying to track Teresa down. I suppose you knew all that, how she changed her name, moved around all the time."

"I have some idea."

"By the time I found out she'd come here, and got here myself . . . well, I missed her. She was already gone." His eyes glistened, and he shifted so he could get his wallet from his back pocket. He pulled out a worn slip of paper and handed it to Chuck. It was a photocopy of Tracy's obituary. "See, that boy at the mission, he was about the right age and all . . . I hoped . . ."

Chuck handed the paper back to him and caught Christine smiling at him. She was right. Again. "Mr. Reynolds, I mean, Ed, Jack *is* her son. We . . . she and I . . . Jack's our son."

He leaned back in the chair and stroked his chin. "So he *was* Teresa's . . ." The old man scanned the obituary held tightly in his hand. "But she . . . it doesn't say she ever married." He rolled his eyes back to Chuck.

"No, she didn't."

The old man nodded slowly and let it go. "I spoke with the boy. He didn't seem to know who he was. Talked about his mother like she was still living."

"My wife and I raised Jack after Tracy's, I mean, Teresa's death. He calls my wife 'mom,' too, but it's out of regard for my wife. He's the last person who would be disrespectful to his mother. He absolutely adored her."

"She was a good mother, then?"

"Jack was the center of her universe."

"She died the day after I was released," Ed said. "Did she know?"

"Did she know you'd been released?" Chuck stalled. Would it serve any purpose to give the details of Tracy's last days other than to grieve him more? What if it caused the old man to change his mind about going to the police? He couldn't risk that.

"Your silence speaks volumes," Ed said softly. "They said I threatened her."

"Did you?"

"I'm sure I did, but I don't remember. Don't remember any of it, exactly. Sometimes I think it's the grace of God that keeps me from remembering." His voice trailed off, then he stood slowly and held out a hand. "Mr. Molinsky, thank you for your time. I'd best be going."

"Oh no," Chuck said, motioning for him to sit again. "Jack's on his way. You can't leave."

"I can't tell him anything." Ed remained standing, his eyes darting to the firm's front entrance as if he were afraid Jack might walk in any minute.

"You've tracked him halfway across the country. He's the whole reason you went into the mission that night. Why wouldn't you want to talk to him?"

"Don't know if I can explain it." Ed eased back into the chair. "Sometimes, forgiveness is a person, you know? If that person doesn't want anything to do with you . . . well then . . ."

"I understand. Believe me." All her life, Shannon proved that Bobbi forgave him, that God forgave him. She undermined that assurance when she took off. She'd be back though. She had to come home.

Chuck leaned forward, trying to bolster the old man. "The whole reason Jack and Brad were out on the street that night—they were looking for you. Brad figured out who you were, and they took out after you. Jack's coming from Columbia. He dropped everything to get here."

"Does he know?"

"Know what?"

"About the, uh . . . about what I did?"

"Yes."

"And he's still coming?" The old man pressed his lips together and shook his head slowly. "You know, he has Teresa's eyes," Ed said gently. "Looks like you, but he has his mother's eyes."

"He also has a very tender, gracious heart. You've got nothing to worry about."

Jack exited the highway and rehearsed for the thirty-seventh time what he would say to his grandfather. His grandfather. He wasn't crazy. His grandfather *was* in the mission that night. He wished he could tell Shannon. It wouldn't help things, but at least she'd know.

Of course the question remained, Where's he been all these months? And why'd he show up today all of a sudden? "Oh, come on," Jack muttered as the light turned red a block ahead of him. "I don't have time for this today. You can give me red lights all the way back, if I can just shoot straight to Dad's office. How 'bout that?" Of course the light didn't change. He rolled to a stop and tapped the steering wheel. "Fine. I'll just sit here."

Soon his mind wandered back to that night back in June. The handshake. Brad tearing out after Ed. He had to jog to keep up with

Brad's long strides. "This is wrong," Brad's last words, then the shot and that sound, that thud.

A quick toot from the car behind him brought Jack back to the present. "Yeah, okay. I'm going." What was he supposed to call the guy? Just Ed? That sounded wrong. Grandpa or something would never work for a stranger. Mr. Reynolds. He'd go with that, at least to start out.

What on earth had they talked about for the last two hours? His mother probably. Jack shook his head. He'd be bound forever to this man by a woman neither of them really knew. Funny how life works out sometimes.

He pulled into the lot at his dad's law firm and parked in one of the visitor spots. No other visitors. His heart caught for an instant. What if his grandfather got tired of waiting? What if he left? No way, Jack reassured himself. His grandfather was in there, and he was going to meet him face to face at last. He threw his Cardinals cap on the passenger seat and smoothed his hair. When he got out of the car, he stuffed his shirttail into his baggy jeans, then he took a deep breath and walked inside.

Even from across the lobby, he could see his dad smile when he walked in. His grandfather never moved. He flinched when Christine called his name.

"I'm so glad you made it here safely," she said. "Don't worry. It's all good. I promise."

"Thanks," he said, without breaking stride or moving his eyes from the man in his dad's office. He wiped his palm on his jeans, then opened the door to his dad's office. The old man snapped around when Jack stepped inside. "You *are* real. I didn't imagine you."

"You're not disappointed, are you?" He had a twinkle in his eyes that reminded Jack of his mother.

"Are you kidding? Ever since that night . . . and here you are in my dad's office . . ." Jack caught himself before he babbled any more. Fat lot of good it did to rehearse his speech on the drive here. Calm down. Act normal. He cleared his throat and stood up straighter. "You came looking for me. You obviously want something."

"I came to St. Louis to find my daughter. I was too late." He looked away.

"I'm sorry," Jack said. "That's a terrible way to find out."

"But I found out she had you. And I thought, well, I hoped . . ."

For forgiveness. Since his mother was gone, his grandfather needed his forgiveness. "You know, I loved my dad before I ever knew him, just because he was my dad. When I found out I had a dad and that he wanted me, that changed my life." His dad winked at him. "Mr. Reynolds, you're my granddad. I love you, too." Jack wanted to hug him, but the old man didn't seem open to that, so he awkwardly slid his hands into his jeans pockets.

"You understand what you're saying? You know what I did, don't you?"

"Yes sir, but this is the way I see it—my mother was a drunk and a prescription drug abuser, but I love her more than anybody understands. I'd give anything to tell her that again." He blinked several times to steel himself before continuing. Seeing his grandfather made him miss his mother more than he had in years.

"Not only that, but I have a sister who left home partly because she couldn't stand to be in the same house with me. Nothing would make me any happier than for her to come home. I love them both because of who they are, not because of anything they did. It's the same with you."

"That's, uh, that's Jesus' kind of love."

"I sure hope so." He motioned toward the office chairs. "You and my dad were the only people who knew my mom. You're the only connection I have to her now. I need to talk to you as much as you need to talk to me."

"Reckon so."

Jack dragged the other chair closer.

"I'm going to leave you alone," his father said as he pushed back from the desk and swiveled his chair around.

"Oh no, Dad. You need to help us both out. You can fill in the gaps."

"Let me at least call your mom, I mean, Bobbi, and let her know you got here safely." He slipped out, closing the door gently behind him.

His grandfather watched his dad for a moment. "You reckon he thinks that offends me? Calling his wife your mother?"

"Maybe."

The old man snapped his head around to face Jack. "I'm, uh, I'm used to mostly talking to myself. You startled me."

"Sorry. But my dad, he does a lot of negotiating so he's very aware of how things come across to other people."

His grandfather nodded toward the lobby where Jack's dad gestured as he talked on Christine's phone. "He teach you about Jesus?"

"Yeah, but my brother Brad was the one that made it all click for me."

"I saw that happen that night, you know? I saw it and I know who it was. I came here to tell him that."

"Are you serious? That'll blow it wide open!" All the details Jack didn't know or couldn't remember no longer mattered. "I can't tell you what this means to me," he said, trying hard not to cry.

"Bet I know." He allowed the corners of his mouth to lift in the slightest smile. "Tell me about your mother."

"Gosh, where do I start? She was beautiful. I know every little boy thinks his mommy is pretty, but she was beautiful." Jack reached in his back pocket and pulled out the only two pictures he had of her. "See? I wasn't kidding."

His grandfather held the pictures, poring over them, blinking ever more urgently, until he swallowed hard and handed them back. "Looks like her mother. Her mother was a beautiful woman, too."

Jack smiled at the photos once more before slipping them back into his wallet. "When I was little, like before I started school, she was home all the time. I don't know what we lived on, but it was great."

"She was a good mother?"

"She was the best."

"But she was a drunk . . . or worse."

"I don't think she was until the very, very end. And I only knew of her having one boyfriend."

Reynolds nodded toward the lobby again. "Him?"

"No. She loved my dad, but he was never her boyfriend. She started seeing a guy she worked with not long after we moved back here. His name was Colin something. I don't think they were serious."

For the next three hours, Jack wracked his brain trying to recall every birthday and Christmas, every trip to a zoo or a theme park, and every book his mother had ever read to him. They paused briefly to eat the sandwiches his dad had sent for, and then his grandfather told what few things he remembered.

Finally Ed Reynolds pulled himself to his feet. "I'd best get going this time. That other meeting, and all." He reached out a hand toward Jack. "You gave me a great gift just now. Seeing you, listening to you, it makes me feel like a curse has been lifted."

Jack shook the old man's hand and grinned. "I don't think I have that kind of power."

"Words have power. I did a lot of damage to your mother with words. Now you've given me renewed hope with yours." He reached across the desk and shook his dad's hand. "Mr. Molinsky, good day to you."

"But wait!" Jack stepped between his grandfather and the door. "Where are you staying? How am I supposed to get in touch with you again? What about Thanksgiving?"

"I know where to find you. Don't worry."

Jack watched him until he disappeared out of the building, then he dropped back in his chair. "I'm exhausted."

"I don't doubt it," his dad said.

"'The curse has lifted,' he said. God's working, Dad. That means Shannon'll be home soon."

"I think that's exactly what it means."

CHAPTER 20
APPOINTMENT

Thursday, November 27, Thanksgiving Day

Bobbi left Chuck asleep and stole downstairs before the day's first light. Today marked the first holiday since . . . well, her first without all her kids there. She blew out a deep breath. If she couldn't even form the words in her mind, how on earth would she get through the day? Plus, if she had any hope of making it through Christmas, she had to do Thanksgiving.

The first scent of coffee drifted from the kitchen as the automatic coffeemaker kicked on right on time. Rather than sit at the kitchen table and watch it drip, she wandered into the study to her favorite corner of the love seat.

Thanksgiving. Grateful heart. Maybe she could fake it for the day. Say all the right things. Smile with plastic joy. Everyone would marvel at her courage and her faith. Chuck would see right through her, though, and he would call her on it. And if he didn't, Rita would.

"Father, I'm going to confess to You right now, I'm having a very hard time being thankful. I know I have Chuck, and Jack and Joel, but it's hard for me not to focus on what I've lost. I don't want to slip back to where I was. I want to trust You. I want to lean on You. I want to hold onto the hope You give, but today it's harder for me to find it. Help me find what's true once more, rather than being controlled by what I feel."

What she felt right now, though, was a craving for that coffee that was surely finished brewing by now. As she passed the desk, she saw a note Chuck had scribbled after talking to Detective Ramirez.

Brad's killer was a twenty-four-year-old drug dealer and gang enforcer. His first arrest came at age thirteen after assaulting a police officer.

Even though Ed Reynolds gave them a description, a name and a license plate, the police hadn't made an arrest yet. The gunman, street smart and with friends in the neighborhood, had disappeared. They couldn't arrest him if they couldn't find him. The detective assured Chuck, in time, they would bring the guy in. A little more patience was all they asked for. As if she had a choice.

In the kitchen, Bobbi poured a cup of coffee and started to take her usual spot at the table, but two Bibles lay open, along with a couple of notebooks. She instantly recognized Jack's tight script. On closer inspection of the other notebook, she felt a quiver, deep in her spirit. Brad. His notebooks.

She set her coffee cup down and tenderly took Brad's notebook, closing it, afraid to allow her eyes to drift across his words. She eased into one of the kitchen chairs and closed the two Bibles, keeping the notebook close to her.

A night owl like Brad, Jack must have come back down to the kitchen to study after she and Chuck went to bed. Of course, now he'd have to find his place again since she had closed all the books. Was Jack struggling with Thanksgiving, too? Surely not. He was probably just reading. He probably read from Brad's notebook all the time. Just like he used to talk to Brad almost every day. Just like she used to.

She laid the notebook on the table in front of her, then reached for the reading glasses she kept in a case by the sugar bowl. "Talk to me, Brad," she whispered, and slowly opened the cover.

PSALM 19:12 WHO CAN UNDERSTAND HIS ERRORS? —
Will I, can I ever really understand how and why my heart and mind conspire in sinful presumptions? Is it as necessary as it seems to understand how and why?

CLEANSE ME FROM SECRET FAULTS — *from the faults I'm unwilling to admit even to myself. To be cleansed, they must be recognized, identified, brought out into the light.*

KEEP [ME] FROM PRESUMPTUOUS SINS – *I'm learning that these are some of my favorites. These are the ideas that I have rights and entitlements from God, that He is obligated, owes me things.*

LET THEM NOT HAVE DOMINION OVER ME — *When I am more focused on myself, how I've been treated/accepted then I get off track.*

BLAMELESS AND INNOCENT OF GREAT TRANSGRESSION — *I want to be but I'm not yet to the point that I am unselfish enough, that I am sold out to that. I want it but I'm not yet willing to do the hard work required to achieve it.*

THE MEDITATION OF MY HEART/ BE ACCEPTABLE — *Even the things I brood over should honor God and not seek to displace Him as Lord.*

She could almost hear Brad in all his frustration, castigating himself this way. He had such high standards and expectations for himself. She had trouble remembering he had any faults, let alone imagining he harbored secret, presumptuous sins.

PSALM 25

*16   Turn Yourself to me, and have mercy on me, for I
am desolate and afflicted.*

*17   The troubles of my heart have enlarged; bring me
out of my distresses!*

*18   Look on my affliction and my pain, and forgive
all my sins.*

*Whether or not the sins are the root cause of all the
pain, it seems that distress at least brings on sin. Sins
of wrong thinking about God. Sins of ascribing
improper, unloving motives to His actions. Sins of
demanding explanations or fixes for the situation.
Instead, it should be a time of examination and
confession, if for no other reason than to break down
the barrier to comfort.*

Bobbi wiped away a tear. How could her son have this insight tailored to her life, her current struggles, including, ironically, getting over his death? God was answering her prayer already, drawing her to the truth that Brad had discovered, comforting her with a mother's mixture of pride and longing. She had to keep reading.

Her little boy, the one with the tousled hair and crooked grin, matured into this astute yet compassionate theologian, and she never appreciated that until now. Until the time she needed it most. She drank in Brad's wisdom one page at a time, oblivious to time, to hunger, to routine, to the rapidly cooling coffee.

Halfway through the book, she came to an entry on Habakkuk chapter 3.

Habakkuk 3:17–19 says "Though the fig tree may not blossom,

> *Nor fruit be on the vines;*
> *Though the labor of the olive may fail,*
> *And the fields yield no food;*
> *Though the flock may be cut off from the fold,*
> *And there be no herd in the stalls—*
> 18 *Yet I will rejoice in the LORD,*
> *I will joy in the God of my salvation.*
> 19 *The LORD God is my strength;*
> *He will make my feet like deer's feet,*
> *And He will make me walk on my high hills.*

Paraphrase: Even though I have nothing now, no hope for tomorrow and no prospect that anything is ever going to change for the better, I WILL CHOOSE to rejoice in God, my God, my salvation. He is my strength and He enables me to walk through these fires with confidence, like it was my natural habitat. I WILL CHOOSE.

Bobbi laid the notebook down on the table and slid off her glasses. "Oh, Brad," she said softly. Did he ever hit the nail on the head with this one. No hope, no prospect for change. Shannon wasn't coming home. And Bobbi also fully expected to be in that minority that succumbed to breast cancer. No fruit on the vines. Rita had seven grandchildren, while she had one by adoption. Even though she dismissed it when Chuck talked about a curse, she wondered herself from time to time if God was cutting off her family line.

She had to choose. Until now, she'd been reacting, then failing miserably. *This is where I am, dear God. I don't see how anything is going to change, how it's going to improve. I can't get moving, or think about the future, because it still seems pointless. I'm going to need Your help choosing to rejoice in You.*

She winced as soon as the tepid coffee hit her lips. Thankfully, her morning pot was good for two cups. She freshened her coffee and leaned against the sink, processing as she sipped. Rita told her the issue was control—she wanted control, especially over her own life and death. She returned to the table and glanced back through the Scripture Brad copied.

Only one of us can be the strength. Either me or God.

Knowing what the "right" answer was wouldn't make it easier to carry through, however. She knew Chuck was struggling with the very same thing. Choosing wasn't about control, though. It was about trust. Again.

When she and Chuck were separated, she felt like God was trying to teach her to trust Him implicitly, before the answers came. The answers did come, along with reconciliation with her husband.

Laurie Dillard suggested that being unable to say good-bye left things unresolved. Bobbi leaned back in her chair, her mind drifting to the waiting room at University Hospital, to the day her mother died. Soon those images were replaced with the ER, and then with Shannon's empty bedroom. Tears formed in Bobbi's eyes, but not from grief. They were angry tears. What she had vented at Brad's gravesite just scratched the surface. Dr. Craig told her years ago that often depression is anger stuffed deep inside, and that she was particularly susceptible to it. She let it get her again.

Dear God, anger and joy can't exist in the same heart. It hurt so much when my mama died. It seemed so senseless and unfair. It made me mad. I felt the same way when Brad died. I kept thinking You couldn't hurt me that way and still love me. I know better. Father, forgive me for harboring this anger. I don't want it anymore. I want to feel what I know, that You do love me, that You will get me through this.

When she raised her head, she saw Chuck standing in the kitchen doorway. "You okay?" he asked.

"I'm much improved." She wiped her eyes and motioned for him to join her at the table.

"I expected to find you in the study." He sat down beside her and took her hand in his.

"I was headed that way, but God had the answers in here." She slid the notebook to him. "Read some of this."

He adjusted his glasses and tilted his head the way he had done since he got bifocals. He quickly read through the first two pages. "This is Brad?"

"He's brilliant, isn't he?"

"He gets that from you." Chuck smiled and flipped through a few more pages. "Did you read this whole thing?"

"Not quite." She pulled the notebook closer and leafed through the pages. "Here, read the one about Habakkuk."

His eyes began to tear up. "This is just what you needed, isn't it?"

"And to hear it from Brad, that was . . ."

"Perfect."

She nodded and wiped away another tear.

He squeezed her hand gently. "You know, I was worried about you getting through today."

"I'm not through it yet, but I think I can do it. I mean, not me. God will walk me through it." She patted the notebook lying on the table in front of Chuck. "Brad told me how."

A few minutes after eleven, Bobbi stood washing up the mixing bowls while she waited on the sweet potato casserole and a pecan pie to finish baking. With Chuck stepping in and helping out, they might actually make it to Rita's on time for a noon meal.

Still pondering what she'd read from Brad's notebook, she jumped when the telephone rang. She cradled the phone on her shoulder and dried her hands. "Hello?"

"Mom, I wanted to check on you," Joel said. "Since this is the first holiday . . . Well . . . I'm not sure we should leave you today. Aunt Rita said we didn't even have to call her if we decided to stay. You just say the word."

"Thank you. I had my own doubts about today, but I took some time this morning, just me and God. Dad and I talked. I think I'll be okay."

"You're pretty amazing."

"Hardly. Listen, sweetheart, if you've got a few minutes tomorrow or Saturday, I'd like to talk to you."

"I can stop by tomorrow after work."

"Perfect," Bobbi said. "You guys enjoy your Thanksgiving. Maybe Abby's parents are coming around finally."

"I'm not sure we're ready for that miracle. Love you, Mom."

"Love you, too, and give my love to Abby and Ryan." As she hung up the phone, Chuck came in from the family room.

"It smells ready," he said. "How much longer?"

Bobbi checked the oven timer. "Ummm, four minutes. That was Joel. I think he was looking for an excuse not to go to Greenways for Thanksgiving."

"I don't blame him. What did you tell him?"

"I told him to go. They might not invite again."

"They might not, anyway." Chuck leaned down to look in the oven. "Your pie looks perfect."

"If you want to hang around and take it out when it's finished, I'll go touch up my makeup. That way we might actually get out of here on schedule."

"Sure thing," Chuck said, but before she could get out of the room, he called her name. "You'd . . . you'd tell me if you were having trouble today, wouldn't you?"

"I'm doing okay. I think I can handle it."

"That's not what I asked."

"Then what is it?"

"You're not going to lie to me, are you?"

"Good grief, Chuck—"

"Bobbi, I hope you're absolutely right. I hope today marks a huge step in healing for you, but considering where we've been these last few months—"

"You don't have to worry."

"Wrong." He crossed the kitchen and took her hand. "Regardless of what happens, how you cope or don't cope, I don't want you to act or pretend."

"I won't."

"Promise me."

"I promise."

Rita rushed to the front door as soon as she heard the car pull up in front of the house. "They're here!" she called to no one in particular. In a last-minute phone call, she tried to persuade Joel to come to dinner, but he seemed convinced his mother would be fine without him. What if she wasn't? Then what?

She swung the front door open. "Hey, you're right on time!" She leaned over to hug her sister tightly. "You look good."

"I feel good," Bobbi said.

Rita hugged Chuck and Jack. "You guys can take the dishes to the kitchen. Gavin and John are in watching some football game, and the girls are on the computer in the den."

"John?" Bobbi's eyebrows arched in surprise.

"John." Rita nodded. "Kara asked me last week what I thought about him coming. Apparently, they've been talking, have had dinner once or twice."

"Are you serious? That's wonderful."

"We're trying to be very reserved. Not let on how thrilled Gavin and I would be if they got back together."

"You? Hiding your feelings?"

"Don't laugh," Rita said. "Miracles happen every day."

She led Bobbi back to the kitchen where Kara was pouring drinks.

"Hey, you made it!" She set the pitcher of tea down and hugged Bobbi.

"On time, even," Bobbi said. "I'm glad John is here."

"It feels right," Kara said. "We'll see what happens."

"Kelly's at Patrick's folks, right?" Bobbi asked.

"Yes, but they'll be here for Christmas," Rita answered as she searched through the silverware drawer for serving spoons. "Danny's even trying to wrangle a few days off. I could have all three of my kids here for Christmas." She smiled broadly until she turned and looked into Bobbi's eyes. "I am so sorry," she said quietly. "That was a stupid, insensitive thing to say."

"It's okay," Bobbi said. "You didn't mean anything by it, and you should be happy to have your kids home."

"But you—"

"Let it go. Please." She picked up her casserole dish and carried it into the dining room.

As soon as she was safely out of the room, Rita turned to Kara. "Will you just smack me the next time I open my mouth?"

"I'm not the one to help you with your mouth," Kara said. "Talk to Dad. He never says the wrong thing."

"I know. It's unnatural."

She and Kara carried the rest of the food to the dining room and called everyone to the table. Heatleys, Molinskys and Isaacs joined hands and Gavin asked a blessing. Rita squeezed his hand tightly when he mentioned those who weren't there, but Bobbi's whispered "yes" reassured her.

Throughout the meal, she stole glances at Bobbi, watching for cracks in her carefully maintained front, but she smiled readily and the long-absent light had returned to her eyes. John and Kara's daughters, obviously thrilled to celebrate the day with both parents, barely let anyone else talk.

Before dessert was served, Chuck leaned over and took Bobbi's hand. She winked at him and mouthed the words, *I'm okay.* Maybe she was.

When Bobbi finished her pie and coffee, Gavin pushed away from the table. "Chuck and I will clean up."

"Gavin, you never pack the leftovers the way I want them done." Rita stood and began stacking dessert plates.

He took her by the arm and looked over his glasses at her. "If you set foot in that kitchen before tomorrow morning . . ."

"What? What are you gonna do?"

"You don't want to find out." He grinned and took the stack of plates from her.

"Can I at least get a fresh cup of coffee?"

"I'll bring it to you. Bobbi?"

"Always. Did the kids leave?"

"They were going to rent a movie. They should be back in a few minutes."

A moment later Gavin returned from the kitchen and refilled their coffee cups. "Let's go sit in the real living room," Rita said. "I never sit in my own living room."

Rita led the way into the front room and switched on the lamp. "Besides, I think Kara and John are in the family room." She took a seat in the corner of the sofa and waited for Bobbi to sit opposite her. "Can I apologize again?"

"There's no need," Bobbi said. "I, on the other hand, need to apologize to you."

"For what?" Rita set her coffee cup down on a coaster.

"Joel told me weeks ago that in order to heal I had to face the pain that I felt and the pain that I've caused." Rita shook her head, so

Bobbi raised her hand. "Let me finish. I've hurt you deeply, and I won't believe you if you deny it." Bobbi smiled gently, then grew serious as she looked Rita in the eye. "I've caused you to lose sleep, to worry and to grieve. I'm sorry, and I'm asking for your forgiveness."

Rita wiped a tear away and moved down the sofa so she could hug her sister. Bobbi was back.

Chuck sat on the edge of the bed, watching Bobbi go through her nightly rituals, still marveling at the way she glided through the day. All he hoped for was a day free of that heavy mantle of grief. Instead, she came alive with a vibrancy he hadn't seen from her in years. If only he could keep the day from ending.

Bobbi kissed his cheek as she passed and pulled down the covers on her side of the bed. "Kara and John seemed to enjoy each other today," she said.

"I was too busy watching you to notice." He nearly melted when she blushed and smiled at him.

"God does good work. It wasn't me." She slid down under the covers and Chuck climbed into bed with her. "You busy tomorrow?" she asked.

And now the bubble would burst. "I, uh . . ." He cleared his throat, stalling, and she raised an eyebrow. He coughed one more time, hoping that would make it more believable. "I figured Jack and I would hang the lights outside."

"So everything is ready for Shannon to come home?"

"Is that okay?"

"It's perfect," she said. "I've got some errands to run in the morning. Could we get a late lunch? Just me and you?"

"Seriously?"

"Seriously."

"I'd leave Jack hanging off the edge of the roof to have lunch with you—late or otherwise."

"Great! Good night." She leaned over to kiss him. "I do love you. You know that, don't you?"

"I never doubted that."

"Never?"

He shook his head. "I wondered if you'd ever be able to tell me again."

"I'm gonna try to make that up to you."

"You already have."

"No, trust me on this."

Friday, November 28

With the wreaths hung and the shrubs decorated, Jack steadied the ladder while Chuck draped the lights across his shoulder. "Want me to do that?" Jack asked.

"What? Climb the ladder? I got it."

"Does Mom know?"

"Of course she knows."

"That you're getting on the ladder?"

"I'll be done before she gets back."

"That's what I thought." Jack grinned, then reset his feet, and Chuck started climbing. Before he got the first strand of lights hung,

Bobbi pulled in the driveway. "This is late?" he called to her once she got out of her car.

"This is Jack on the roof?" She crossed her arms across her chest and tilted her head the same way she did when she caught the kids in something.

"I'll just finish this up." Chuck slipped the lights over the hooks and climbed down the ladder. "Do I need to change clothes?"

"Good grief, no. Jack, are you set for lunch?"

"There's leftovers and pie. I'm good."

"It's like having Joel home again," Bobbi said, teasing him. "I'm not sure how long we'll be."

"I think I can trust you guys," Jack said, easing the ladder away from the porch roof. Chuck took one end to help him carry it back to the garage. "Dad, I got it. Go."

"I'm driving," Bobbi said, getting back into her car.

"You sound like a woman on a mission," Chuck said when he got in the car.

"I am." She backed out of the driveway, then honked and waved at Jack before driving away. "Looks like you got a lot done on the lights."

"They all worked first try. That sped things up." He watched Bobbi get her sunglasses from the visor case and slip them on. "Can I ask you something?"

"Sure."

"Is this for real?"

"Is what for real?"

"You."

"I really caused some deep scars, didn't I?" At the next red light, she raised her sunglasses. "I promise I'm not acting, Chuck. I feel good. Better than I have in months."

"Brad's notebook did that?"

"It was the catalyst. Things seemed to click for me yesterday."

Especially after yesterday he wanted to believe her. He wanted to accept that everything was back to the way it should be, but he needed more proof, so he risked a question. "What about Shannon?"

Bobbi sighed deeply, and he tensed, fearing he'd blown it. "I don't know yet," she said. "For the longest time I convinced myself she wasn't coming home, that she was gone for good."

"Why would you think that?"

"General hopelessness, I guess."

"But now you think she's coming home?"

"I said I don't know yet. My answers seem to be coming gradually, in stages. I'll get back to you." She glanced over at him and smiled.

"So, where are we going?"

"To lunch."

"Where? This is the road out to the lake. There aren't any restaurants on this road."

She looked over the rim of her sunglasses at him. "Sometimes you need to sit back and enjoy the ride and stop trying to figure everything out."

"But why are you going to the lake?"

"Chuck! Stop! Just ride."

He dutifully spent the rest of the drive to Dixson Lake silently watching his wife. When she pulled onto the boat ramp and turned off the car, he asked, "So do we get out?"

"I think so." She got out and rounded the car to him. She took both his hands in hers, her eyes brimming. "I want to apologize to you. I've made your burdens so much heavier. I am so sorry. Can you forgive me?"

"Of course," he said. "You brought me all the way out here for that?"

"No, I brought you out here for this." She pulled a small envelope from her coat pocket and handed it to him.

"What's this?"

"Open it, silly."

He ripped the end off the envelope and removed a business card. "Oncology Associates, Dr. Stephen Kremer." Flipping the card over, he continued reading, "Wednesday, December third, ten thirty a.m."

CHAPTER 21
CONNECTION

Just before three o'clock, with the Colorado-Nebraska game at halftime, Jack wandered into the kitchen for a second piece of pie. If Colorado could hold on to their lead, that would move Missouri one step closer to the Big 12 championship game next weekend. He poured a glass of milk for himself and put his slice of pie in the microwave. Aunt Rita had gone traditional on them this Thanksgiving, baking a pumpkin pie instead of the usual fruit pie.

As he pulled the warm pie from the microwave, he heard the front door open. "I'm in the kitchen!" he called. When his parents walked in, he teasingly scolded, "Now when I said I could trust you guys, that didn't mean I expected you to take advantage of me. It doesn't take three hours to eat lunch."

His mother smiled at his dad. "He sounds just like you."

Jack grinned. "Dad, Colorado is up at the half. We're still in."

"What about Oklahoma?" he asked.

"Killing State. Two touchdowns so far."

"Excellent. Did you finish the pie?"

"Not yet. Here." He handed Chuck the warm piece of pie and got a plate from the cabinet. "You didn't get dessert with your two-hour lunch?"

"Why would I buy dessert when Rita's pie is here?" He took a large bite.

"Chuck, why don't you go get a good seat on the sofa for the game." His mother pointed his dad toward the family room.

"Huh? Oh, right." His dad shuffled toward the door, taking another bite of pie on his way out.

His mother opened the refrigerator and got the last piece of pie out and slid it onto Jack's plate. "I promise I won't keep you from your game," she said, "but I need to talk to you for a second."

"You're going to the doctor, aren't you?"

"How'd you know?"

"The look on Dad's face when he came in. He looked like he'd won the lottery, and since Shannon wasn't with you, you going to the doctor was the only other thing I could think of that would make him that happy."

"You're pretty sharp." She smiled, the weariness finally gone from her eyes. "I have an appointment Wednesday morning. That's not all I wanted to say. Jack, I want to apologize to you."

"Why?"

"I hurt you deeply, and I haven't been much of a parent lately. I've been so self-absorbed that I haven't been there for you. I'm sorry."

He smiled gently and hugged her. "Thanks. That takes a lot of guts, apologizing to your kids."

"Dad and I have lots of practice apologizing over the years, and not just to our kids."

"Well, I think you and Dad are just about the two most incredible people I know."

"I love you." She kissed his cheek, then hugged him again. "I couldn't have done this without my boys."

"How's that?"

"You and Joel both had the guts to tell me the tough things I needed to hear, and Brad's notebook . . ." She looked away and swallowed hard. "Brad's notebook had some insight I needed."

"Isn't it funny? You and Dad taught us all that stuff growing up. Now you're getting it back when you need it."

"God's wonderful that way. Now, go watch your game."

"It's worth a million bucks to see you smile again." He winked at her, then picked up his piece of pie and headed to the family room.

As Bobbi watched him walk away, her mind drifted back to her own irrational fears about Jack, fears that he would be a wedge between Chuck and her, that he had his mother's unbalanced vindictiveness, that he would be a tormenter to Shannon. Instead, God gave them a gentle, thoughtful, fiercely loyal young man. Amazing.

She glanced at the clock on the microwave. Plenty of time before Joel stopped by. She walked back out to her car and retrieved a small shopping bag from her trunk. She carried it upstairs to her bedroom, and sitting on the edge of the bed, she pulled a devotional book from the bag, *Great Is Thy Faithfulness*, the very book she'd been reading from when Brad was killed. She carefully turned to the last page she'd read, slipped the receipt in for a bookmark, and laid the book on her nightstand.

Bobbi sat at the kitchen table paging through the stack of Black Friday ads from the morning paper. A few things caught her eye as possibilities for Jack or Shannon. She whispered a prayer of thanks for that small miracle. Two days ago, the thought of Christmas was more than she could manage.

"What's the score?" Joel called as he stepped through the kitchen doorway.

"Twenty-one to seventeen," Jack called back. "But Nebraska has the ball."

"I didn't hear you come in," Bobbi said, pushing back from the table.

"Don't get up." Joel hung his jacket on one of the kitchen chairs and leaned down to hug her. "But before football," he said, taking the chair next to hers, "you were going to tell me how wonderful you feel."

"Is it that obvious?"

"You were one hundred and eighty degrees different on the phone yesterday. The house even feels different today."

"Let me pour us some coffee and you can tell me what else I'm going to say to you," Bobbi said, teasing him. "How was Thanksgiving?"

"It was good, actually. Rob didn't say anything snide, and Angela was very gracious."

"Was Abby's brother there?"

"Perfect Josh? Of course. And perfect Amber with perfect little Zachary."

"You sound snide now." She set a cup in front of him and rejoined him at the table.

"I just get frustrated with them. Home should be the place where you can count on unconditional love. With Abby, it's the only place she doesn't get it. I hate it for her."

"Do you think Shannon's afraid we'll judge her somehow? Is that why she's staying away?"

"You tell me," Joel said, taking a long drink from the coffee.

"What are you talking about?"

"You know better than anyone what's going on with Shannon. You've been the prodigal, Mom."

"What?"

"You walked away from God because He hurt you. You refused to have anything to do with Him for weeks, but then something brought you back."

Bobbi leaned back in her chair. "Joel, how do you know these things?"

"It's not any special insight. Basically, I don't think before I speak." He smiled broadly. "So when is your doctor's appointment?"

Bobbi rolled her eyes at him. "At least I could surprise Dad. It's Wednesday."

"Still with Dr. Kremer? He's the best."

"Yes, that's who Dr. Karsten recommended." She took a sip from her coffee. "Listen Joel, I want to ask for your forgiveness."

"What on earth for?"

"I've been difficult these last few months. I've caused you a lot of grief, and I'm sorry."

"If it makes you feel better to apologize, then I accept, but you didn't have to. I understand."

"You played a big part in snapping me out of this, you know. You weren't afraid to be brutally honest with me and with Dad. We needed that. I don't think either of us was thinking especially clearly."

"Yeah, it's tough being the only sane one in the family."

"Hey, I'm sane!" Jack carried his pie plate in and put it in the dishwasher. "Nebraska scored. Now they're up twenty-four to twenty-one."

Joel grimaced. "This is nerve-wracking."

"You should go watch the game," Bobbi said.

"I'm recording it. I can watch it when I get home, provided Jack doesn't blow the ending for me."

"Sorry," Jack said, and disappeared back into the family room.

"So what are your plans for Christmas?" Joel asked.

"I have no idea," Bobbi answered. "I hadn't thought much past this week."

"Great! You can come to our house then."

"Are you sure Abby wants us?"

"It was her idea. She wants to do it for you, you know, to take some of the pressure off."

"I'm good now. I can do Christmas."

"Mom, let Abby do this for you."

"All right. Christmas is at your house."

Bobbi shook her head as she watched Chuck back out of the driveway. Incorrigible. She specifically, explicitly stated she did not want anything for Christmas, and yet as soon as they finished off the Thanksgiving leftovers, Chuck announced he and Jack were headed to the Galleria.

She settled in the corner of the family room sofa and clicked through the channels on the muted television. The shows couldn't steal her attention away from Joel's comments. Did she know Shannon better than anyone?

Was she as hardheaded as Shannon seemed to be? That unreasonable? Probably. Dying from cancer had made perfect sense to her, but it was completely insane. Whatever Shannon was doing must make perfect sense to her.

She closed her eyes. What else? What else might by cycling through Shannon's mind? Probably the same kinds of things that dragged through her own mind during the last few months.

No options. *Shannon must feel like she has no other options when, in fact, options are everywhere.* She also likely believed no one understood what she felt, that her hurt was worse, or at least different, than everyone else's.

But something brought you back, Joel said. Not something. Someone. More than one, actually. Did Shannon have anyone to challenge her? If not, what would bring Shannon home? In the Biblical story the prodigal son came home after he came to his senses, "came to himself."

It had to be her decision, though. No one would be able to convince Shannon to come home, just like no one could convince her to change her mind and go to the doctor. Not until she couldn't fight anymore. Not until she was ready to let go of her anger and her shame. Not a moment before.

Dear God, did You worry about me like this? At least You knew where I was, and You knew I'd come back. I know You want me to trust You, rejoice in You in spite of everything, but could You just let me know she's okay? Can I ask for that much grace?

Shannon Molinsky sat in the food court at the Galleria staring at the stream of people passing by without really focusing on any of them. Thankful to have someplace to go besides her cold, empty apartment, she wondered how many more days she could hang out here before mall security started checking up on her.

Her Thanksgiving celebration consisted of splurging on dinner at Denny's, if slinking into the restaurant alone to grab a carry-out dinner that she had to keep her coat on to eat could be called splurging. Hardly. Not when everybody else was at Aunt Rita's. She was tempted . . . so tempted to just show up yesterday, but . . . she didn't have answers to the questions they'd ask. Why'd you leave? Why'd you stay away so long? What were you trying to prove? Those answers, so clear-cut back in July, were a tangled November mess.

Plus she had her own questions. Could she go home? Could she face her dad? Would her mother forgive her for what she'd done? And Jack . . . would Jack ever speak to her again? Was there any real reason to stay away, or had she simply backed herself into a corner that she couldn't get out of?

She finished off the cappuccino, her last splurge, her last spare cash for the month, and took a notepad and ink pen from her purse. She wrote down headings for two columns, *Stay away* and *Go home.*

"Stay away, that's easy." She quickly wrote, *Don't have to face Mom, Dad, Jack, or anyone else.* Then her pen hung in midstroke. There was no second reason. Surely there was more to it than that.

As she stared out across the rush of people, the crowd seemed to part. That old brown leather jacket . . . It couldn't be . . . It was! Her dad and Jack were headed her way. Panicked, she grabbed her purse and knifed through the food court into the nearest store. They stopped at the counter at Subway. While their backs were turned, she slipped out of the store and hurried to the nearest exit.

She ran to her car, then collapsed against it. Her breath came in great gasps until her heart rate slowed down and her hands stopped shaking. She glanced back at the mall entrance and burst into tears. *Why did I run? Dad . . . He would've said, "Shannon, thank God you're okay! Let's go home." I am so stupid.*

She pulled her coat tight around her and wiped her eyes with the heel of her hand. Then she remembered the list. She left her list on the table. What if her dad found it? She hadn't listed any reasons to go home yet. What would he think?

Get a grip. There's a very slim chance they would find the list. Even if they did, who's to say they'd read it, and then figure out it was mine? She unlocked the driver's side door, and with another lingering look at the mall entrance, she toyed with the idea of going back inside. Not . . . yet.

"Let's grab a seat for a minute and rethink this," Chuck said, handing Jack a Coke and a package of cookies. "All the ideas I had for your mother are a bust. I need some inspiration."

"And I need cookies." Jack dropped into a chair at a nearby empty table. "Oh, hey, somebody left their shopping list or something." He set his Coke and cookies down and picked up the slip of paper. He glanced at it, then handed it over. "Dad," he said weakly, "read this."

"What—" He recognized the handwriting immediately. Shannon.

"You think that's really—"

"It's hers," Chuck said. "The question is, how long ago."

"It couldn't be more than a few hours. With the mall this busy, they'd have to clean the tables constantly."

"Come on." Chuck grabbed his drink and hurried off.

"Lost and found?" Jack asked when he closed the distance between them.

"I'm going to have her paged. Maybe she's still here somewhere." He cut through the crowd until he arrived at the information desk. He didn't have time to wait for the lady at the desk to look up. "Hi, I need your help. My son and I found some personal papers at the food court that belong to my daughter. Could you page her for me?"

"What's her name?" the lady asked, pen poised to write.

"Shannon Molinsky."

Chuck strained his eyes, looking down each concourse leading to the information desk. His heart fluttered every time he saw a young girl with long dark hair, but for thirty minutes, he and Jack watched and waited in vain.

"Do you want to leave the papers here?" the lady at the desk asked gently.

"No, I'll see her soon enough," Chuck said. "I just thought if she was still here, that would simplify things. Thanks for trying."

The lady nodded, and Chuck walked away, headed toward the entrance where his car was parked. "Dad, I'm sorry," Jack said just before they stepped outside.

"It's not all bad, Jack. We know she's here in town, and we know that she's thinking about coming home."

"Bobbi!" Chuck called even before he got the front door open. "Bobbi, where are you?"

"Back here," Bobbi called from the family room. "What's wrong?"

"Nothing." He strode back through the house, leaving Jack to lock the car and shut the front door. He met Bobbi in the kitchen, her face pale with worry. He grinned and put Shannon's slip of paper in her hand. "Here, read this."

"What is it?" Bobbi turned the paper around and immediately her eyes brimmed with tears. "Where did you get this?" she whispered.

"It was on a table in the food court at the Galleria. I had Shannon paged, but she either wasn't there any longer or she wouldn't answer the page. Do you know what this means?"

"That she can't think of a reason to come home?"

"It means she *is* still in St. Louis somewhere, and she's thinking about coming home. She's just about had enough."

Bobbi blinked but said nothing. She wasn't buying it.

"Honey, think about it. If Shannon was living some great exciting life, she wouldn't be trying to reason out whether she should come home. Plus, if she was surrounded by friends, she wouldn't be making lists like this at the mall."

"How do you know she wrote it at the mall?"

"The pen was still there."

"Why would she leave her pen?" Bobbi studied the note again, then her eyes widened. "Chuck, you don't think she saw you, do you? Maybe that's why she left everything. She saw you and she didn't want you to find her."

"Oh, Bobbi, if I was that close . . ."

"Mom! Can you believe it? She was there!" Jack bounded into the kitchen. "It won't be long now!"

She held the paper like it was a rare treasure. "This is an answer to prayer. I asked God just this evening to let me know she was okay, and He did." She wiped a tear away.

Chuck took her in his arms and kissed her forehead. "He's going to answer all those other prayers, too. Soon."

Wednesday, December 3

Chuck reached for Bobbi's hand at the first red light on the way to Dr. Kremer's office. "Your hands are freezing cold."

"Nerves."

"About what he's going to tell you? Surgery, maybe?"

"No, it's what I have to tell him."

"Honey, you don't owe him any explanations. It's none of his business why you cancelled your appointment."

"Appointments," she said. "But it's not about him. It's about me. I have to face it all." She turned and looked out her window, and spoke more softly. "Besides, Shannon . . . I don't want Shannon to make it home and find out I didn't have the courage to tell my doctor the truth. Not when she . . . I know what she has to face in order to come home, and I don't want to be a poor example."

"Impossible." He kissed the back of her hand. "You're my hero."

She glanced at him with a half smile, her face flushed. "I think you could do better, but thank you all the same."

When they arrived at Oncology Associates, Dr. Stephen Kremer welcomed them with a handshake and showed them into his private office. St. Louis Cardinals memorabilia filled the small space. Chuck leaned close to Bobbi and whispered, "I like him already."

Bobbi shook her head as she settled in one of the chairs.

Dr. Kremer took his seat behind the desk and folded his hands. "You disappeared on me, Mrs. Molinsky."

She dropped her eyes, and Chuck laid his hand on hers, hoping to bolster her. "I did, and I'm sorry." She raised her head and spoke with such dignity. "I lost my son this summer. He was murdered not far from the mission he ran downtown. Then a few weeks later my daughter left home under less than ideal circumstances and we haven't heard from her since."

Chuck squeezed her hand, and his own throat tightened as she continued.

"This diagnosis was more than I could deal with, quite frankly, and for a while, dying didn't sound like such a bad idea."

"Mrs. Molinsky—"

Bobbi raised her free hand to cut the doctor off and caught Chuck's eye with the slightest smile. "I'm okay now. I'm ready for this fight." She took a deep breath. "So what am I in for?"

"You always have options, of course, but I'm going to give you my recommendation. I want you to go for another mammogram just to make sure nothing has changed significantly, then we'll do surgery, take what we have to, but nothing more, and follow that up with radiation. In most cases, that takes care of breast cancer for ten or twenty years."

"Which at my age is a pretty good prognosis."

"Yes, ma'am."

"What's your timetable on this?" Chuck asked.

Dr. Kremer pulled his desk calendar closer. "Let's say two weeks, the seventeenth."

"That soon?"

"There's no reason to wait, really." He turned and addressed Bobbi again. "That will give us time to get the mammogram done. You'll be in good shape for Christmas, then we can start the radiation on the second of January."

"How long does that last?" Bobbi asked.

"Six weeks," Dr. Kremer said, almost apologizing. "It's very effective, though."

She counted on her fingers. "So that takes us through mid-February."

"All better by your birthday," Chuck said. "We can throw a big party."

Bobbi frowned at him, then she sighed. "All right, put me on your schedule."

Shannon settled into a booth at a burger place not far from her apartment, courtesy of holiday overtime pay and a coupon. Eating out at a restaurant, especially a fast food one, used to be so ordinary, no planning and no triple-checking the finances.

With her back to the door, she kept a close eye on the reflections in the restaurant's plate glass windows. It would be insane if her dad walked in here, but after the near-miss at the Galleria, she vowed to stay on her toes.

Before she could get the second bite of her cheeseburger down, Dylan Snider ambled through the door. A wave of nausea rolled over her, followed by the heat of shame and anger. As desperately as she wanted to go throw up, she didn't dare move. Nothing was worth the risk of being spotted.

Too late.

"Shannon? I almost didn't recognize you."

"Dylan, I don't have anything to say to you." She started wrapping her cheeseburger up and preparing her escape.

He slid into the booth across from her. A new tattoo peeked over the neckband of his shirt and he wore a heavy gold chain. "After I helped you out, came to your rescue? I'm hurt."

"You used me, took advantage of me—"

"Sweetheart, you used me."

"I used you?" She rolled her eyes in disbelieving disgust.

"Absolutely. After you got what you wanted, got set up in your own place, I never heard from you again. You know, I thought you genuinely liked me. That's what you said after we went out."

"That was before you—"

"You could have said no. You could have stopped it. I didn't do anything you didn't want, so let's just drop this and start the conversation over." Shannon clenched her jaw and glared at him. "There, now how are you? Still got your own place?"

"Yeah, living the high life," Shannon muttered.

"You know, your dad is totally furious at you."

"How do you know?"

"He came to my house. After what you did to your mother, he couldn't wait to get a hold of you."

"Are you serious?" No one could deny how protective her dad was, especially when it came to her mother.

"Oh yeah, he was yelling, all red-faced. He even grabbed me by the shirt and slammed me up against the house 'cause I wouldn't tell him where you were."

During those days before she left, he was close to that kind of anger. It wasn't much of a stretch to imagine him losing it. "I'm sure he's calmed down by now."

"I don't know. I think they got rid of your car and everything. It's like you're erased."

"That's crazy."

"Maybe, but ole Jack's moving into the law firm, you know, like he's primed to take over."

"Jack's going to seminary."

"He's already working at the firm, Shannon."

Dylan had to be wrong. Her only hope, her only way out of this mess was if her family would take her back unconditionally. If they really had disowned her, her list of options just became frighteningly short. She reached in her purse for her cell phone. It had a few emergency minutes left on it. A text message would only cost a few pennies to send and would only use a few seconds. "Excuse me a second," she mumbled as she quickly punched in a message to Katelyn, asking if Jack was working at Benton, Davis & Molinsky.

"That's not one of those pay-by-the-minute phones, is it?" Dylan asked.

"So?"

"Why didn't you say you needed cash?" He reached for his wallet.

"Because I don't. I don't need your money."

Ignoring her, he took out a stack of bills, folded them and slid them across the table to her. "Please, I'd feel better if you'd let me help you out."

"You were just griping that I'd taken advantage of you, and now you're wanting to give me money? You don't make any sense."

"Neither do you, telling me how great your life is when I know better. I bet this is the first meal out you've had in weeks."

"I'm busy," Shannon said softly. "I work a lot of overtime."

"Just what I thought. You can use this, can't you?"

She'd rather die than admit that to him, but the prospect of a month with full heat was extremely appealing. She picked up the cash and stuffed it in her purse.

"I'm just sorry you had to wait this long. I mean, your dad sure isn't breaking a sweat to help you out."

"Only because he doesn't know where I am."

"Like you're that hard to find. I found you and I wasn't even looking. Look, if he cared as much as he said, he'd already have you home. I think you're better off away from him." He tapped the table, then stood up. "Listen, I gotta get going. You know my number."

She closed her eyes, squeezing off the tears. He had to be lying. He had to be. Her phone buzzed, and she fumbled to flip it open. Katelyn sent back a one-word reply—yes.

Dylan . . . he was right. She *had* gone too far, burnt her bridges. She turned off her phone, wrapped up the cheeseburger and trudged back to her apartment, even more lonely, even more hopeless.

Across town, Katelyn Isaac groaned in frustration. "Shannon turned her phone off."

"Shannon!" Kara picked up her own cell phone and began dialing Bobbi and Chuck's number. "You're texting Shannon? Does anybody else know you've been in contact with her?"

"This is the first time. She just sent me a message, I replied, and now it's shut off."

"What'd she want?" Kara listened to the Molinskys' phone ring.

"She asked if Jack was working for Uncle Chuck."

"That's it?"

"I know. It's weird. After I said yes, I tried to tell her about her mom, but the message bounced."

"Aunt Bobbi? It's Kara. Katelyn just had a text from Shannon. We're on our way over, and we'll explain everything. It's not much, but it's a little ray of hope."

Bobbi clutched the drapes and peered up the street, almost afraid to blink. When she saw the car turn onto their street, she rushed to the front door, barely aware that Chuck followed her.

"Aunt Bobbi." Katelyn trotted around from the passenger side of Kara's car. "Shannon sent me a message asking if Jack was working for Uncle Chuck. He is, isn't he?"

Chuck nodded. "Over Christmas break." He shut the front door behind Kara, then took his place at Bobbi's side.

"Okay," Katelyn said. "So I sent back a yes. Then that was it. The next message bounced back."

"What did you send?" Bobbi asked.

"I told her about your cancer."

"Katelyn, sweetheart, I have a request. If she contacts you again, don't tell her—"

"Bobbi, will you stop it!" Chuck said, exasperated. "Stop being a martyr! She needs to know you have cancer and she needs to come home because of it."

"Shannon needs to figure this out, resolve this for herself, on her own. She can't feel pressured or forced into the decision. I don't want her manipulated."

"It's not manipulation to inform her."

"Katelyn, tell her she can come home. Offer to go get her, offer to have any one of us go get her, but don't tell her about the cancer." Bobbi glanced at Chuck. "Please. Trust me on this one."

Chuck crossed his arms across his chest and shook his head.

"She's sending out feelers. She's trying to figure out what the mood is at home, whether or not she can come back, how she'll be received, especially by you."

"Then why'd she ask about Jack?" Chuck asked. "That doesn't make any sense."

"To see if you guys feel the same. If you're working together, you have to be in agreement."

"Wow," Katelyn said, eyes wide. "You're good. I would have never figured that out."

"Don't mess with mothers," Kara said, laying a hand on Katelyn's shoulder. "We know way more than you think."

"I guess. So what else can I say if she texts me again?"

"Tell her we've shopped for her for Christmas, that we're expecting her. She can come home anytime." She turned to Chuck and reached for his hand.

"That her dad stopped being angry with her about three seconds after she left," he said.

"Oh, here," Katelyn said, handing them a piece of notepaper. "That's the number she texted from. Maybe you can catch her sometime."

"Thank you," Bobbi said, taking the slip. "Thank you for coming over. You made my day."

"We'll keep praying," Kara said. "Maybe we're getting close."

"I think so," Bobbi said.

"Oh, what did the doctor say?" Kara asked. "Didn't you go today?"

Bobbi nodded. "Surgery on the seventeenth, then six weeks of radiation starting January second."

"Goodness, that's soon."

"There's no reason to wait. I'll be glad to have it behind me."

Shannon slumped into the chair at her kitchen table and dug the wad of Dylan's money from her purse. She laid the money out on the table and stared at it. She could really use it. There was at least one fifty-dollar bill in there. Even if all the others were ones, it was still a lot of money.

There's nothing wrong with accepting a gift. Even from him. Right?

Except it wasn't a gift. He was buying her off. When she took the money, that was like saying everything was okay. He would think everything was okay now because he gave her money. Like he paid her for having sex with him. Which made her a . . .

She snatched the money up and threw it in the trash without counting it.

CHAPTER 22
RESILIENCE

Wednesday, December 17

Chuck gave up pacing the tiny hospital waiting room and dropped into the chair beside Jack. He checked his watch once more, but it was only three minutes later than the last time he looked. Rita and Gavin sat in the chairs across from them, while Glen Dillard sprawled in a corner seat.

"You okay, Dad?" Jack asked.

"Yeah, I just hate waiting. I figured somebody would've let us know something by now."

"It's only been forty minutes."

"It's not 'only,'" Rita said, winking at Jack.

Chuck tried to focus on Headline News playing on the waiting room television, but it started to repeat itself. He shifted in his chair and stretched out his legs.

"Want me to send Gavin after some coffee or a Coke or something?" she asked.

"I don't think I could drink it," Chuck said.

"This is a real straightforward surgery, Dad," Jack said. "Mom's gonna be fine."

"I know, I know. Mom said I should have been the one sedated for the surgery." Chuck stood again and slowly walked the length of the small waiting room. Out of the corner of his eye, he saw Rita pointing toward the door and he turned to see Dr. Kremer. He quickly crossed the room to shake the doctor's hand. "This is good, right?"

"Excellent," Dr. Kremer answered. "Everything went very smoothly. She did great. We're going to keep an eye on her until she comes out of the anesthesia. You want to come back and be with her when she wakes up?"

"Please," Rita said, with a teasing smile, "he's making us nuts. Get him out of here."

"I'll call Joel," Jack said as Chuck followed Dr. Kremer out the door.

Dr. Kremer led Chuck through a series of doors marked Authorized Persons Only to a recovery room where Bobbi lay, still sleeping with various monitors tracking her vital signs. "She should be coming around any minute now," Dr. Kremer said. "We planned on forty-five minutes for the anesthesia, and we beat that by several minutes. There's a chair there, and the nurses will be in and out, so don't hesitate to let them know if you need anything."

"Thank you," Chuck said, pulling the chair closer to Bobbi's bedside. He wrapped his hand around her fingers, careful not to touch the intravenous line in the back of her hand. "Dear Jesus, thank You for answered prayers," he whispered.

As he watched her, his mind drifted back to the night she'd spent in the hospital following the shock of Brad's death. She had endured so much, not just in the last few months, but through her whole life—her mother's death, her father's emotional collapse and alcoholism, his infidelity, Tracy, raising Jack, besides Brad and Shannon. She was an amazing woman.

Her eyelids fluttered and opened halfway. "Hey, gorgeous," he said softly.

"You sound like my husband, but I think you're in the wrong room, sir," she said with a weak smile.

"Dr. Kremer said everything went very smoothly."

"Good. I couldn't tell."

"Smart remarks," Chuck said. "Now I know you're okay."

"How long was I out?"

"Forty-some minutes. Can you feel anything yet?"

"It's not completely numb," Bobbi said as she gingerly raised her left hand and rubbed her right shoulder. "My fingers are moving, aren't they? I can't see them."

"You want to sit up?"

"Not until they tell me to. I'm trying to do everything I can in hopes that this time the anesthesia won't make me so sick."

"Oh, right, I forgot about that. You told them, didn't you?"

"Yes, and they said that things had improved tremendously since Shannon had been born, and since we weren't under such time pressure as with a C-section, I should be in much better shape this time around. We'll see."

"Mrs. Molinsky, you're awake," Dr. Kremer said as he walked into the recovery room. "How do you feel?"

"Fine, I guess. Drugged."

"Can you sit up?"

"Probably," Bobbi said, grabbing the bedrail with her left hand. Chuck slid an arm behind her to help ease her up to a sitting position. "Thanks," she said with a wink.

"Dizzy or anything?" the doctor asked.

"Not bad. It'll go away in a few minutes."

He made a note on her chart. "They'll go over all your post-op care with you here shortly. My pager number is on there. Please feel free to use it. Mr. Molinsky, that goes for you, too. Call, even if it's the middle of the night."

"Thank you," Bobbi said. "I'll be fine."

"No doubt," Dr. Kremer said. "They're going to bring you a painkiller, and then I wrote a prescription for more if you need them. You shouldn't have excessive pain, so if you do, something else is going on, and we need to know about it." He slipped her chart under his arm. "Now, are there any questions I can answer?"

"Can we move the radiation to the fifth?" Bobbi asked.

"To Monday? Of course. That's when I meant to start it anyway." He smiled sheepishly. "I would have caught that at your follow-up."

"I'm sure," Bobbi said. "I thought Friday was an odd day to start."

"Speaking of your follow-up, would you rather come in next Tuesday or Friday?"

"Tuesday."

"Tuesday it is. If there's nothing else, Mrs. Molinsky, I'm very pleased with how things went. I think you're all set."

"I'm glad to hear that," Bobbi said. Dr. Kremer shook Chuck's hand, then left them alone.

"You got plans for the second? Is that why you don't want to start the radiation?" Chuck asked.

"Not really."

"We'll have to go out. Once you start radiation, you may not feel like doing anything for a while. Jack will still be home. We can get Rita and Joel to go with us. Make a big deal out of it."

"I think I'd like that," Bobbi said.

Dragging in to work, Shannon found a note on her locker advising her to stop by the supervisor's office before she started this morning. Great. That was the last thing she needed. She told herself over and over, it was probably about some overtime for the holidays. Mrs. Wolfe knew she could always use some extra cash, and filling up those hours . . . well, nothing could fill them. She knocked tentatively on her supervisor's office door. "You wanted to see me?"

She smiled and waved Shannon in. "Yes. Don't worry, it's nothing bad."

"Good," Shannon said, easing the door closed. A heavyset woman with skin the color of her mother's coffee sat in the chair across the desk from the supervisor.

"This is Esther Parker," Mrs. Wolfe said. "She's going to be helping you out."

"Great!" Shannon said, reaching to shake hands. Esther was the same age as her mother, Shannon guessed, maybe younger, with kind but tired eyes. "Oh, did Richie talk to you about me working afternoons or evenings in the restaurant?"

"He did. I don't have a problem with it as long as you keep up in housekeeping."

"Thanks. The extra money will come in handy."

"Esther's worked in hotels before, so you'll just have to show her the way we do things," Mrs. Wolfe said. "I think you'll get along fine." She turned to Esther. "Do you have any questions?"

"No, ma'am," Esther said quietly. "I'll just get started."

"All right, ladies," Mrs. Wolfe said. "Have a good day."

Shannon held the door for Esther and walked her to an elevator in a back hallway. "I'm Shannon Molinsky," she said, offering her hand again. "I don't think that was an official introduction back there."

"Molinsky . . . ," Esther mumbled. "You're not kin to that preacher boy, are you?"

"Brad? He was my brother." Shannon pushed the button for the elevator, then looked away. "He was killed this past summer. Did you know that?"

"No, baby, I'm sorry."

Shannon immediately felt a twinge of homesickness, shame and guilt. "What did you call me?"

"Baby. It's just a habit. I didn't mean anything—"

"No, it's . . . My mom always calls me baby. . . . I guess it sounded funny to hear someone else say it."

The elevator door slid open and they stepped on. Shannon pushed the button for the eighth floor, where she started every morning. "You have family?"

"It's just me and my mama now. I had a son, Julius, but he's been dead . . . oh, thirteen years now, I guess."

"Esther, that's too bad."

"It'll be all right. My boy's in heaven. You know, it was your brother what got him there. He told him all about Jesus."

"Really? That's awesome." The elevator door slid open once again, and they stepped off. Shannon led Esther to the storage closet where the housekeeping cart was kept. She flipped through her keys and unlocked the closet.

"You know, I don't think he was faking, either," Esther said. "I think that boy really cared about us."

"Oh, he did. That mission was his whole life. We used to tease him about being married to it." Shannon wheeled the cart out and pushed it to the end of the hallway and knocked on the first room door. "Housekeeping," she said, leaning closer to listen for movement in the room. Hearing none, she unlocked the door. "This one's a check-out, so it gets the full treatment."

"So what's a rich white kid like you doing here changing bed sheets?" Esther asked bluntly.

"What? Oh, I needed a job."

"Ain't no jobs out in the suburbs?"

"Look, it's complicated," Shannon muttered.

"You ran away from home, didn't you?"

"I didn't run away. Little kids run away from home."

"And little kids got sense enough to know when to go back home," Esther said, her hand on her hip. "I'll take the bathroom in this one."

Shannon jerked the sheets off the first bed, then pulled the cases off the pillows. How weird. Of all the people to show up here, working with her, it was somebody who knew Brad. She stripped the second bed and began rearranging the items on the nightstand.

"All right, kid, come in here and show me where the little shampoo bottles go!" Esther called.

"You're done already? No way!"

"Mmm-hmm," Esther said, nodding. "I got a system."

"I guess so," Shannon said. "Let's see, lotion, shampoo, conditioner on that side." Shannon pulled three small bottles from her front pocket and set them on the left side of the sink. "Two soaps, a mouthwash and a shower cap on this side. Oh, they need the coffee stuff, too. It's out on the cart." She stepped out in the hall and returned moments later with Styrofoam cups and small packages of coffee.

"You ever try this stuff?" Esther asked.

"No, my mom's a big coffee drinker and my brothers like it, but I never really got a taste for it."

"So your daddy was the one who made you mad," Esther said, nodding again.

Shannon slapped her hands against her thighs. "How could you possibly know that?"

"Cause you never mentioned him."

"I never mentioned any sisters either."

"If you had any sisters, you'd be living with them and not working here."

"What are you, psychic or something?"

"No, but I've seen a lot of living, baby. Lotta living." Esther turned off the light in the bathroom. "You miss your mama, don't you?"

"My mom is the strongest, most incredible woman there is. Nothing rattles her."

"I bet her baby girl leaving did."

"Maybe," Shannon said quietly. She left the bathroom and threw a set of fresh sheets on the bed, then picked up the first pillow and began stuffing it in a pillowcase. Esther helped her finish the beds and they checked off the rest of the room without much more conversation.

After working the rest of the morning in near silence, Esther spoke gently, "If you miss your mama, and you know how much it hurt her for you to leave, why you still here? You can't be that mad at your daddy." Shannon looked away without answering. "Mmm, mmm. Say no more, baby. Say no more." Esther raised her hand and shook her head.

"I didn't say anything."

"You don't have to. You got messed up with some boy, some bad boy, and now you're too ashamed to go home and face your mama. Mmm, mmm, mmm."

"Esther, stop it!" Shannon was only partly kidding. "You can't know all this stuff!"

"Come on, it's lunch time. Let me buy you a cheeseburger outta the machine downstairs. Make it up to you."

"Thanks, but I packed a lunch today."

"Then you at least need a Coke. Come on." Esther locked the cart back in the closet.

"Wow, just one floor to go," Shannon said as they got on the elevator to go downstairs. "It's much better working with you, Esther."

"In spite of everything?"

Shannon nodded. "It's good to have somebody else to talk to." Esther followed her to the break room where Shannon pulled an insulated lunch container from the refrigerator. Esther took out a coin purse and began making her selections from the vending machines.

Joining Shannon at a table, she unwrapped her sandwich and opened her bag of chips. "If I haven't made you too mad at me, can I tell you a story about your brother?"

"You didn't make me mad, and I would love to hear your story," Shannon said.

"Brad led me to Jesus, Shannon. Just after Julius died, he came to my place. Sat on my couch and talked to me. Oh, and I argued with him. Told him I was too far gone, it was too late, all that kind of stuff."

She looked away, tears forming even after so many years. "He read to me out of Joel, of all places. God says, 'Turn to Me now while there's time.' Then Brad says to me in that preacher voice, 'Now's the time, Esther. Now.'"

"Wow, he was good," Shannon said.

"He was. But you know what God says right after that? He says, 'I will restore, I will give back to you what you lost, what the locusts ate.' Now, God don't have a time machine, I know, and He ain't gonna bring Julius back from the dead, but He did give me my self-respect back, my purpose, my hope. I gotta reason to get up in the morning, and it ain't cleaning hotel rooms."

Esther smiled and raised her eyebrow. "Baby, I'm sure you ain't supposed to be here. God don't want you here. He wants you back home with your mama and your daddy."

"I know," Shannon admitted, her voice barely audible over the rattle of the heating system.

"Then what's stopping you?"

Shannon sighed deeply. "You nailed it awhile ago, I'm ashamed. I'm afraid to face my mom and dad and tell them what I did."

"Love is stronger than shame, baby. I promise you. Love is stronger."

CHAPTER 23
BREAKTHROUGH

Thursday, December 25

Just after six a.m., Abby Greenway Molinsky started the water for a hot shower. For once she managed to wake up before her husband. Joel functioned perfectly well on four hours of sleep a night, but just for Christmas, he seemed to have switched off his internal alarm clock. Her son, on the other hand, was a typical teenager and likely wouldn't rouse until nine thirty or ten.

She and Joel always had Christmas breakfast in bed, with the first one awake responsible for fixing it. Abby had already started the coffee and put the turkey in the oven for Christmas dinner later that afternoon. Even though her parents would be here, she was calm, actually anticipating the meal. Joel's parents were coming. They'd done so much for her, accepted her into the family with open arms, and she was glad to have the chance to pay them back in some small way. They would temper anything her parents might say or do. She hoped her mom and dad would take notes today, notes on how to accept flawed, failed people, daughters especially, with grace and dignity.

Before getting in the shower, she pulled out a small calendar that she kept in one of the bathroom cabinet drawers. Since she and Joel had run into fertility issues, she kept a careful watch on her cycle, but with the rush of activity this past week, she'd mentally lost track. Today marked the third day she was late. She counted and recounted, backwards and forwards, tapping the calendar a little harder with each pass. She'd never been three days late . . . except when she was pregnant with Ryan.

"No way," she said, trying to suppress a smile, coaching herself not to get too excited. With her hands trembling, she dug through the cabinet under the sink, finally locating a home pregnancy test kit far in the back. Before opening the package, she debated whether or not she should wake Joel. If this was it, he would want to be in on it. But if it wasn't, she would rather he didn't know anything at all than to tell him once again, "not this month."

She fumbled with the package, tearing it open, destroying the box in the process. Then, unfolding the instruction sheet, she read it carefully three or four times before following the steps to the letter. Simple, straightforward. Too nervous to shower now, she paced as she watched the clock on the wall tick off the seconds. The first line appeared in the test window, which only heightened Abby's anticipation.

She sat down on the edge of the tub, almost dizzy. "I can't watch this." Another minute passed. "One more minute, just to be sure." At last, she grasped the edge of the bathroom sink, and pulling herself up, she picked up the test stick. "JOEL!"

Shannon stood on the porch of Esther Parker's home, promptly at noon. Esther's house blended in with the other cracker box houses packed closely on the street. Only the paint color on the porch, front door and shutters distinguished the houses from one another. There were no yards to speak of, and the houses were barely as wide as the cars parked in front of them. Last Christmas, Shannon wouldn't have been caught dead in a neighborhood like Esther's.

Before she could even raise her hand to knock, Esther opened the door. "Come in, baby. Come in!" She was dressed in her Sunday best, with every hair in place, bright lipstick and a string of pearls.

"You didn't tell me this was a dress-up dinner," Shannon said, suddenly self-conscious in her jeans.

"Look, you do Christmas your way. I'll do it my way and neither one of us has to feel bad about that, all right?"

"Your mom's not here," Shannon said, glancing around the living room.

"No, and I gotta confession. She's at Uncle Mont's and I promised I would be there by three."

"You should go then."

"It ain't three yet. We got plenty of time. Come on."

"Everything smells great," Shannon said, breathing in deeply.

"It'll taste good, too. Just wait."

"Can I help you with anything?"

"Don't you know how to be a guest at somebody's house?" Shannon smiled and nodded. "Then have a seat at my table." As soon as Shannon slid into one of the chairs at the kitchen table, Esther began setting bowls and platters in front of her. Ham, sweet potatoes, greens, corn, cranberry salad and a basket of warm rolls. Shannon, suddenly overwhelmed by the meal, real food cooked by someone who cared about her, began to cry and then sob.

"Baby, what's wrong?" Esther asked gently, as she knelt and wrapped her arms around Shannon. "It'll be all right." She patted the teenager's back, rocking ever so slightly, all the while whispering, "Shhh, it's all right, baby."

With her tears exhausted, Shannon pushed away from Esther. "I'm sorry, I don't know what happened," she said, wiping her eyes.

"You're missing your mama," Esther said, reaching for a box of tissues.

"I guess," Shannon admitted softly.

"Call her."

"What?"

"Call your mama, right now."

"I can't do that," Shannon protested. "They have caller ID. They'll find me."

"First of all, I got a blocker on my number. Second, even jailbirds call their mamas on Christmas. Just tell her you love her." Esther pulled the receiver down from the wall phone and handed it to Shannon. She held the phone carefully, almost reverently. "You remember your phone number, don't you?"

"Yes. I just . . . I don't know what she'll say."

"Baby, there is nothing on this earth your mama wants any more than to hear from you."

Shannon swallowed hard and dialed, then lifting the receiver to her ear, she listened to it ring . . . and ring . . . and ring, then the answering machine picked up. Shannon clicked off the phone and held it out for Esther. "She wasn't home."

Esther crossed her arms across her chest, refusing to take the phone back. "Then where is she?"

"Oh, probably my brother's or my aunt's."

"Call her there."

"I'm not tracking her all over town. I don't want to talk to a bunch of people, even if they are relatives."

"I'm not taking the phone back," Esther said firmly.

"You want me to leave a message?"

"At least."

"Fine," Shannon muttered. She dialed home again and waited through the three rings, but when her dad's answering machine greeting came on, she choked. After struggling through a few broken words, she ended the call and held the phone out for Esther again. "There. Are you happy?"

"Are you?"

Shannon sighed and looked around the kitchen, blinking back tears. "No."

"You want me to call your daddy to come get you?"

"No."

"Mmm, mmm, I don't understand you, child."

"A couple of weeks ago, somebody told me my dad was still furious with me. He doesn't want me home."

"Now that's a lie," Esther said, uncrossing her arms and placing her hands on her hips. "I don't know who told you that, but it's a flat-out lie. Your mama and daddy are married, right?"

"Yeah, so?"

"Your daddy could not be that mad at you and still live with your mama every day. He couldn't. He couldn't watch her be all torn up about you being gone and not want you home. I'm telling you, somebody's lying to you, girl." Esther took a seat at the table beside Shannon. "Baby, it's just like what Brad read to me a long time ago. 'Now's the time.' There's no sense to waiting."

Shannon took a deep breath and weighed things out. She knew in her heart that Esther was right, but the guilt and the fear of facing her dad's anger, or worse, his disappointment, were too heavy. "Esther, do you think God could let me know things were okay at home?"

"How so? What do you want Him to do?"

"I want Him to send my dad to get me," Shannon said through tears.

"Baby, you just said your daddy doesn't know where you are."

"God knows where I am. If He wants me home, if my dad wants me home, then God should be able to take care of the details."

Abby couldn't resist straightening a fork as she passed by the dining table on her way back to the kitchen. The table had been set for hours, and aromas of roasting turkey, baking bread and the cinnamon candle in the living room mingled through the house. Joel stood at the kitchen table carving the turkey, like he'd stepped out of a Norman Rockwell print. Everything was perfect. "Do you know what you're going to say?" she asked him.

"Yeah, I think I've got it. Ryan said he can play it cool." He laid the carving knife aside and slipped his arms around his wife's waist, and kissed her gently. "I love you. I wish you could feel it."

"I don't think I've ever seen you like this," Abby said, blushing.

"Two days after I met you. It was just like this, I promise."

"It took you two whole days?"

"I was pretty sure you thought I was a dork after that first time I talked to you."

"Are you kidding? I couldn't believe you talked to *me*."

"Yeah, and look where it got me!" Joel said, his blue eyes twinkling. "I can't wait to see the look on Mom's face."

"You won't have to wait long," Abby said, glancing out the kitchen window. "I think that's them."

"My mother, always painfully punctual," Joel muttered.

"Not just yours. Mine pulled in right behind them."

"Good, that means they have to leave first," Joel teased.

Abby punched him in the arm as she left the kitchen to let everyone in. She gently hugged Joel's mother, taking care not to squeeze. "I can't believe you had surgery a week ago! You look great."

"I feel good," Bobbi said, "although afternoon television is enough to challenge your sanity." Joel had followed Abby into the entryway and hugged both his parents and Abby's mother, then shook hands with Rob Greenway. Jack followed moments later with two shopping bags full of wrapped presents.

"Let this man through!" Joel exclaimed, pushing the door open wide for his little brother.

"Hey thanks! Merry Christmas," Jack said. He leaned over and kissed Abby's cheek.

"Merry Christmas, Jack. You can just set those by the tree." She pointed toward the living room where the Christmas tree silently blinked.

"Abby, everything smells wonderful," Angela Greenway said, handing her coat to her daughter. Abby caught Joel's eye and hoped he was the only one who noticed she didn't hug her parents.

"Thank you, just make sure you get ahead of Ryan, or else I can't guarantee any food will be left. I think he must be going through a growing spell. I can't fill him up these days."

"Josh was that way," Angela said, "and I think Zachary will probably end up like his daddy."

Joel rolled his eyes ever so slightly and Abby smiled.

"Everything is ready, so come ahead and we can say the blessing and eat." She led the way to the dining room. Her parents were last in so they ended up at the far end of the table away from Abby and Joel. Jack and Ryan became the buffer between them and the Molinskys.

Joel slipped into his seat and looked across at his father. "Dad, would you ask the blessing?"

"Yeah, sure," Chuck said, sitting up a little straighter and clearing his throat. He reached for Bobbi's hand and bowed his head. "Father in heaven, thank You. Thank You for the great gifts You've given us, for Jesus Christ, for our salvation, and for our family. Thank You for Abby and Joel and Ryan and bless them for their hospitality. Bless this wonderful meal. Bless Shannon especially today. In Jesus' name. Amen."

Abby squeezed Joel's hand. That was it. The opening her parents needed. Right on cue, Angela Greenway broke the silence. "So Shannon isn't with you?"

"Shannon has been away from home since this summer," Bobbi said.

"Away from home?"

"A prodigal." Joel's mother didn't flinch.

"That must be very difficult for you."

"It has been, but God is working."

"Where does that come from? That kind of rebellion?"

Abby's stomach tightened, but Joel's blue eyes twinkled.

"We're all born with it," Bobbi said. "And a parent's job is to model the grace that God gives every one of us so our children find Him early in life. If we love them unconditionally, then they can trust that God loves them unconditionally as well."

Joel winked at Abby, and Ryan tried his best to hide a smile as he took a drink of his tea. "Angela," Joel said with as much charm as he possibly could, "would you care to start the potatoes around?"

"Of course." She dipped from the serving bowl of mashed potatoes and passed it to her husband. "But doesn't God have standards that He expects us to meet?" she asked without missing a beat.

"How can we expect to meet any standard set by a holy God?" Chuck asked.

Abby's father laid his fork down and raised his head slowly. She knew he disapproved of Chuck Molinsky almost as much as he disapproved of her. "So you're saying we shouldn't try?" Rob Greenway said.

Ryan rubbed his cheek so he could grin at Jack from behind his hand.

"Not at all," Chuck said with a smile. Abby leaned back in her chair to watch as Joel's dad got his lawyer posture. "I'm saying, my worth in God's eyes is not dependent on my ability to live up to His expectations. My worth and acceptance comes from the fact that He is my Father and Christ is my Savior."

"So, let's just say, Shannon comes home. You're not going to punish her?"

"No."

"What's stopping her from doing something like this again, then?"

"Not a thing."

Her father shook his head slightly, smiling a condescending smile. "You see? Kids will always take advantage of you." He glanced in Abby's direction and she felt her face flush. He never missed an opportunity.

"So you wouldn't let Shannon come home?"

"Sounds like she's made her choice to me." He took the next serving dish from his wife and passed it along. "I mean, look at Abby. Do you think it's an accident that God has denied her any more children?"

Abby dropped her eyes, shamed by her father again, but Joel's dad, with kindness and grace, took up for her.

"No, I don't think it's an accident at all," he said, "but I hardly think God is denying them children."

"Children are a blessing from the Lord, Chuck. No children, so obviously there's no blessing."

"All right, then. What's it going to mean when Abby and Joel do have more children?" Her father didn't answer. "Is it too much to believe that God could bless your daughter? That He's pleased with her? That He's using her?"

"God doesn't use sinners." Abby knew that tone. Her father intended that to be the killing blow, but Joel's dad smiled and leaned up to the table.

"Rob, what other choice does He have?"

The setup was too perfect. She knew Joel couldn't keep it quiet any longer. He grinned and took her hand. "Say, Abby and I have been talking. We think this is going to be her last year of teaching for a while."

"Why on earth would you quit, Abby?" her mother asked.

Bobbi looked at Abby, her eyes brimming with tears. She knew before Joel said it. "Abby's going to stay home with the baby. She's pregnant!"

Chuck glanced behind Bobbi as he unlocked the front door of their house. "What are you looking for?" she asked.

"Nothing. I was just checking to see if your feet were touching the ground."

She smiled at him. "My goodness, that's the best news I've had in about a hundred years. A baby, oh, I can't wait!"

"My favorite part," Jack said, then he lowered his voice, "'So what's it gonna mean when they do have children?' And they are! Everything you said about God blessing Abby, being pleased with her! I loved it. That was too sweet."

"Abby so needed to hear something like that." Bobbi handed Chuck a hanger from the closet for his coat. "I'm glad you stood up for her."

"I had to. Rob's just wrong. Besides, standing up for Abby . . . I felt like I was standing up for Shannon, too."

"I wish Shannon could have heard you."

He dropped his eyes. "Yeah. Listen, we've done well today. I, uh, I don't want us to fall apart now. I'm gonna go start your coffee."

"Thank you," Bobbi said. "I'll meet you in by the Christmas tree."

"Is this a married-people-only thing?" Jack asked.

"Of course not. You want some coffee?"

"Yeah, if it's not too strong. Mama's boy coffee, you know." He pulled the front door open. "I'll bring in the bags."

"Thank you, sweetheart. I hope you don't think that's all you're good for, lugging bags in and out."

"It's just makes me wish for the day that I have teenagers of my own," Jack teased.

Bobbi kicked off her shoes, took a seat in the corner of the sofa and pulled an afghan around her. She closed her eyes and took a deep breath, soaking in the day, savoring the thoughts of being a grandmother. When she opened her eyes again, she noticed the message light on the phone blinking. Unwrapping herself, she walked over and pushed the playback button.

"Mom . . . it's Shannon. I'm okay . . . I love you . . . I'll be home soon."

"Baby," Bobbi whispered, clutching the arm of the recliner. "Dear Jesus, she's okay . . ."

"Bobbi?" Chuck was there, reaching an arm around her and easing her down into the chair. "You didn't hear me, did you? Did you faint?"

She shook her head and held out the phone to him, choking the words out. "Shannon called."

Tuesday, December 30

Shannon paced the short hallway outside Mrs. Wolfe's office waiting for Esther to come out. Mrs. Wolfe was going to split them up. Esther was getting her own floors. That's the only thing it could be. *Please, let it be about union dues, or insurance, or anything else. I need Esther.*

The last week had been the worst since leaving home. Leaving that phone message for her mother touched off something much deeper than homesickness or shame. She hadn't slept since then. Her appetite was gone, even with Esther's fabulous leftovers, and everything made her jumpy. If she lost Esther, too . . .

Just then Esther came out of the supervisor's office and Shannon pounced. "What'd she say?"

"I get my own floors next week."

"That stinks."

"Why? You ain't gonna be here next week."

"Why wouldn't I be?"

"You gonna be home."

"Don't start that prophet stuff. I'm not in the mood today."

"Tell me when I been wrong about you. One time even. Tell me. I'm listening."

Shannon shook her head and pushed the button for the elevator. "Esther, can I ask you something?"

"Uh-huh."

"What's it feel like when God's dealing with you?"

"You never had God deal with you?"

"I don't think so."

"Never?"

"No, that's why I'm asking you."

"Miserable."

Shannon raised her eyebrows. "That answers that, then."

They stepped on the elevator and when the doors closed, Esther spoke. "Listen, baby, you best get things settled with God before He gives up."

"I didn't think God ever gave up."

"All right, I ain't no preacher," Esther said in frustration. "He doesn't give up, but He ain't gonna beat a dead horse, either. If you aren't gonna listen, He's gonna quit talking."

"You think He just wants me to go home?"

"You gotta answer that one."

"How?"

"You read, you pray and you wait."

"I don't have a Bible," Shannon said.

"I can fix that," Esther said with a smile. When the elevator door opened, she quickly got the housekeeping cart from the closet and knocked on the first door.

"We're supposed to start at the other end of the hall."

"Shush," Esther said, unlocking the door. She breezed in and quickly returned carrying the Gideon Bible from the room.

"You want me to steal a Gideon Bible?" Shannon asked.

"It ain't stealing. They want you to have them. They told me so. Besides, when you're back home you can send and have it replaced."

"What am I supposed to read, then, Madame Prophet?"

"Joel chapter two."

"If you say so," Shannon said, stowing the Bible on the cart. "Tonight before I go to bed." At this point, she'd try anything.

Jack loosened his tie and kissed his mother's cheek on his way to the refrigerator.

"Don't get too much," she cautioned. "Dinner will be ready in a few." She lifted the lid for the large pot and the aroma filled the kitchen.

Jack settled on pouring a large glass of milk and took a seat at the kitchen table. "Smells good. Roast?"

"Beef and noodles, and I made cornbread."

"Awesome." Jack gulped his milk and leafed through the morning paper still lying on the table.

His mother returned the lid to the pot and took her usual spot at the table. "So how is it, working for your dad?"

"It's good, but he mostly has me working for Chad Mitchell so nobody thinks I'm getting special treatment."

"So even wearing a tie every day is okay?"

"Yeah, I don't mind, really. My ties are a lot cooler than Dad's, anyway."

"Is he making you work tomorrow?"

"Yep, but there's a television in the conference room, so I can at least keep up with the games."

"I thought Missouri already played their bowl game."

"They did, but that doesn't mean I don't want to watch the other games." He took a large gulp of milk.

"Oh, sweetheart, I almost forgot." She shuffled through a stack of catalogs and junk mail in the center of the table. "You got a letter today."

"Who from?"

"I have no idea." She glanced at the envelope before handing it to him. "No return address, but it's postmarked St. Louis."

Jack frowned and tore open the envelope. He unfolded a half sheet of lined paper, written in a ragged scrawl.

Dear Jack,

The police are through with me for now, so I'm moving on. I know you're disappointed, and I can't explain to you why it has to be this way. Reckon if there's a trial, I might be back. Hard to tell.

You're a great man, Jack, just like your father.

Ed

He enclosed a photograph of a young family, a man, a woman, and a little girl who looked barely old enough to be in school. The edges were worn and the colors were faded. Jack studied the picture, lightly touching the little girl's face.

"Everything all right?" his mother asked softly.

He handed her the letter. "He's leaving town."

"Honey, I'm sorry."

"Yeah." Jack pressed his lips together and handed over the photo. "He sent me this."

She studied it several minutes, then she smiled. "She looks like you, like you looked when you first came."

"I thought I looked like my dad."

"You do, but I can see a lot of your mother in you, too. Especially at that age." She handed the photo back. "Is that the only one you have?"

"I have two old ones now, and the one from Penner Hewitt. The rest of 'em are up here." Jack pointed to his temple. He stuffed the letter back in the envelope. "It's like he doesn't want to associate with me."

"He's spent his life alone. We can't expect him to take up with a family overnight." Jack frowned and shook his head. "Can I say one more thing that won't help?" she asked.

Jack smiled. "Sure."

"He's right. You are a great man. Now."

He grinned. "Well, coming from a great woman, I reckon I have to believe it."

"Smart boy."

Shannon collapsed on her bed after her shift in the hotel's restaurant. The Gideon Bible peeked out of her bag. "Not tonight," she mumbled. She knew if she closed her eyes, she would sleep until morning. Esther would understand. One night wouldn't make that much difference.

But . . . Esther would ask her first thing tomorrow morning. She sighed and rolled over, then yanked out the Bible. Joel chapter 2, as promised. "I hate the Old Testament," she grumbled, wading through the verses in the King James. "This doesn't even make any sense." Then, a verse caught her eye and she sat up on the bed.

> *Therefore also now, saith the LORD, turn ye even to me with all your heart, and with fasting, and with weeping, and with mourning: and rend your heart, and not your garments, and turn unto the LORD your God: for he is gracious and merciful, slow*

to anger, and of great kindness, and repenteth him of the evil.

Then farther down almost to the end of the chapter, she read a verse that made her smile.

And I will restore to you the years that the locust hath eaten, the cankerworm, and the caterpillar, and the palmerworm, my great army which I sent among you.

"Esther's locusts," she said.

And ye shall eat in plenty, and be satisfied, and praise the name of the LORD *your God, that hath dealt wondrously with you: and my people shall never be ashamed. And ye shall know that I am in the midst of Israel, and that I am the* LORD *your God, and none else: and my people shall never be ashamed. . . . And it shall come to pass, that whosoever shall call on the name of the* LORD *shall be delivered.*

Thursday, January 1

Chuck slapped at the clock before he roused enough to realize it was the doorbell ringing and not his alarm. He blinked several times, forcing his eyes to focus on the clock. Two thirty. Who . . . ? He felt Bobbi throw off the covers on her side of the bed. "Honey, just stay here. I'll handle it."

"No way, mister. What if it's Shannon?"

"Ringing the bell? Why wouldn't she come on in?" He pulled on a robe, slid his feet into a pair of sneakers he kept by the bedside.

"Who knows?" She yawned and pulled on her own robe.

Jack staggered out of his room and met them at the top of the stairs. "Who's at the door?" He squinted and tried to mash his hair down.

Chuck flipped on the porch light and peered through the side panel. "Good grief, it's John."

"John Isaac?" Bobbi said.

"Yeah." Chuck disarmed the security system and opened the door. "John, come in. What's wrong?"

"Nothing!" John said with a grin Chuck would remember for the rest of his life. "I found Shannon!"

CHAPTER 24
HOMECOMING

Found. Shannon. Bobbi grasped the console table in the entry hall as that hope, once given up, now transformed itself into tangible reality. John . . . found Shannon. He knew where she was.

"Found her? Where?" Chuck asked, already reaching in the hall closet for his coat.

"Hang on." John took Chuck's arm. "You can't go get her right this minute."

"Why not?"

"I know where she works. I don't know where she lives." He pointed toward the living room. "Can we sit down?"

Bobbi managed to nod and stumble backwards out of his way. She switched on the light and motioned John to the recliner while she sat on the edge of the sofa. Chuck slid in beside her and took her hand. He rubbed his hand across the back of hers gently, trying to warm it and ease the tremors. Jack leaned against the arm of the sofa.

"Where is she?" Bobbi asked. "How'd you find her?"

"Dumb luck," John answered.

"Providence," Bobbi corrected.

"Right," John said, nodding. "Durham Chemical hosted a big New Year's Eve party at the Palladium downtown—"

"One of the big casino hotels?" Chuck asked.

"Yeah," John admitted, dropping his eyes. "Anyway, I was in there this evening checking on the arrangements when I saw Shannon working in the restaurant."

"What'd you say to her?" Bobbi asked.

"Nothing. I was afraid to approach her, you know? I was afraid she might take off again." He shifted in his seat. "Should I have said something?"

"No, you did the right thing," Chuck said.

"I asked the hotel people about her. She works in housekeeping, too. She's due back at eight in the morning."

"I'll have her home in time for breakfast," Chuck said quietly, hugging Bobbi tightly to him.

"Finally," she whispered, and relaxed into tears. Chuck held her, then kissed her and hugged her again. The siege was over.

"John, I don't know how we can ever pay you back," Chuck said after letting a long deep breath go. He stood and shook hands with John.

"I'm just sorry I didn't get out here sooner. That party was kinda my baby. I couldn't get away."

Bobbi stood and gave him a hug. "You don't know what this means to me."

"No, but I have an idea what it means to get back someone you love." He grinned and held his left hand up, showing off his wedding band. "Kara and I . . . we're . . . we did the courthouse thing the day after Christmas."

Bobbi hugged him again. "That is wonderful, John. I'm thrilled for you and Kara and the girls."

John smiled again. "Glen and Laurie said they'd help us out."

"I love Glen and Laurie. They've meant so much to us over the years."

John nodded toward the door. "I'm gonna get going. We'll be praying."

"Thank you," Chuck said. He closed the door behind John and swept Bobbi into his arms. "She's coming home today!"

"Can it really be? After all this time?"

"I think you can let yourself believe it."

Bobbi did. She collapsed against him, letting her emotion, her fear and anxiety give way to joy, relief and blessed anticipation. Six hours. That was less time than she labored to bring Shannon into the world, and now after six bleak months they would bring her home again. Thank You, Jesus. Thank You, Jesus. Thank You, Jesus.

Chuck laughed through his own tears, kissed her and rocked her in his arms until Jack cleared his throat. Jack. She had completely forgotten Jack was in the room. She turned to him and smiled. "We're getting her back."

He nodded and grinned. "Since we're all up, I'll, uh . . . I'll go make your coffee."

Shannon put the key in the ignition and gripped the steering wheel. "Now Hondas are supposed to be extremely reliable. Lately, you seem to be forgetting that. Next payday, we'll go get a nice oil change and make you feel all better, but today you need to hold up your end of the deal."

She turned the key and the engine growled, then turned over. "See, I knew you had it in you. Now we'll drive to work and you can take the rest of the day off."

She, on the other hand, would work and try her best not to think about her mom, or her dad, or her brothers. Last night, watching that stupid ball drop, surrounded by the drunks in the hotel bar, she felt so isolated and forgotten. But then she got angry. She was here, alone, because she chose that. Nobody threw her out. She left. She refused to call home even. She was the one hiding. It was her own stupid fault.

Her plans made so much sense that Saturday morning. Dealing out punishment for her injustice. Giving her dad what he deserved. Right. How stupid.

Last night, when sleep wouldn't come, she kept trying to imagine what it was like when her dad had to come home and face her mother after he cheated. Or when he confessed it all in front of the church. What was it like to stand there alone and face all the people he'd hurt, the very people he loved most? He always said Phil Shannon told him what to say, but still. He had to say it. If only she had a Phil Shannon.

The downtown was dead, but the red lights still directed the nonexistent traffic. "Of course," Shannon muttered as she eased to a stop. When she moved to lower the sun visor, she caught sight of her own name in her peripheral vision. Her name. On a billboard.

SHANNON

IT'S OKAY TO COME HOME!

LOVE, DAD

She clamped a hand to her mouth. How many other Shannons could there be in the city? Was there anyone else that message was aimed at? Or was her dad that nuts? She smiled as tears spilled onto her cheeks. He was totally nuts.

The driver behind her tapped his car horn. "Green light, right," she muttered. She couldn't wait to tell Esther. If her dad really put up that billboard for her . . .

Chuck kept a close eye on his speedometer, fighting the impulse to blast his way downtown, but he promised Bobbi he would obey the speed limits. That was the first of her conditions for letting him come alone. She also made him tell her what he planned to say. He'd rehearsed that since June. He was going to beg for Shannon's forgiveness and ask her if she would come home. Finally, he agreed not to mention the cancer. She wanted to handle that once Shannon was settled in back at home. He went along with her wishes immediately. He had to. He needed to bring Shannon home himself.

He checked the scribbled sheet of directions he held against the steering wheel, but he couldn't make out the street names. Grabbing his glasses from his shirt pocket, he used his teeth to open them up. "Here we go," he whispered as he double-checked the streets and exited the highway. Ten more minutes and he'd be at the Palladium.

Jack watched his mother pace, alternating between wringing her hands and hugging herself each time she passed. "Can I do anything for you?" he asked.

"No, sweetheart." She smiled and patted his knee. "I'm afraid this is how it's going to be until I hear from them."

"You wanna read the paper?"

"No." She peeked out the front window again, and Jack shook his head. His dad wouldn't be back for at least an hour.

"Do you care if I read it?" he asked.

"Of course not."

Jack slouched against the arm of the sofa and read through the sports section first, catching all the updates from bowl games and the last games of the NFL season. To kill a little more time, he began reading through the local section, the part he usually skipped. "Mom, you better take a look at this."

She took the folded paper from him and visibly flinched when she read the article.

SLU student arrested on four counts of sexual assault

St. Louis University freshman Dylan Aaron Snider, 19, was arrested Tuesday evening on charges he sexually assaulted four females. Two of the victims are under eighteen and two are college students, all of whom may have been involved in a relationship with Snider. St. Louis police filed the charges after an investigation prompted by a 15-year-old victim coming forward. The complaint alleges that Snider offered the girl marijuana in exchange for sex and when she refused, engaged in nonconsensual sex. The other victims' complaints are similar. If convicted of felony sexual assault, Snider faces a maximum seven years in prison.

Chuck screeched to a stop in the registration lane at the Palladium. He flipped his emergency blinkers on and breathed a quick prayer. "Dear God, please let this be it." He slipped his glasses back in his pocket and got out of his car. He intended to go floor by floor until he found her. If that failed, then he'd get the hotel management involved.

Inside the lobby, he punched the button for the elevator and checked his watch. Eight fifteen. When the elevator door slid open, he hit 22 and waited. He'd start at the top and work his way down. On the nineteenth floor, he caught up with two housekeepers who told him Shannon usually started on eight.

On the elevator back down to the eighth floor, he tried to rub some feeling back in his icy hands and wished he had a drink of water. What if she wouldn't come home with him? The phone message, like the note, was for Bobbi. What if she still wanted nothing to do with him?

He'd take her home anyway.

When the doors opened, he bolted off to the left, down the dimly lit hallway. He made a right at the next hallway and then stopped cold. There she was. Shannon. His baby girl. Her back was to him, her focus on the clipboard in her hand. The woman working with Shannon didn't seem to notice him either.

He didn't want to startle her, so he stopped fifteen feet from her. "Shannon." He spoke softly, gently, the way he used to do when he'd wake her up for school. The other woman broke into a wide smile, nodding in his direction. Shannon seemed frozen for a moment, then she dropped the clipboard in the laundry bag and turned around in the slowest of slow motion.

He closed the distance between them in four long strides. Shannon fell into his arms and sobbed. The prepared speech evaporated from his mind. "Baby, I love you. I'm sorry. I'm so sorry." He kissed her forehead, her hair, and rocked her in his arms as he held her, mingling his tears with hers.

She dug her fingers into his jacket, clinging as if her life was at stake. "Daddy, I'm sorry . . ." She hadn't called him Daddy since the third or fourth grade.

"Shhh, it's okay. It's all okay." As he patted and rubbed her back, she seemed so thin now. His heart ached with guilt for all that she'd been through in the last few months, all of it faced alone.

"But I . . . you don't know, Daddy, I—"

"Doesn't matter. Nothing matters except I found you, I love you, and I'm taking you home."

"I can come home?" She looked up in his face with heartrending disbelief and wiped her eyes.

"Of course you can come home. Right now."

"So the billboard . . . you did that?"

"You saw it?"

She nodded and wiped her eyes again. "This morning."

"I meant it. There's no reason for you to stay away anymore."

She stiffened and pulled away from him. "Wait, we have to talk first." Her eyes darted to the other woman then back to him. "Daddy, I . . . uh . . . I did something . . ."

"If it's about Dylan, I know, and it doesn't matter."

"You know? How?"

"He told me."

She hung her head. "And you still want me to come home?"

He took her by the shoulders and leaned down to catch her eyes. "Honey, I love you. I love you because you're my little girl, not because of what you do or don't do." Shannon looked away and wiped her eyes. "I loved you just as much the day you left home as I did when we brought you home from the hospital, probably more even." He took her in his arms again. "That has never changed."

"But you were so mad at me."

"I know, honey. I wish I could take back every bit of it. I hurt you, I hurt your mother because I lost my temper with you. I am so sorry. Can you forgive me?"

"Me?"

"Yes, I'm asking you to forgive me. I was wrong, Shannon. I didn't listen to you. I assumed the worst—"

"About that . . . Dad, there's something else."

"What?"

"Daddy, I'm not saved."

Bobbi shuddered violently when the telephone rang, but she snatched it up and answered it immediately. "Chuck?" Jack watched her eyes, anticipating.

"No, ma'am. This is Detective Rick Ramirez. Is this Mrs. Molinsky?"

"Yes, I'm sorry. I was expecting someone else." She shook her head at Jack.

"I'm sorry to bother you this early on a holiday, but I thought you'd want to know the state police picked up Antoine Miller."

"Are you serious?" She held the phone down and mouthed to Jack, "Brad's killer. They got him."

"Yes, ma'am. The DA's been on him already. He wants to plead out."

"What does that mean exactly?"

"He wants to make a deal, a plea bargain."

"He murders my son and . . . and he gets to bargain? How is that right?"

"It guarantees Miller goes to prison."

"So it's this or nothing."

Ramirez sighed. "No, but it would save you the strain of a trial."

"Well, thank you. Thank you for all your hard work, and for keeping us posted." Bobbi set the receiver back and looked at Jack. "That was Detective Ramirez. Antoine Miller was arrested. He's trying to negotiate a plea deal."

"Negotiate? That's just wrong. Brad—"

"Brad would be ashamed that the guy was going to prison at all," Bobbi said with a sigh. "God will have to fix it now."

"Mom, I'm sorry." Jack draped an arm around her shoulder.

"Shannon's still coming home. Nothing is going to take away from that."

Chuck took his daughter's hands. "Honey, what are you talking about? Of course you're saved. I was there—"

"I never really believed it. I mean, I thought I did. I said all that stuff . . . but it wasn't real."

Just then the other woman spoke up. "Here, let's get you all outta the hallway." She unlocked the closest room and held open the door.

"Good grief, Esther. I'm totally rude," Shannon said. "Daddy, this is Esther Parker. She . . . she's a lifesaver."

"Thank you," he said as he walked past her, shepherding Shannon into the room. "I'm Chuck Molinsky, Shannon's father." He held out his hand, and Esther shook it vigorously.

"Yes, you are," Esther replied with a smile. "Nobody gonna bother you in here. Take your time."

"Thanks," Shannon said as Esther eased the door shut. "She knew Brad. That boy Julius that he talked about, she's his mother, and Brad led her to Jesus. How crazy is that?"

"It's not," Chuck said. "That's the way God works. Now listen, I want you to understand something. Just because you . . . made some mistakes—"

"Dad, God has never dealt with me like He has since Christmas." She dropped onto the bed. "I can't sleep. I can't eat. I can't think about anything else."

"That still doesn't mean—"

"Then Esther told me to read Joel chapter two." She waved her hand toward the door. "That's what Brad used on her, and it's got this part in there about 'turn to Me with all your heart.' I've never done that, Daddy. Not like that."

"Then what's stopping you?"

She tried to smile as tears filled her eyes. "I had to be sure you would take me back. If you wouldn't . . . I didn't see how God would either."

"Oh, honey." Chuck knelt in front of her and took her hands. "How could you think I wouldn't take you back?"

"It's a long story." She pushed the tears away with her fingertips. "Then I was coming to work this morning and I saw this billboard some psycho put up." She laughed through the tears that choked off her words.

He smiled at her. "And then you knew?"

She nodded. "I knew you were coming today. I knew it."

"Honey, God wants you back home even more than I do."

Shannon nodded and pushed her hair back behind her ears. She took his hands, bowed her head, and with a quiver in her voice, she prayed. "Dear God, I'm a mess. I've sinned against You, against my parents. I'm sorry." She sniffled and let go of his hand to wipe her eyes again. "I want You to take that all away, for real this time. I want to live Your way from now on."

Chuck wanted to pray with her, pray for her, but he couldn't concentrate on anything but the sound of her voice and the touch of her hand. Finally.

She raised her head and smiled at him with a sparkle in her eyes just like her mother's, and he hugged her to himself. "Thank You, Jesus. For bringing her back. All the way back."

"I want to go home." He kissed her and kept one arm around her, then pulled his cell phone out and handed it to her. She quickly punched in the number. "Mom? It's Shannon. I'm with Daddy. I'm coming home."

Miles away, in her suburban St. Louis living room, Bobbi collapsed into the recliner before Jack's eyes.

"Mom? Was that Dad? Is she coming home?"

"Thank You, Jesus," she murmured. "Thank You, thank You, Jesus."

"She's on her way?" Jack asked.

"Yes!" She popped up out of the recliner and threw her arms around his neck, then kissed him on each cheek. "She's on her way! Dad's got her, and they're on their way home!" She realized she was still holding the telephone. "I need to call Joel." She stared at the handset, then handed him the phone. "Here, dial for me, then give me back the phone."

Jack smiled, pushed two buttons and handed her the phone. "He's number five on speed dial, Mom."

"Yeah, I know. I can't think right now." She held up the phone and listened to it ring. "Joel . . . answer . . ." She paced to the entry hall and back. "Joel! She's on her way home. Dad's got her!" She smiled broadly and nodded. "See you in a few. I love you, Joel." She clicked off the phone. "Oh, Rita. Which one is she?"

"Four."

"Right." She hit the buttons and nodded while she waited. "Gavin! Chuck's got Shannon! They're on their way home right now! I know, God is good. . . . You absolutely should come over. . . . No, bring them, too. Love you guys." She laid down the phone and looked at the mantel clock. "How long has it been?"

"Five minutes, maybe."

"How much longer, then?"

"Today, twenty or thirty." He pointed to the front window. "You know, you can pace over there and still see out the window." Bobbi picked up a throw pillow from the recliner and tossed it at him. "I was just trying to help," he teased.

"Oh, Glen and Laurie! I should call them."

"They're not on speed dial." Jack took the phone and called the pastor's number, then handed the phone to his mother once again.

"Glen? This is Bobbi . . ." Tears choked off her words once again. She took a deep breath and swallowed hard. "Chuck has Shannon. They're on their way home."

This is what freedom feels like, Shannon thought as her dad took the on-ramp out of the downtown. Light. Safe. Unburdened. Sheltered. Her father reached over and squeezed her hand again. "You nervous?" he asked.

"It's a little of everything. Anxious, ashamed, exhausted, excited." She sighed. "Then I keep thinking things went smooth with Mrs. Wolfe. I'm not sure my landlord will be so easy to deal with. There's still five months on the lease."

"Don't worry about any of that. There's plenty of time to handle all that stuff. Right now, I just want you to focus on one thing." When he pulled up to a stop sign, he looked into her eyes. "Focus on how much the people in your life love you. I don't want you to think about anything that's happened in the last six months. None of it. Today, you soak in that love. That's what's real."

"Why didn't I see that before? Why did I have to go through . . . this before I understood that?"

He smiled at her. "You got more of my genes than any of us realized apparently."

"Can I ask you something?"

"Anything."

"What was it like when you told everybody, you know, about the affair?"

"Terrifying . . . Sickening."

"Great."

He gave her a gentle smile. "Yeah, like that. But you'll see what love really is. It's not just some gooey emotion. It's deep and it's intense. And you see that it's you that they love, to the core of your soul, not what you do or what you do for them."

"Wow."

"You don't take it for granted anymore. When somebody chooses to love you, that means something."

"I love you, Dad." He patted her knee and turned onto Danbury Court. Shannon saw her mother standing on the porch, waving. "She looks beautiful."

"You ought to see her up close." Her dad grinned and then honked the car horn like a maniac.

Her mother left the porch and ran to the edge of the driveway by the road. She wasn't going to wait for them to pull in. Before he brought the car to a complete stop, Shannon threw the door open and jumped out of the car into her mother's waiting arms.

"Baby . . . I love you."

"Mom, I'm so sorry . . ."

"Shh . . . Doesn't matter. Not now."

"But, Mom—"

"You're home. You're safe and you're home."

"But I—"

"Came home." She kissed her and hugged her once more, then she turned and pointed to the front porch where her brothers stood. "Now, I think those boys are anxious to see you."

Joel met her halfway up the walk, lifted her off the ground with his hug and spun her around like she was nine again. "Welcome home, Squirt."

"Thanks, Jellybean."

Jack stayed on the porch, though. She couldn't blame him. They weren't on the best terms when she left. She took a deep breath and walked carefully up to the porch. "Jack, what I said to you . . . I'm so sorry. Can you forgive me?"

"I need to ask your forgiveness, too," he said.

"What for?" He pulled her spark plug wires from behind his back and smiled sheepishly. "That was you? I thought it was Dad!"

"After the things you said about my mother . . . well, I was pretty angry with you."

"Oh, Jack." Her own hateful words flooded back into her memory. "I was . . . I'm sorry. There's no excuse for ever talking about another person like that, especially someone you love so much. If things are not the same between us, I understand."

"I doubt they'll ever be the same."

Shannon nodded with resignation.

Then he grinned. "Can't they be better?"

She returned his smile and hugged him. "They already are. Much, much better." Her parents and Joel stepped up on the porch as she let go of Jack. When she reached for her mother's hand, she noticed the cars lining the street. "Who's here?"

"Come and see." Her mother pushed open the door for her.

Before Shannon saw anyone she smelled breakfast. Pancakes. And bacon and sausage. And coffee. Home. Aunt Rita was making breakfast, and all her cousins were there. Even Danny. Seeing him made her miss Brad, but not in a bad way. He had a greater homecoming than this one.

Katelyn squealed as she hugged her, bursting with the news of her parents' remarriage. "What else did I miss?" Shannon asked.

"Joel and I are expecting," Abby announced, and Joel and Ryan beamed.

"Seriously?"

"Just found out Christmas Day."

Shannon hugged Abby and Joel again, whispering in her brother's ear, "I hope it's twins."

Even Pastor Glen and Miss Laurie were there. "We're glad you're home safe," Laurie said.

"Thank you. Pastor Glen, we need to talk if you have some time in the next day or two."

"You bet. Just let me know."

Her mother, never more than an arm's length away, laid a hand on her shoulder. "Baby, let me have your coat, and we can sit down for Aunt Rita's breakfast feast."

But she was wearing her housekeeping uniform and had no intention of sitting through her homecoming breakfast with everybody staring at it. Even the prodigal son got to change clothes. "Ummm, actually, I think I'd like to run up and change. Into my own clothes, you know."

"Of course," her mother said and followed her up the stairs. After a moment's hesitation and a deep breath, Shannon opened the door to her bedroom and stepped inside. That wonderful home-from-vacation smell wrapped around her, and every detail was just the way she remembered it. "We didn't move anything," her mother said.

Shannon dug through the box in the back of the closet until she found an old University of Missouri sweatshirt that had belonged to Joel. Then she got jeans and her favorite old sneakers. She quickly threw off the uniform and got dressed. Even the smell of the fabric softener was wonderful.

Her mother stood against the doorframe, smiling, on the verge of tears again. "Mom, I'm so sorry."

"Not today." Her mother hugged her tightly. "Nothing but good stuff today." But as she let go, her mother winced.

"What?"

"Nothing."

"Liar," Shannon said with a raised eyebrow and a grin.

"All right. Sit down." Her mother sat on the bed and patted the spot beside her.

"You're kinda scaring me."

"The scary part is over." Her mother reached for her hand, a kind seriousness in her deep brown eyes. "I wasn't going to tell you this for another day or two, and I threatened everybody downstairs not to breathe a word of it."

"Mom, just say it."

"I had surgery on the seventeenth to remove a small tumor from my right breast. It was cancer. Radiation starts Monday."

"MOM!" She . . . cancer . . . radiation? She leaned forward, trying to catch her breath, trying to make the bed stop spinning. "And I . . ."

"Had no way to know. Shannon, it's okay." Her mother pulled her over into her arms. "The surgery was a complete success. I feel fine. A few little treatments and we'll move on like it never happened."

"But Mom . . ." The tears of guilt and shame came with no way to stop them. No rationalizing or justifying this one. As if the direct pain she caused weren't enough.

"Baby, I know everything inside you is telling you 'shame on you.'"

Shannon nodded. "And that's the nice stuff. The rest is worse."

Her mother smiled and pushed the hair back from her face. "Don't listen to it. The people who love you aren't shaming you. Don't do it to yourself."

Bobbi cleared the throw pillows from the family room sofa, making room for the family to settle in for an afternoon of watching the bowl games. Shannon said she wanted everything to be like a normal New Year's, so football and snacks became the order of the day.

Just then, Shannon shuffled in, her hands stuffed in the front pouch of her sweatshirt. Bobbi motioned for her and hugged her. "How was your nap?"

"Best sleep I've had in months," Shannon said, dropping onto the sofa. "Where's everybody at?"

"Abby and Joel took Ryan and Jack to get snacks and Dad's making tea. And coffee, I hope." She joined Shannon on the sofa and pulled the afghan around her shoulders. "Are you warm enough?"

"I'm fine, thanks."

"You know, you have Christmas presents to unwrap."

"I don't deserve—"

Bobbi pointed a finger at her, but the reproof was only halfway teasing.

"I mean, I'll get to them later."

"Much better." She smiled and patted Shannon's knee.

"So tell me some more stuff. What's everybody been doing? What about the police? Did they ever find the guy that shot Brad?"

"Oh my goodness! You'll have to get Jack to tell you. His grandfather showed up at Dad's office one day in November."

"No way!"

"He did. He saw the shooting. He had the guy's name and he went to the police."

"And?"

"And they called this morning. I haven't even told your dad yet. Chuck!"

He stepped in the doorway "Yeah? Oh, hey, sweetheart."

"Detective Ramirez called. They arrested Antoine Miller."

"Honey, that's great!"

Bobbi frowned. "He's trying to negotiate a plea deal."

"I need to talk to the prosecutor," Chuck muttered. "We can do better than that."

"Speaking of prosecutors," Bobbi said, "is the paper in there?" Chuck returned a few minutes later with the morning newspaper, and Bobbi shuffled the pages around. "Here. You'll both want to read this," she said, pointing to the article on Dylan Snider's arrest.

"Just when I'm about to lose faith in the justice system," Chuck said, "they come through."

"Joel said one of those girls was a patient of his. He may have to testify."

"I'd love to testify against that punk."

Then Bobbi noticed Shannon sinking back against the sofa, chewing on her bottom lip. "Baby? Everything all right?"

"I feel a little sick."

"I shouldn't have had you read it. I'm sorry."

"No . . . I just . . . I believed him, and everything he ever said was a lie. He said I was amazing, that I was special."

"Those are true," Chuck said, and she shook her head.

"Yeah, but he . . . I mean, I let him go too far, and then . . ."

"Oh baby." Bobbi took her in her arms again, sharing silent tears with her daughter. She rubbed Shannon's back and spoke gently. "You've been through a horrible experience. I wish coming back home could magically erase all that hurt, but I know it doesn't.

We'll work on it, though, and the healing will come, I promise you that. Healing will come."

At the close of the day, after draining the last of the coffee into her mug, Bobbi joined Chuck on the love seat in the study. He slipped his arm around her, and she nestled even closer. "Kids asleep?" he asked.

"I know Shannon is. Jack's light was still on."

"I think you were more beautiful today than I've ever seen you. There were times when I had to stop what I was doing and just watch you."

"Laying it on a little thick, aren't you?"

He shook his head. "No. You had your family all around you . . . I don't know . . . you just glowed."

"It was quite a day."

"We've had a few of those over the years, haven't we?"

"Probably have a few more before it's all said and done."

He shifted so he could stretch out his legs. "You know, we need a fireplace in here. That would make it perfect," he said.

"It's close enough."

About The Author

Image by: Mary Rose

After working several years as research chemist, Paula Wiseman was blessed with the opportunity to stay home with her children and follow the writer's path. *Contingency: Book One: Covenant of Trust Series*, her bestselling debut novel, won two Indie Excellence Awards and was a Readers Favorite Winner in Christian fiction. *Indemnity*, the follow-up, was also an Amazon bestseller and #1 Hot New Release. When she isn't working on new projects, Paula blogs on matters of life and faith at www.paulawiseman.com.

CPSIA information can be obtained at www.ICGtesting.com
Printed in the USA
BVOW070336020113

309597BV00002B/578/P